Summer Exhibition Illustrated 2019

A selection from the 251st Summer Exhibition
Edited by Jock McFadyen RA

Summer Exhibition Illustrated 2019

Royal Academy of Arts

Sponsored by

Contents

Sponsor's Foreword

The Royal Academy of Arts Summer Exhibition is a truly remarkable event, significant for its longevity – it has now run without interruption for more than 250 years – and for its role as the world's largest open-submission exhibition. Each year it creates an opportunity for artists from all backgrounds to be associated with a momentous cultural event which commands international attention. Inevitably, this results in a vibrant selection of surprising and often challenging submissions from some of the world's most exciting contemporary artists.

Visitors to this year's exhibition will find an intriguing array of works assembled under the curatorial stewardship of the acclaimed British painter Jock McFayden RA who, as part of his contribution, has installed an animal-themed 'menagerie' in the Wohl Central Hall. The exhibition reaches throughout the RA's galleries, exploring themes of light and time, and then spills out beyond the building itself with sculptural work in the courtyard and a colourful installation on nearby Bond Street.

Insight's association with the Summer Exhibition has now continued for more than a decade. We are honoured to play a role in its enduring success and I have personally always found it to be an inspiring forum for encountering new work by both established and emerging artists. We hope everyone who experiences this year's selection will share our enthusiasm for this truly unique display of artistic endeavour.

Abdallah Nauphal
Chief Executive Officer

Sponsored by

Insight
INVESTMENT

Part of BNY MELLON

President's Foreword
Christopher Le Brun

To follow the great success of last year's Summer Exhibition, which marked the 250th anniversary of the Royal Academy, was never going to be an easy task. We were delighted by the enthusiasm with which visitors greeted that show, making it the most popular for a hundred years and underpinning the Summer Exhibition's continued role in an increasingly complex art world with so many different opportunities to see and enjoy contemporary art.

The reception of last year's exhibition gave a sense of confidence to the committee, with the painter Jock McFadyen as chief co-ordinator this year. This is detectable in the overall feel of the exhibition, as well as in the individual focus of each of the galleries. With an overarching emphasis on art that reflects the world we live in, members of the committee have taken this theme in different directions. The architect Spencer de Grey has examined the sustainability of modern architecture, illustrating how practices have long focused on reducing the carbon footprint of their buildings through innovative methods of sourcing and construction. Barbara Rae reflects the same urgent concerns in her gallery, which contains both abstract and figurative works that celebrate the beauty of the outer regions of the world and remind us of the fragility of the planet. A grouping of wild and domestic animals in the Wohl Central Hall further reminds us of humankind's responsibility to nature.

Hughie O'Donoghue balances these themes in his gallery, which is mostly occupied with considerations of human existence. The depiction of the human form can also be seen in Timothy Hyman's room where drawings are strongly featured with each work selected for the quality of its draughtsmanship. Anne Desmet and Barbara Rae reveal very different aspects of contemporary printmaking, and between their galleries they have assembled a rich selection of techniques and themes. In the Lecture Room Stephen Chambers has delivered a masterclass in hanging works together that provide an array of different modes of expression. This is balanced by the denser pattern-dominated hang by Jock McFadyen in Gallery III, the largest and grandest of the Academy's spaces. Richard Wilson has overseen sculpture across the entire exhibition, carefully placing works which chime with the context and theme of each gallery.

On the Summer Exhibition Committee for the first time this year are Bob and Roberta Smith and Jane and Louise Wilson. The constant renewal of the Summer Exhibition is dependent on these fresh perspectives. The Wilsons have brought their knowledge and sensitivity for light-based work to their gallery, whereas Smith has focused on the outer limits of the human imagination and contemplative cosmology. The combination of the skill, hard work and dedication of the entire committee has resulted in a particularly thoughtful exhibition this year.

In addition to thanking the Summer Exhibition Committee, it is a pleasure to yet again acknowledge an immense debt of gratitude to our long-term sponsors Insight Investment.

Introduction
Jock McFadyen RA

Twenty-two years ago at 'Sensation' Marcus Harvey's picture of Myra Hindley was attacked by members of the public in the RA's galleries. Eggs and ink were pelted, the media went viral and anyone who had not yet heard of the YBAs simply hadn't been paying attention. Today Marcus Harvey's powerful new work *The Victory* is hung prominently in the 2019 Summer Exhibition and many of the artists exhibited in 'Sensation' are now Royal Academicians.

But the RA has always included artists who make challenging work, as previous generations from the 1950s, 1960s and 1970s to the recently elected Turner Prize-winner Lubaina Himid prove, and a number of Academicians have huge international reputations. The quality of artistic life at the RA hasn't changed, but the business of art outside the walls of the Academy has.

In Mike Leigh's 2014 film *Mr Turner* we saw that in the eighteenth century the Royal Academy's Annual Exhibition was a display of new work by Royal Academicians shown alongside new work by artists who were not Royal Academicians. The exhibition has been running continuously for the past 250 years and is always extremely popular. Nearly 300,000 people visited the show last year. In the art business there is the suspicion that if something is popular then it might not be much good. But hang on a minute: Picasso is popular and he's pretty good, and so is Andy Warhol, and Tate Modern always seems to be rammed and it's not bad either...

Until recently one might have been forgiven for thinking of the Summer Exhibition as an easy target for snooty critics and a joy to thousands of visitors who wouldn't dream of visiting the Venice Biennale or popping over to Art Basel Miami. And some people still think it's just a show of pictures of cats and dogs, and maybe I did too. Before I was elected to the Academy seven years ago I didn't send in my pictures and rarely visited the show, but I was behind the curve. Now I am passionate about the exhibition and consider it one of the most important survey shows of contemporary art in the world.

Critics are rarely snooty about the international art fairs, yet they are curated by dealers. Guest curators might participate but even they can only curate artists presented by the dealers. Survey exhibitions in museums of contemporary art are invariably curated by academics who in turn are often influenced by dealers, so the wheel turns and a self-fulfilling narrative emerges. The unfolding story of art.

In the last few years the wheel has come full circle. Many commentators have drifted towards the journalistic end of criticism while the art fairs get even closer to the banality of international money. The auction houses too have become rather boring with their ever-breaking sales records, to the point where the 'best' works appear to be by artists who rarely change or experiment or, better still, are dead. After all, clients

Wim Wenders Hon RA
Armenian Alphabet, Armenia
C-print
178 × 373 cm

Thomas Houseago
Blue Owl
Aluminium
H 243 cm

Tom Hunter
Dinosaur Island
Silver gelatin print
92 × 122 cm

need to be able to recognise a signature work from 100 feet in a crowded evening sale after a few drinks. Over in the public sector, museums feel the squeeze and dumb down to interactive over-explanation and the horrors of headphone culture as funding dwindles. And what was cool isn't cool any more…

What is easily forgotten is the fact that the Summer Exhibition is curated by artists.

This distinction is fantastically important and should lend the event the shock of authenticity, making it worthy of critical attention each year. But old prejudices die hard. Despite this there is now a groundswell of serious artists eager to place work in the Academy's Summer Exhibition and they bring with them an equivalent number of collectors and viewers who are able in one visit to see the greatest cross-section of recent art by living artists in an exhibition that lasts for two months. Moreover this work is displayed in beautiful top-lit galleries in a palace in the middle of one of the world's great cities. Classical architecture and contemporary art are no strangers and the combination offers up a dramatic counterpoint similar to that of the Venice Biennale. This, and the fact that proceeds from sales help to fund one of the world's only free art schools, compound the exhibition's significance and reiterate the concept of an academy as a self-supporting hive.

So welcome to the 251st Royal Academy Summer Exhibition. This year it is my turn to co-ordinate the committee of artists and one architect, all of whom I admire in different ways and for different reasons. The theme for this year is art that describes the world today. And this art need not be figurative or graphic – after all it is 76 years since Mondrian painted *Broadway Boogie Woogie*. I also want to celebrate the

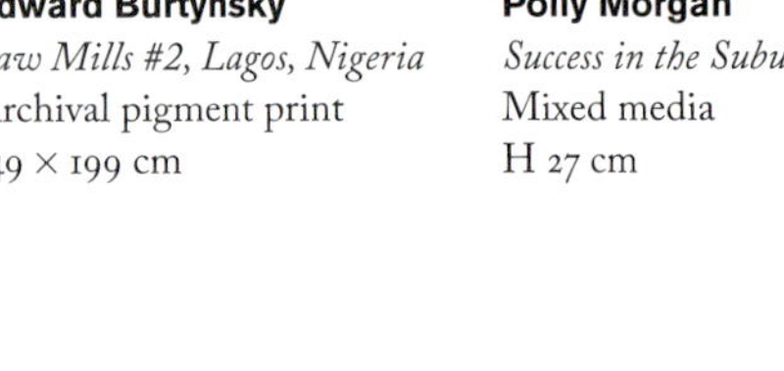

Edward Burtynsky
Saw Mills #2, Lagos, Nigeria
Archival pigment print
149 × 199 cm

Polly Morgan
Success in the Suburbs
Mixed media
H 27 cm

significance of photography and to this end I have asked the great German filmmaker and Honorary Academician Wim Wenders to make a separate display of his stunning large photographs in the McAulay Gallery, and a number of other important photographers will be found throughout the show, including Edward Burtynsky and Hannah Collins with her monumental black-and-white photographs *Nelson Mandela's Teenage Home, National Monument* and *The Road to Mvezo – Nelson Mandela's Birthplace*. The Annenberg Courtyard will host as ever a spectacular display of recent sculpture, this year by Thomas Houseago.

I have made a room of animal art – a menagerie – to pay homage to the first known art. Cave painting. I'm also facing down the hackneyed view of the Summer Exhibition as a showcase for pictures of cats and dogs. Well they are all here this year! Cats, dogs, horses, fish, snakes, and a rhinoceros too. To this end I invited a number of artists whose work I admire, among them Tom Hunter, Polly Morgan and Charles Avery. The menagerie idea morphed coincidentally with Spencer de Grey's theme of architectural sustainability, which in turn morphed serendipitously with Barbara Rae's recent visits to the Arctic and her passion for that landscape. I'd like to claim that this is all part of some grand design but the truth is that these interconnecting themes spread like a small bushfire to the bemusement of the hanging committee. A bit like making art in fact.

Co-ordinating the Summer Exhibition is the curatorial equivalent of action painting and that too is part of the excitement of this most mercurial and important annual exhibition.

FRAGILE

The Black Mailers
Smile
REVELATION CHAMPIONSHIP ROLLAWAY

Wilson
174X125

MY SON CHANGED MY ART. I CAUGHT
ALGORITHM
NEON
26362

UP UP
SIDE SIDE
DOWN
JOIN THE DOTS

COMUNE DI MILANO
Parco Certosa
1

Charles Avery
Untitled (Duculi)
Bronze
H 145 cm

Kenny Hunter
Black Swan
Bronze
H 80 cm

Prof Cathie Pilkington RA
Messenger
Mixed media
H 152 cm

Derrick Guild
Clara with Van Dyck Eye
Oil and chain
135 × 174 cm

Karen Knorr
Brief Encounter, Palazzina Cinese
Pigment print
122 × 152 cm

Fiona Essex
Dog Sitter
Acrylic and pastel
13 × 18 cm

Ian Angus
The Elephant in the Room
C-type print
57 × 90 cm

Peter Jones
Zebra (After Stubbs)
Oil
45 × 45 cm

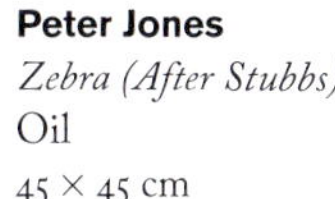

Mieke Douglas
Mesa
Archival print
60 × 84 cm

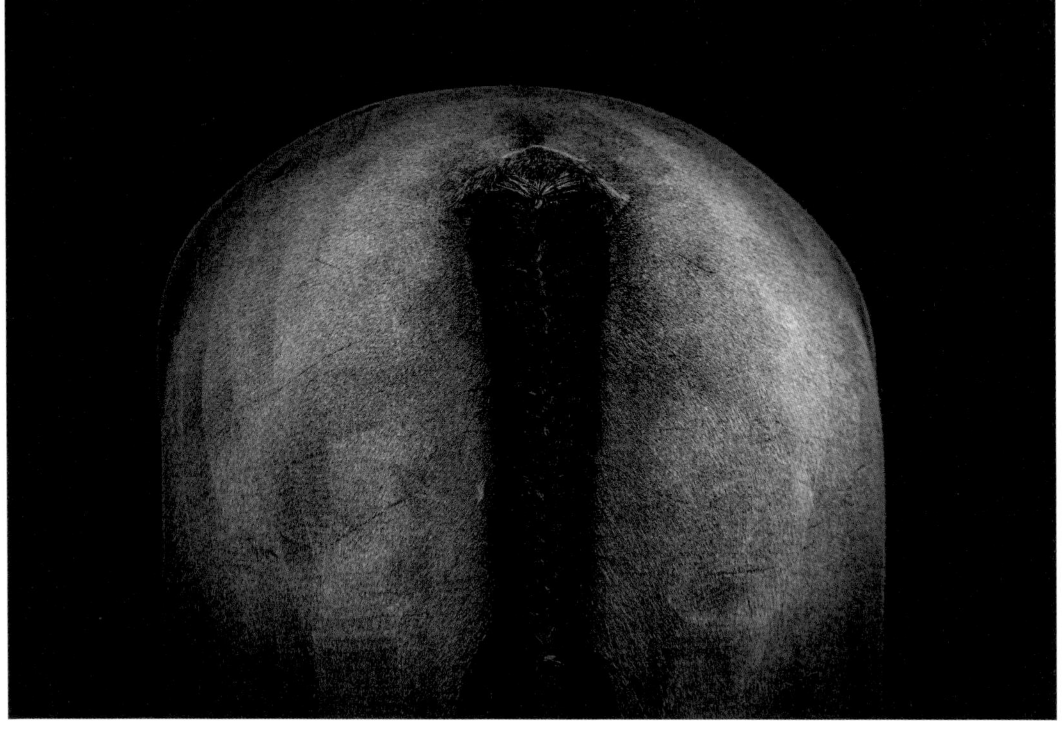

Gillian Singer
Animal
Plaster and paint
14 × 17 cm

Fiona Scott
Pot Dog
Oil
80 × 80 cm

Anna Dickerson
The Robin's Breakfast
Acrylic
25 × 31 cm

Mat Collishaw
Gasconades (Letsdothis)
Pigment and screenprint
53 × 42 cm

Christopher James
Macaw
Acrylic
28 × 16 cm

Kate MccGwire
Viscera
Mixed media
H 180 cm

Terry Setch RA
On the Rocks
Encaustic wax and pigment
25 × 34 cm

Anselm Kiefer Hon RA
Fünf Jahre Lebte Vainamoinen auf der Unbekannten Insel auf dem Baumlosen Land
Mixed media
280 × 380 cm

Marc Atkins
Aimless 105
C-type archival print
76 × 102 cm

Peter Abrahams
Pears on a Newspaper
Archival pigment print
77 × 115 cm

Jock McFadyen RA
Poor Mother
Oil
151 × 211 cm

Andrew Hardwick
Moor, Valley and Distant Heavy Black Smoke
Mixed media
91 × 214 cm

Hannah Collins
Nelson Mandela's Teenage Home, National Monument
Pigment print
244 × 350 cm

John McLean
Tocsin
Acrylic
130 × 100 cm

Trevor Sutton
Atelier
Oil
92 × 198 cm

Tess Jaray RA
Promise
Acrylic
178 × 142 cm

Dr David Tindle RA
My Birthday Flowers
Acrylic
69 × 61 cm

Ken Howard OBE RA
New York
Oil
31 × 31 cm

Jeffery Camp RA
Viper's Bugloss at Beachy Head
Pencil and watercolour
38 × 48 cm

Diana Armfield RA
Sheep Up the Nant Hir
Oil
38 × 37 cm

David Hepher
Hey Wayne on the Meath Estate
Mixed media
285 × 502 cm

Anthony Whishaw RA
Flower Piece
Acrylic collage
101 × 101 cm

Basil Beattie RA
Flaming Ladder (Ladder Series)
Oil and wax
155 × 125 cm

James Butler MBE RA
Sir Bobby Moore
Bronze
H 56 cm

Hugh Mendes
Obituary: Joshua Reynolds
Oil
35 × 25 cm

Tom Phillips CBE RA
Pale Fire
Pastel
76 × 62 cm

Frederick Cuming Hon D Litt RA
Fowey Estuary, Dawn
Oil
51 × 61 cm

Olwyn Bowey RA
Cardoons
Oil
84 × 80 cm

Anthony Eyton RA
Horse on Piano
Oil
33 × 51 cm

Bill Jacklin RA
Dance of the Clouds and Breezes with Dog
Oil
127 × 140 cm

Isaac Julien CBE RA
The Miracle (Radioactive Avatar #14)
Inkjet print and foil
84 × 60 cm

Ishbel Myerscough
Lily and Quaye
Oil
123 × 158 cm

LLERY

CONNECTIONS
CCCS

Tracey Emin CBE RA
I Just Wanted to Sleep with You
Bronze
11 × 14 × 37 cm

Hugh Buchanan
Goldsmiths Bench
Watercolour
38 × 74 cm

Fiona Banner RA aka The Vanity Press
Full Stop Seascape; Klang, Courier, Nuptial
Graphite
24 × 30 cm

Bill Woodrow RA
Untitled
Woodcut
107 × 78 cm

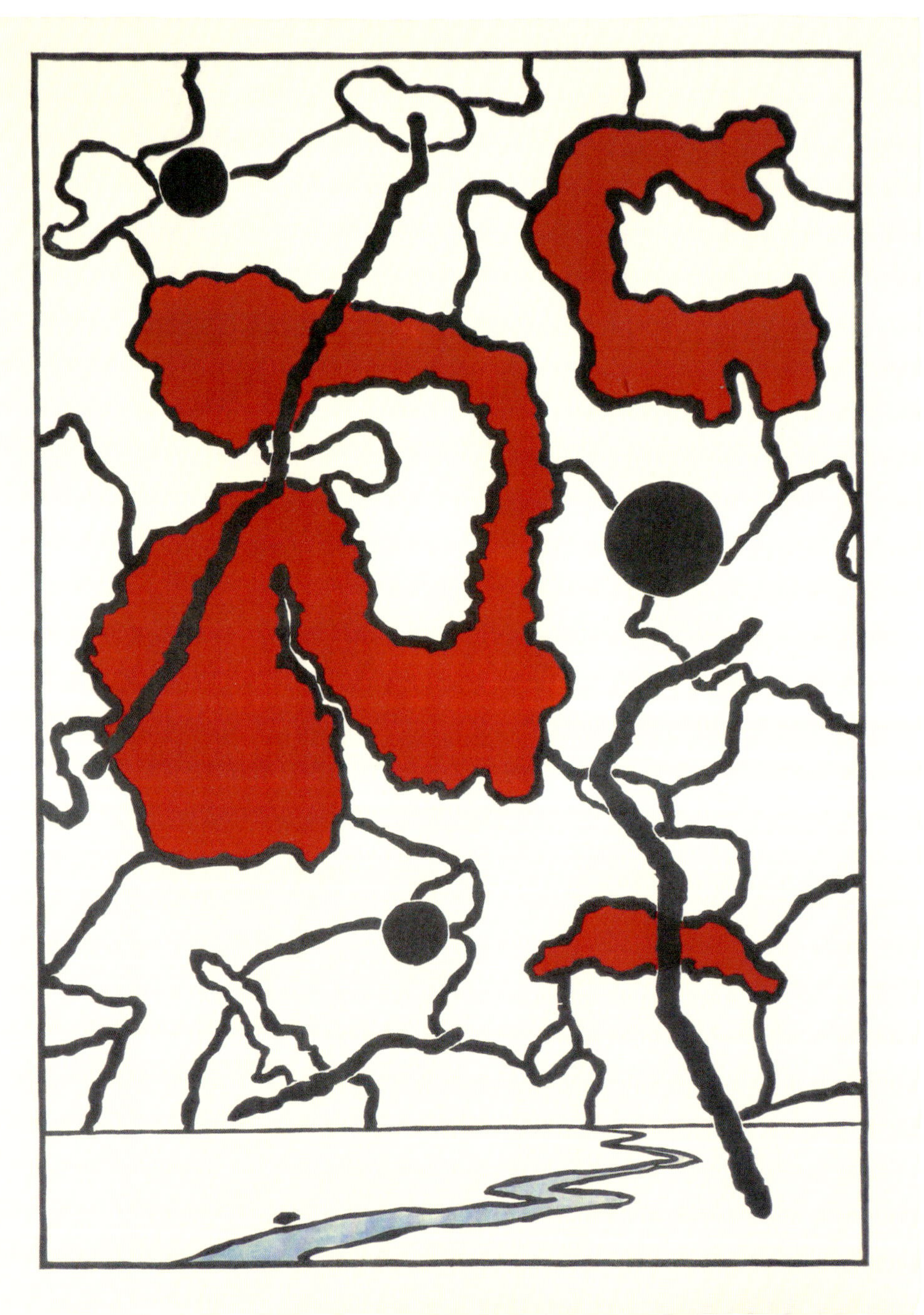

Jason Barron
Graffiti Standard with Socket
Digital print
46 × 94 cm

Katarzyna Green
Hungover
Masking tape
40 × 50 cm

Prof El Anatsui Hon RA
Untitled
Ink and gold leaf
132 × 132 cm

Prof Bryan Kneale MBE RA
Untitled – Black on Grey Wash
Acrylic
100 × 70 cm

William Tucker RA
Marist VIII
Monotype with charcoal
50 × 32 cm

Martin Pover
Carceri. Tiergarten Berlin
Photographic print
100 × 100 cm

Dorothy Cross
Medusae III
Luminescent print
38 × 60 cm

David Remfry MBE RA
Chandelirium
Oil
76 × 76 cm

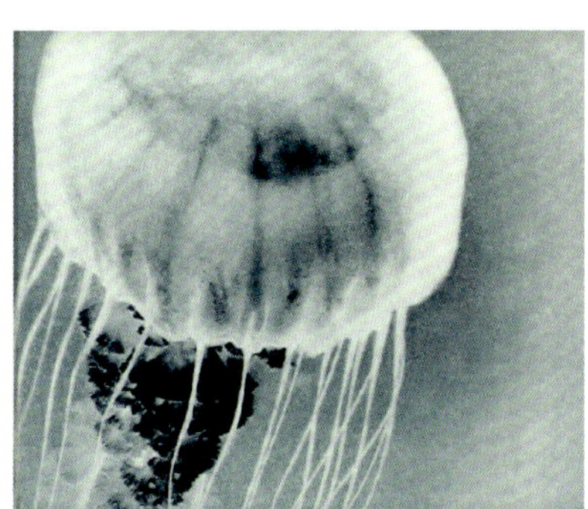

Sir Michael Craig-Martin CBE RA
Savarin Can
Digital inkjet print
42 × 30 cm

Alfred Griffiths
Mars Bar
Pen, ink, watercolour and pencil
20 × 30 cm

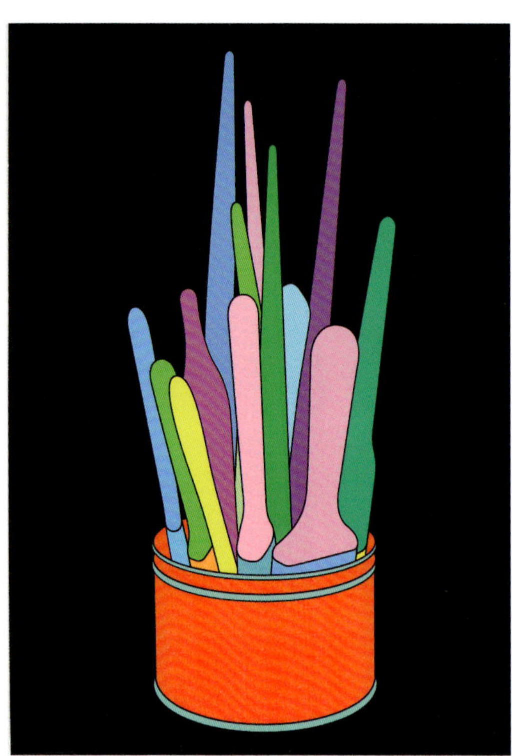

Richard Deacon CBE RA
For Michael
Wood
H 84 cm

Zatorski + Zatorski
The Dream of the Pearl Diver's Widow
Giclée print
94 × 115 cm

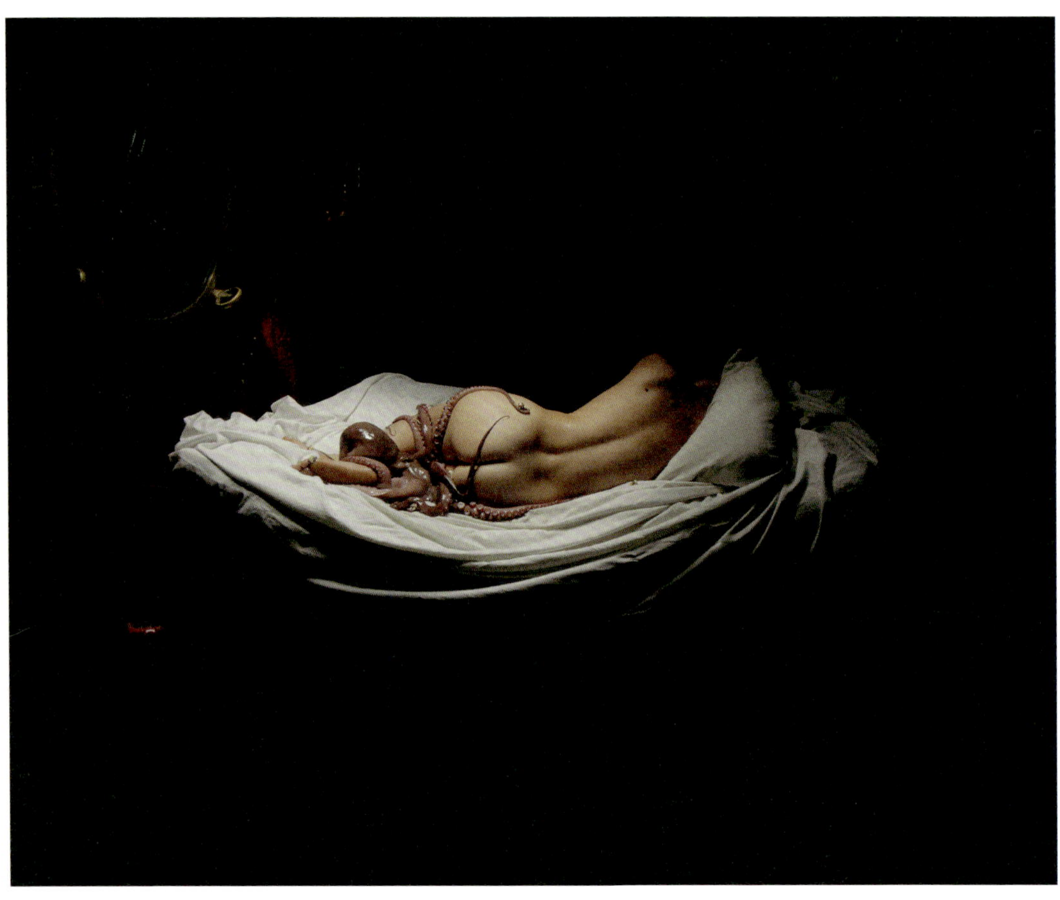

Richard Woods
Delightfully Landscaped Gardens
Screenprint and woodblock
64 × 86 cm

Prof Phyllida Barlow CBE RA
untitled: catch; 2019
Hessian scrim, paint, plaster, PVA and steel
46 × 40 × 35 cm

Cathy Lewis
Orlando
Marble
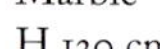
H 120 cm

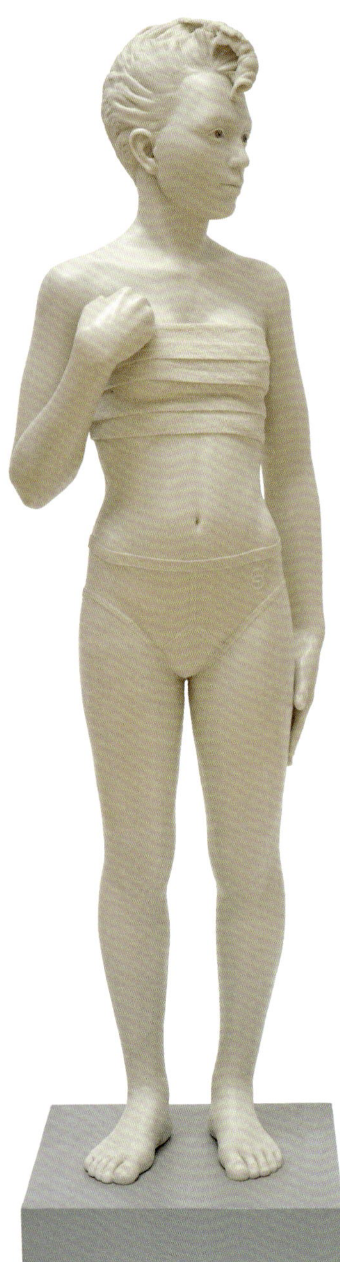

Richard Wilson RA
Red Shells
Wood, metal and formica
H 104 cm

Peter Randall-Page RA
Entomology VII
Aquatint
33 × 24 cm

Luke Caulfield
Performance Documentation
Chris Burden Shout Piece
Oil
150 × 110 cm

Ksenija Vucinic
A Portrait of a Couple – Part 2
Acrylic
50 × 70 cm

Sarah Ball
Self (II)
Oil
100 × 100 cm

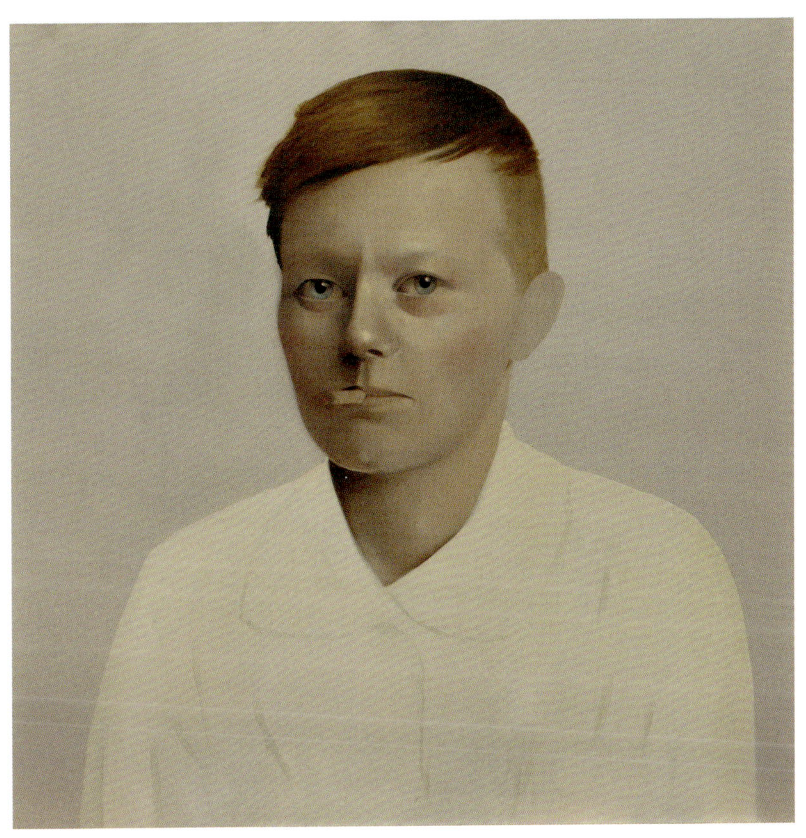

Wolfgang Tillmans RA
Liam and TM Jumping Up the Cliff
Inket print
206 × 138 cm

William Marsden
Anthon Raimund
Photographic print
178 × 127 cm

Fabian Peake
Torque at the Edge
Oil
84 × 117 cm

Cristina Rosa-Cervelló
Don't Forget Venezuela (Diptych) (detail)
C-type print
40 × 59 cm

Daniel Libeskind Hon RA
Occitanie Tower, Aerial
Digital print
33 × 48 cm

Prof Sir Peter Cook RA
Walled Village
Print from ink and watercolour
40 × 50 cm

Sir David Adjaye OBE RA
IFC, Dakar, Senegal
Digital print
119 × 84 cm

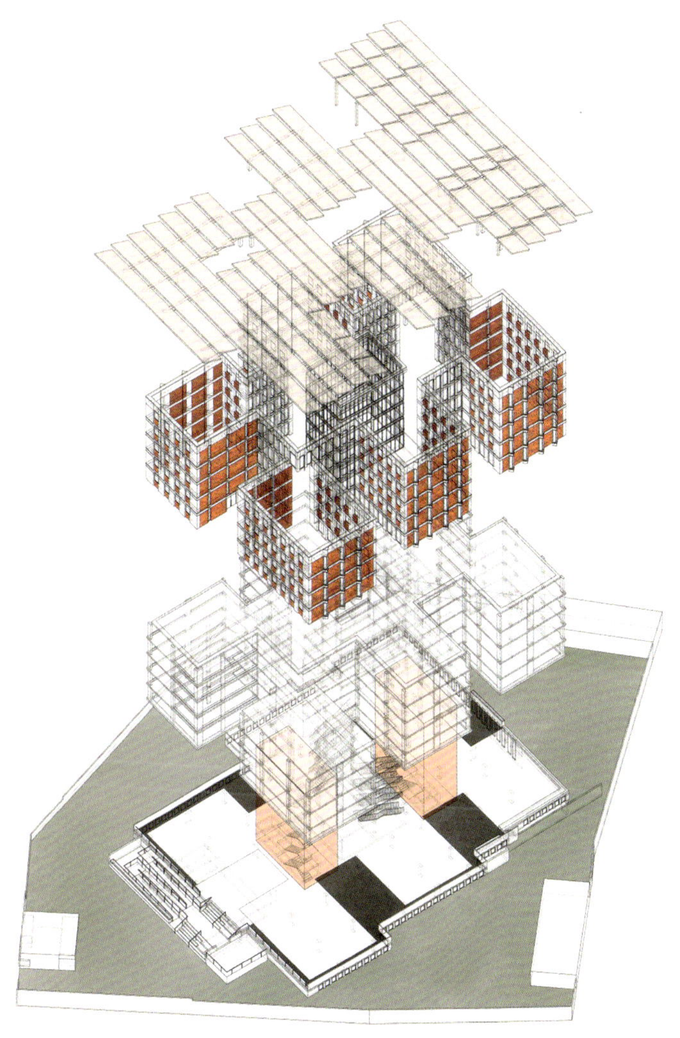

Spencer de Grey CBE RA
Amaravati High Court Complex, India
Pulpboard and SLA print
H 34 cm

Lord Foster of Thames Bank OM RA
Snowdon Aviary, London Zoo
Timber and acrylic
H 32 cm

Piers Gough CBE RA
Arterial Road
Plywood and Perspex
H 20 cm

Edward Cullinan CBE RA
Straight from the Wood
Hand-drawn digital print
42 × 59 cm

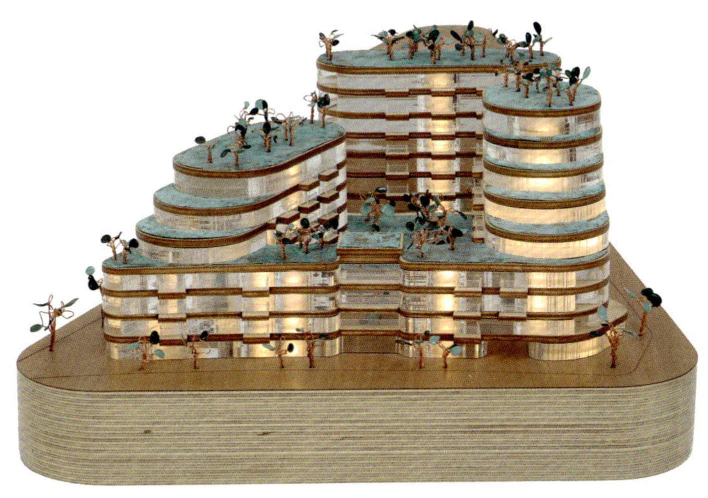

Alex Flint
Silver River House
Mixed media
H 35 cm

Studio MUTT and Roger Zogolovitch
Pottering Shed
Mixed media
H 20 cm

Chun Ting Ki
Yen Town – The Last Unpolluted Territory
Digital print
137 × 102 cm

円都総図

Paul Koralek CBE RA
Roofs in Camden
Pencil
14 × 20 cm

Eric Parry RA
Cambridge Assessment Initial Massing Model
Timber
H 19 cm

Prof Trevor Dannatt OBE RA
'ARE U DEAF?' 'WOT ME?'
Collage
32 × 47 cm

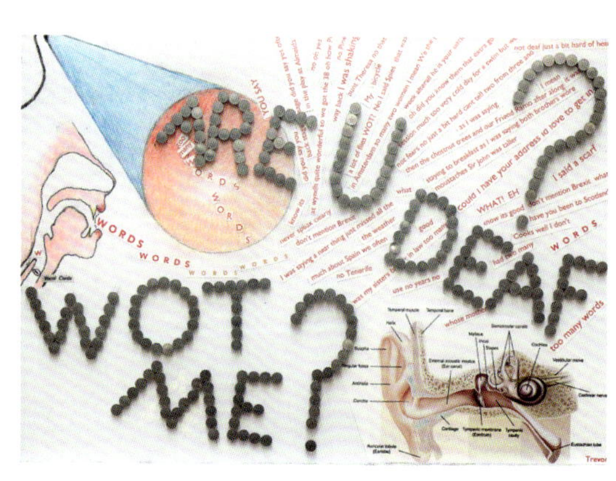

Eva Jiricna CBE RA
Living with Waves
Photograph
46 × 65 cm

Caruso St John Architects
Bremer Landesbank, Bremen
Photograph
60 × 70 cm

Thomas Heatherwick CBE RA
UK Pavilion Rods with Seeds from the Millennium Seed Bank at Kew in Cardboard Box
Acrylic and seeds
H 33 cm

Lord Rogers of Riverside CH RA
The Leadenhall Building
Acrylic
H 142 cm

Prof Gordon Benson OBE RA
Graphic Topography B
Digital print
80 × 60 cm

Prof Chris Wilkinson OBE RA
Proposed New Compton and Edrich Stands at Lord's for MCC
Acrylic, model board and stainless steel
H 31 cm

Louisa Hutton OBE RA and Matthias Sauerbruch (Sauerbruch Hutton)
M9, Mestre
Fine-art print
38 × 64 cm

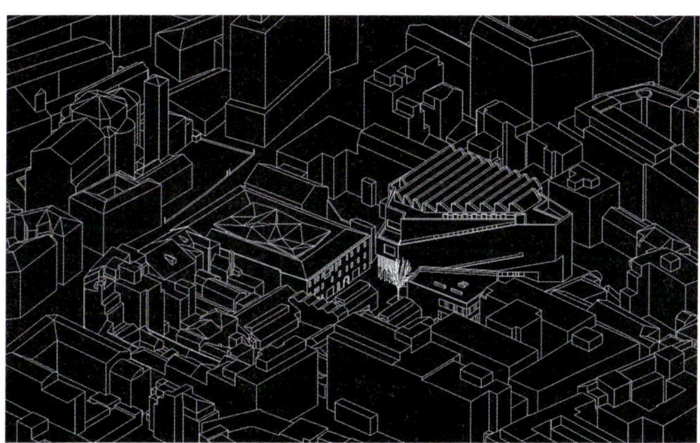

Senator Renzo Piano Hon RA

Emergency Children's Surgery Centre, Entebbe, Uganda
Digital drawing
84 × 119 cm

Ahmad Angawi with Stanton Williams

Three Letter Studies for the British Museum Albukhary Foundation Gallery of the Islamic World
Giclée print
60 × 30 cm

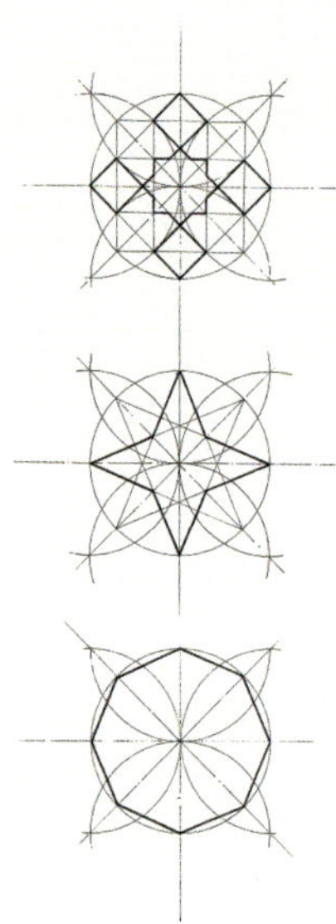

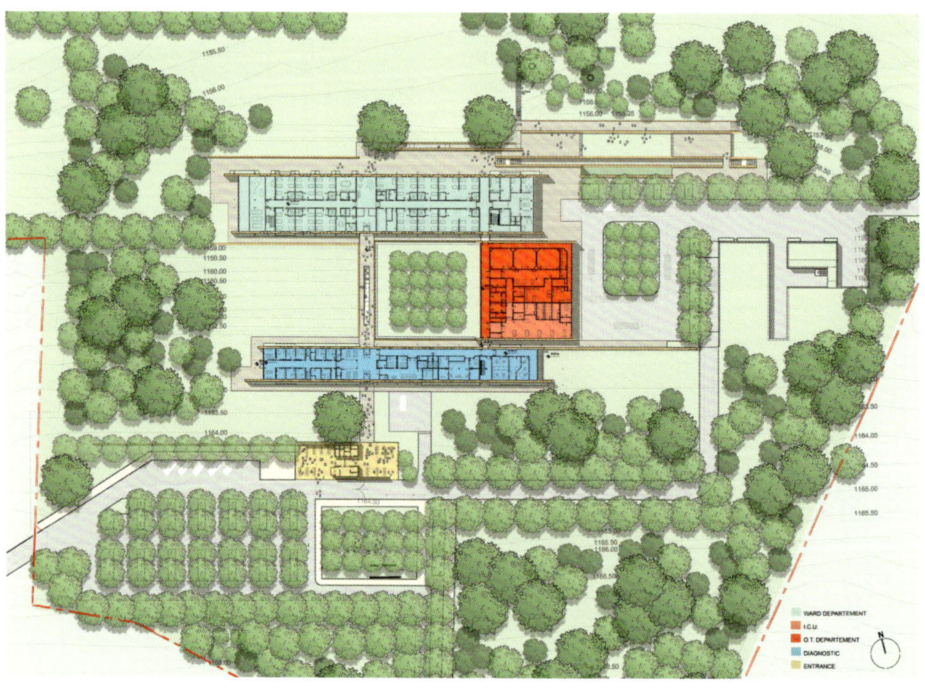

Sir Nicholas Grimshaw CBE PPRA
Terra World Expo 2020 Sustainability Pavilion
Timber and plastic
H 37 cm

Sir Michael Hopkins CBE RA
Smith Campus Center, Harvard University
Timber and plastic
H 50 cm

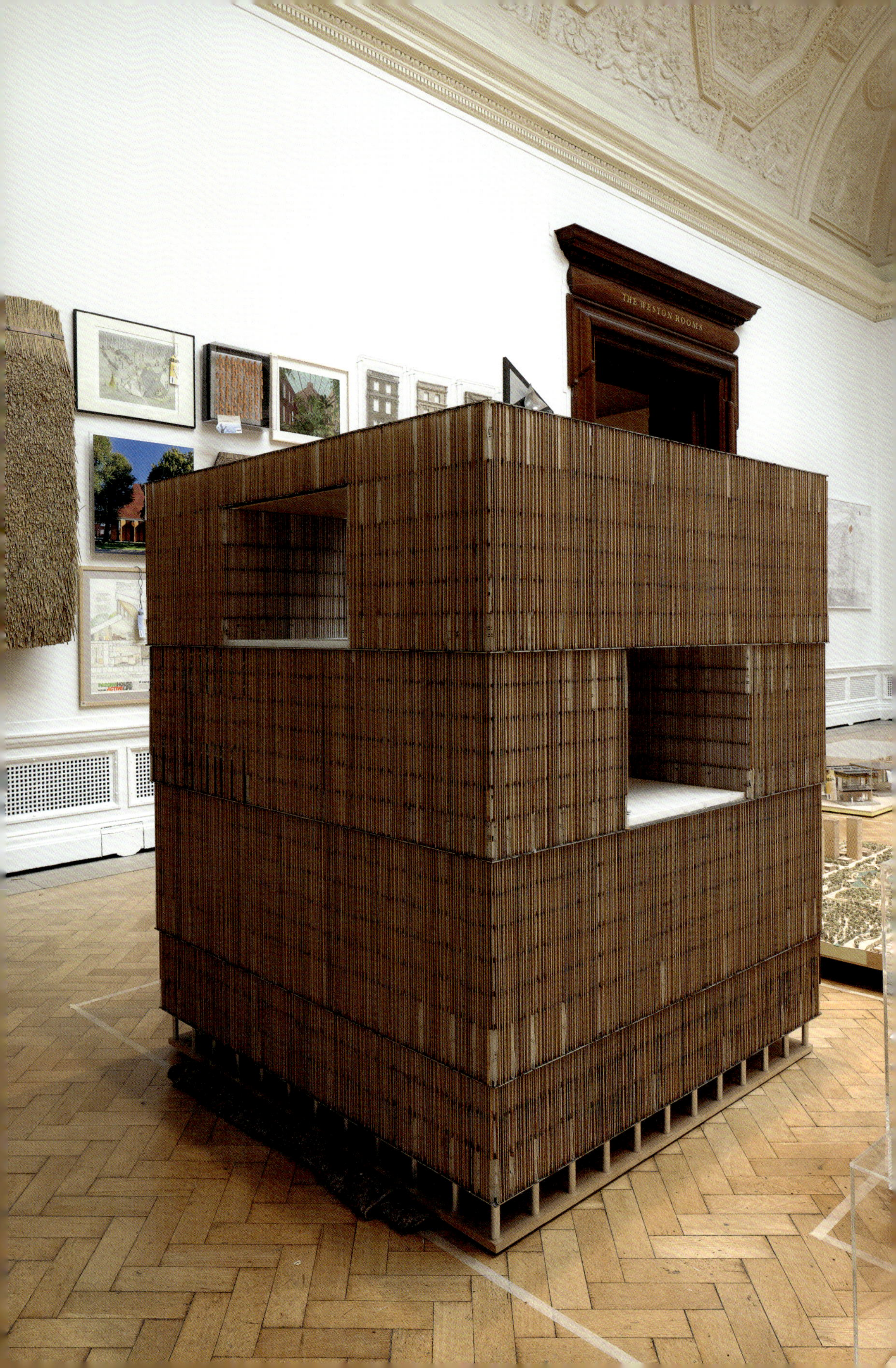
THE WESTON ROOMS

James Turrell Hon RA
MORS-SOMNUS (07),
Medium Diamond Glass
Glass and L.E.D.
137 × 137 cm

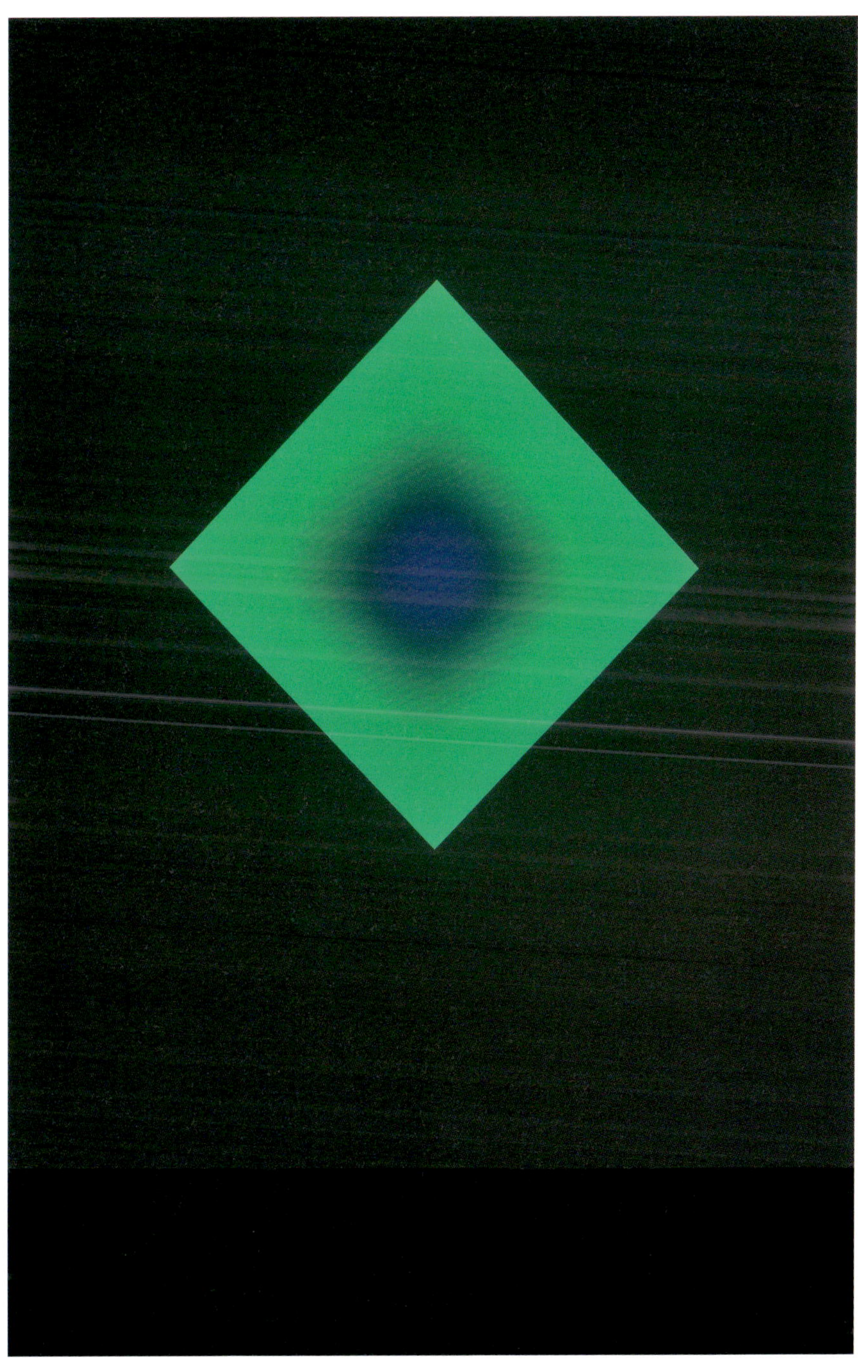

Mick Moon RA
Anticipating
Mixed media
122 × 122 cm

Prof Michael Sandle RA
Hymns Ancient and Modern
Ink
97 × 147 cm

Stuart Mackenzie
Species: Coelacanth (Diptych) (detail)
Monotype
100 × 175 cm

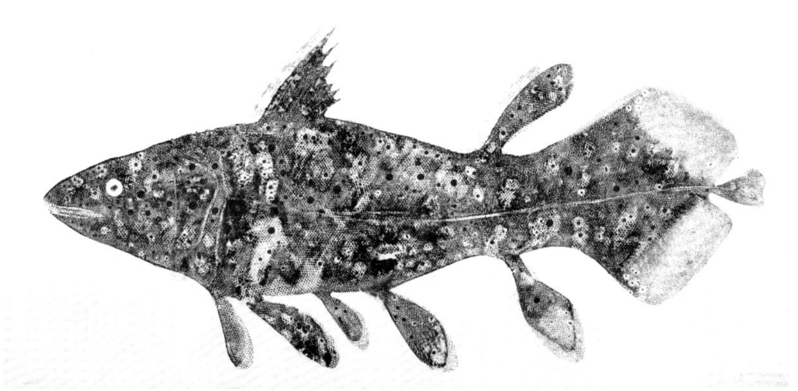

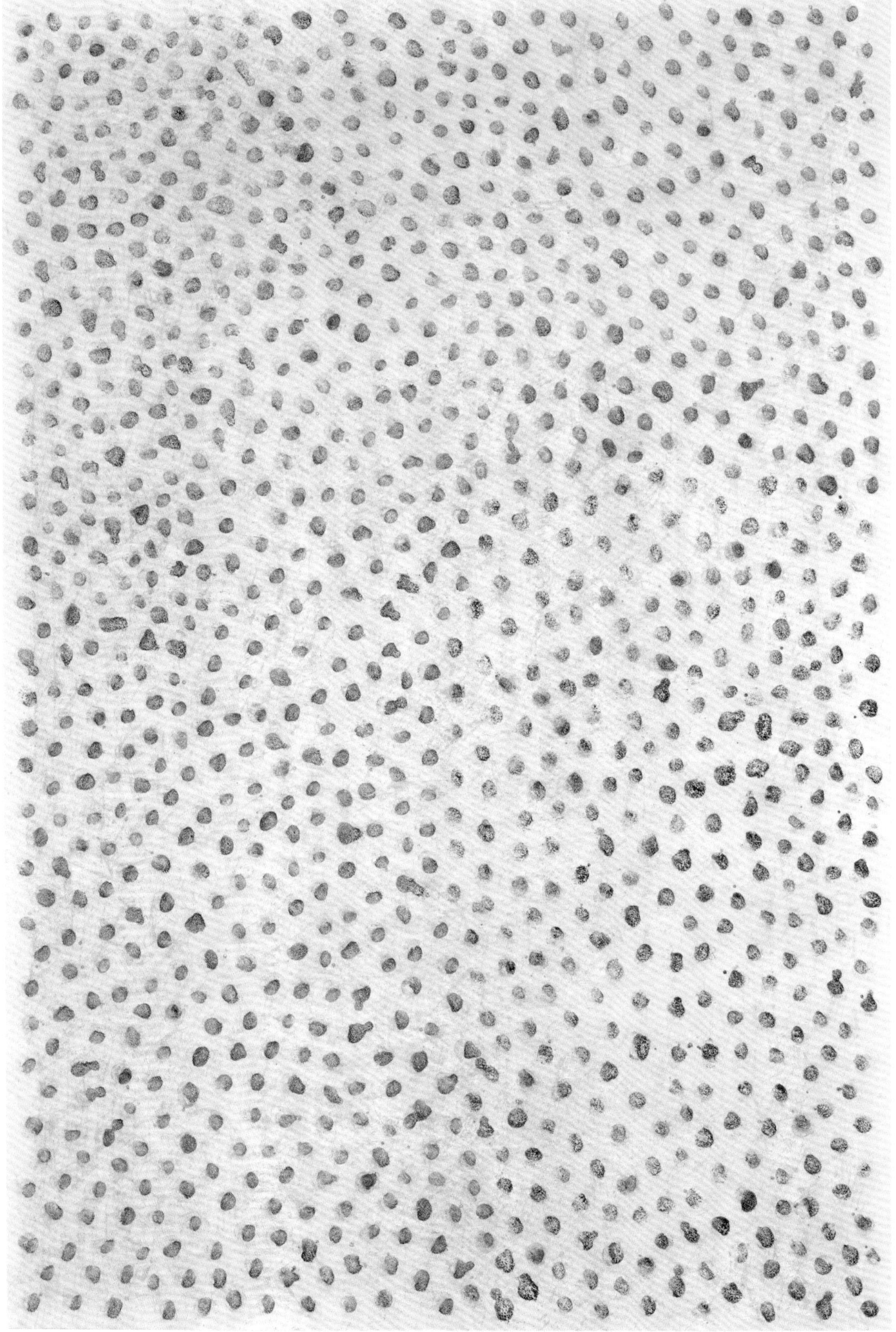

Rebecca Salter RA
Untitled AR2
Mixed media
142 × 98 cm

David Nash OBE RA
Blue Tree
Pigment
66 × 88 cm

Dr Barbara Rae CBE RA
Ilulissat
Mixed media
183 × 183 cm

Nicholas Jones
An Austere Beauty, Iceberg Off Cape Mercy, Baffin Island
Acrylic
138 × 138 cm

Claudia Legge
Ice Road
Photograph
72 × 89 cm

Covadonga Valdes
Arch 2
Oil
50 × 60 cm

Prof Ian Ritchie CBE RA
Steness Stones 18
Woodcut
55 × 55 cm

Charlotte Knox
Canvey Island
Watercolour
56 × 76 cm

Jim Dine Hon RA
The Artichokes
Lithograph
104 × 79 cm

Prof Humphrey Ocean RA

Sparrow
Gouache
46 × 72 cm

Moorhen
Gouache
46 × 72 cm

Black-headed Gull
Gouache
46 × 72 cm

Dunnock
Gouache
46 × 72 cm

Tim Shaw RA

Raven I
Photopolymer etching
33 × 28 cm

Sir Richard Long CBE RA
Spring Tide
Screenprint
102 × 72 cm

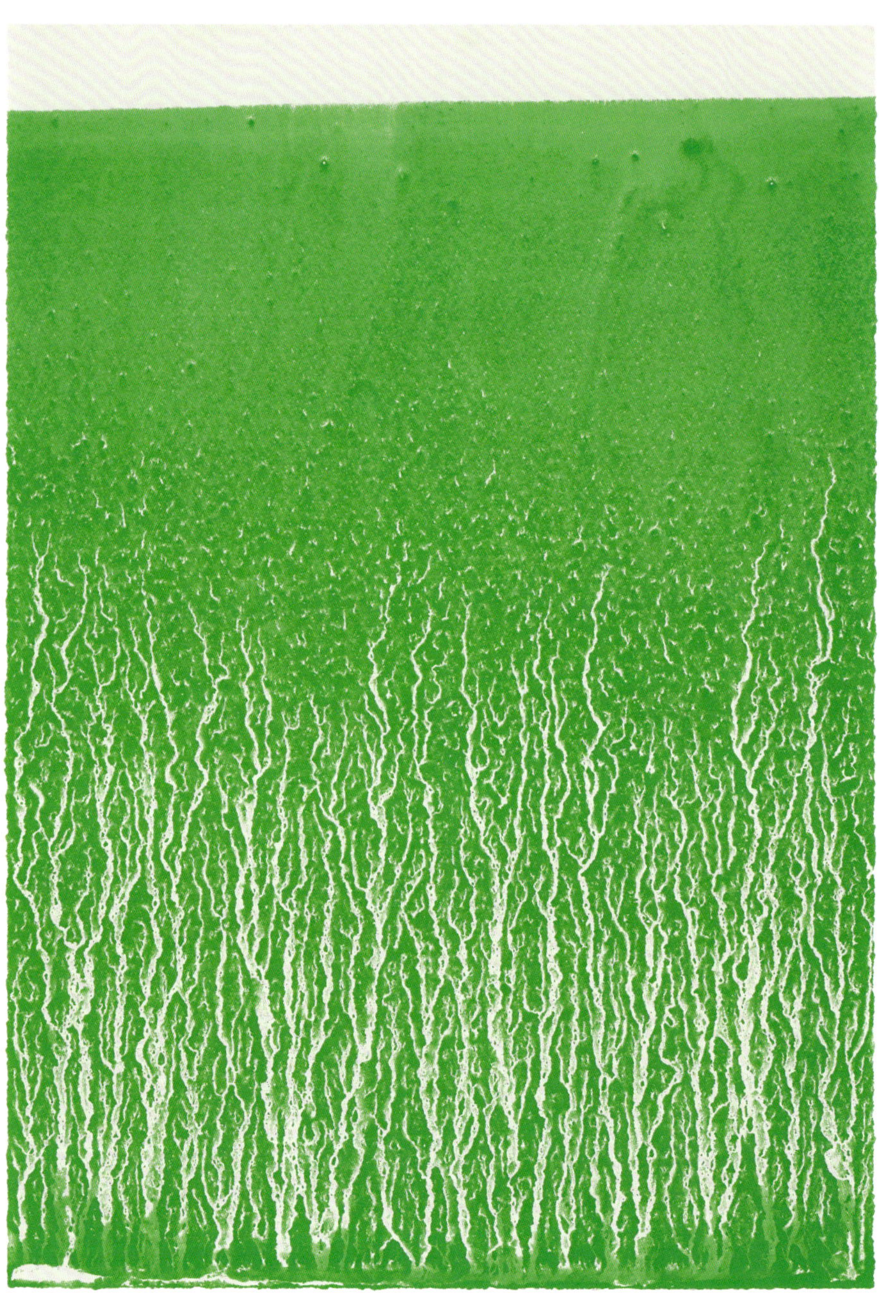

Antony Gormley RA
Release I
Etching
34 × 27 cm

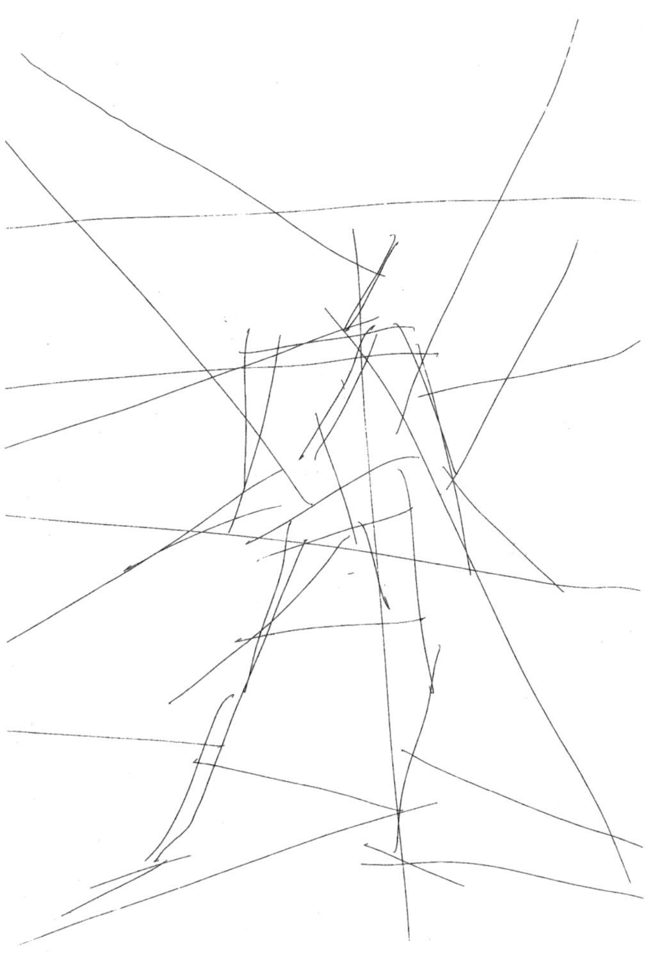

Cornelia Parker OBE RA
Poison and Antidote Drawing
Rattlesnake venom,
anti-venom and ink
61 × 61 cm

Emma Stibbon RA
Caldera Overlook
Woodcut
214 × 372 cm

hunting
the
noumenon

Adrian Wiszniewski
Crail III
Laser woodcut
89 × 85 cm

Gary Hume RA
School House
Lithograph
99 × 64 cm

Timothy Hyman RA
Ezekiel Draws the City
Acrylic
153 × 238 cm

Peter Darach
The Wishing Tree
Oil
244 × 305 cm

Louise Soloway Chan
Drawing with Timothy Hyman RA
Ink and pen
31 × 21 cm

Alexander Gilmour
Drawing of Jeffery Camp RA
Graphite
30 × 21 cm

Frances Borden
SP05
Oil
18 × 13 cm

Paul Fenner
Toussaint in the Undergrowth
Oil
91 × 61 cm

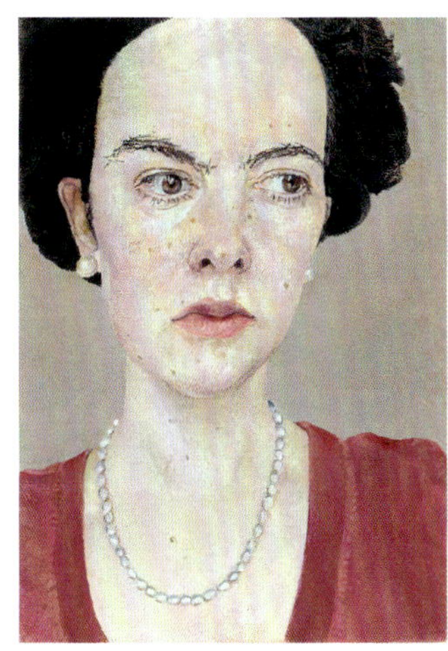

Nathan Cash Davidson
The Archer
Oil
210 × 120 cm

Prof Brian Catling RA
Unshriven with Company
Egg tempera
30 × 30 cm

Mick Rooney RA
Children of the Storm
Gouache and tempera
29 × 53 cm

Anthony Green RA
Mary Cozens-Walkers' World
Oil
170 × 167 cm

Prof Chris Orr MBE RA
Albert and the Mudlarks
Engraving
56 × 76 cm

Philip Sutton RA
Hello Don Quixote
Oil
102 × 102 cm

The late Dr Leonard McComb RA
Verrocchio Village, Tuscany
Watercolour
42 × 52 cm

Dame Elizabeth Blackadder DBE RA
Orchidaceae Laeliocattleya Chinco 'La Tuilerie'
Etching
60 × 52 cm

Melissa Kime
Superman Has Delivered!
Oil
140 × 110 cm

Sonia Lawson RA
Homage to Courbet
Oil
92 × 72 cm

Michael Ajerman
Conversation
Oil
61 × 76 cm

Eugenie Vronskaya
Self-portrait as an African
Oil
68 × 51 cm

Su Blackwell
Cutters and Smugglers
Mixed media
H 29 cm

Claire Douglass
The Garden of Earthly Delights
Acrylic
123 × 257 cm

Neil Bousfield
The Last Laugh
Relief engraving
23 × 32 cm

Lesley Hilling
Natural History
Mixed media
30 × 18 cm

Roy Willingham
Southwark Arch, Expansion II
Paper, card and wood
22 × 17 cm

Anne Desmet RA
Seems Like Heaven
Linocut, lithograph and monotype
33 × 33 cm

Rachel Heller
Untitled
Crayon
65 × 52 cm

Isabel Rock
Lucky Sailor
Woodblock and acrylic ink
120 × 150 cm

Grace McMurray
George Michael
Glitter and velvet ribbon
41 × 31 cm

Emily Allchurch
Babel Britain (After Verhaecht)
Transparency on L.E.D. lightbox
130 × 142 cm

Veta Gorner
The Edge of All Extremity
Lithograph
48 × 38 cm

Peter Ford
Urban Archaeology 4
Relief print
38 × 61 cm

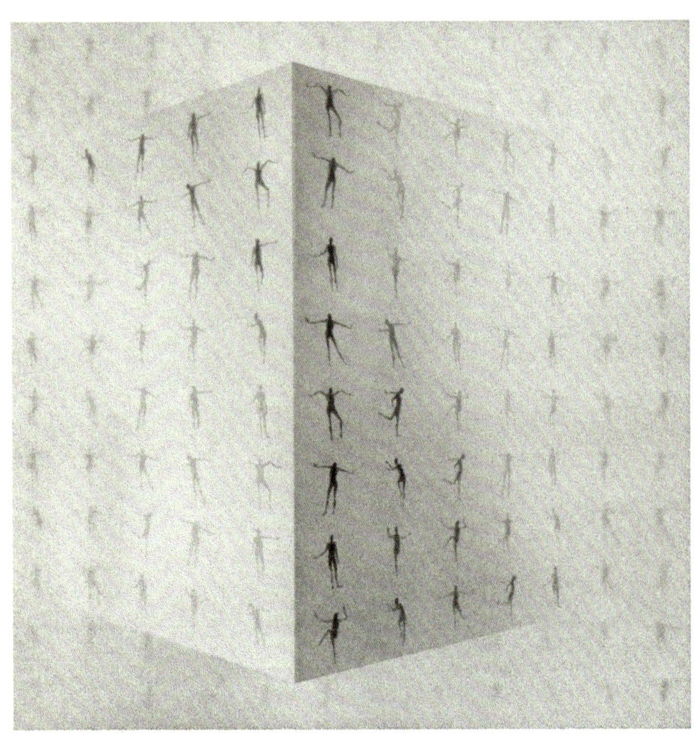

Prof Norman Ackroyd CBE RA
The Pool of London
Etching
14 × 16 cm

Peter Freeth RA
Evening in the Suburbs
Aquatint
20 × 15 cm

John Maine RA
Epicentre
Whinstone
H 170 cm

Tomma Abts
Untitled (Diptych)
Watercolour
Each 30 × 21 cm

Thomas Joshua Cooper
St Kessog, Looking North, Loch Lomond, A Teaching Site, Inchtavannach, Argyllshire, Scotland. St Kessog was the First Patron Saint of Scotland (460–520 CE)
Silver gelatin print
40 × 47 cm

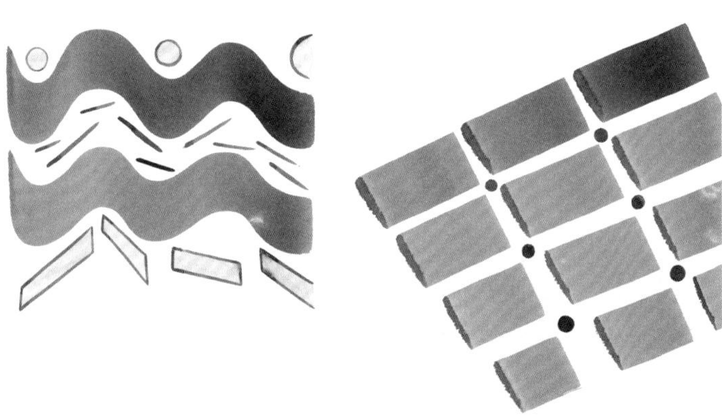

Kenneth Draper RA
Ocean
Mixed media
70 × 70 cm

Ron Arad RA
D.F.W.T.M. 2
Glass fibre and polyester gelcoat
H 84 cm

Nigel Hall RA
Drawing 1781
Acrylic and charcoal
80 × 70 cm

Prof Alison Wilding OBE RA
Midas
Wood, wire and paint
18 × 25 cm

ART MAKES CHILDREN POWERFUL
TWO ROADS DIVERGED IN
UP UP
TAKE IT AROUND
SIDE SIDE
AND AROUND
DOWN
JOIN THE DOTS

MY SON CHANGED MY ART. I
MY 4 YEAR OLD SON MAKING A
SAID WHATS THAT? HE SAID
DRAWING DAD. I DRAW A LOOP
LINE THROUGH THE LOOP THEN ON TO THE
AND SO ON UNTIL I HAVE
PAGE. I SAID WOW THATS
YOU HAVE CREATE AN
A RECIPE. AN INSTRUCTION,
FRENCH WOULD CALL IT A
HE SAID IF YOU LIKE THAT
LOVE THIS

Frank Bowling OBE RA
Ella and Her Mum Zoe's Visit
Mixed media
238 × 290 cm

Paul Crook
Orange Stairway
Acrylic
95 × 125 cm

Mali Morris RA
Ghost
Acrylic
200 × 220 cm

Jason Thompson
Armoury
Enamel paint
76 × 66 cm

Eileen Cooper OBE RA
Reach
Woodcut
27 × 19 cm

Jessica Voorsanger
Eye of the Tiger
Mixed media
102 × 81 cm

Murae Van Reede Van Oudtshoorn
Memory in Motion
Platinum palladium print
60 × 47 cm

Bob and Roberta Smith OBE RA
The Blue and Orange Amazing Painting
Signwriters' paint and acrylic
56 × 46 cm

Prof Paul Huxley RA
Joseph's Coat
Acrylic
239 × 239 cm

Jennifer Durrant RA
Ghirlanda Series: White Strip
Acrylic
112 × 152 cm

Vanessa Jackson RA
Passing Light
Oil
183 × 152 cm

John Wragg RA
Looking Out
Acrylic
76 × 60 cm

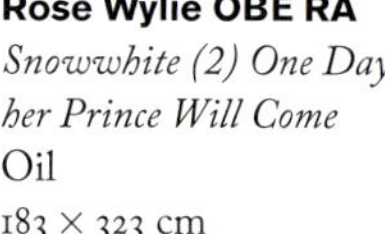

Rose Wylie OBE RA
Snowwhite (2) One Day her Prince Will Come
Oil
183 × 323 cm

SOMEDAY
WILL
COME
7
14
SOME
WILL

Christopher Le Brun PRA
D1
Oil
150 × 105 cm

Tony Bevan RA
Self-portrait (PC191)
Acrylic and charcoal
162 × 302 cm

Ian Davenport
Bluebonnet
Acrylic
200 × 200 cm

Joe Tilson RA
The Stones of Venice, La Campana di San Marco
Mixed media
122 × 113 cm

Audrey Grant
Woman IX
Oil
30 × 25 cm

Prof Chantal Joffe RA
Night Self-portrait
Oil
28 × 21 cm

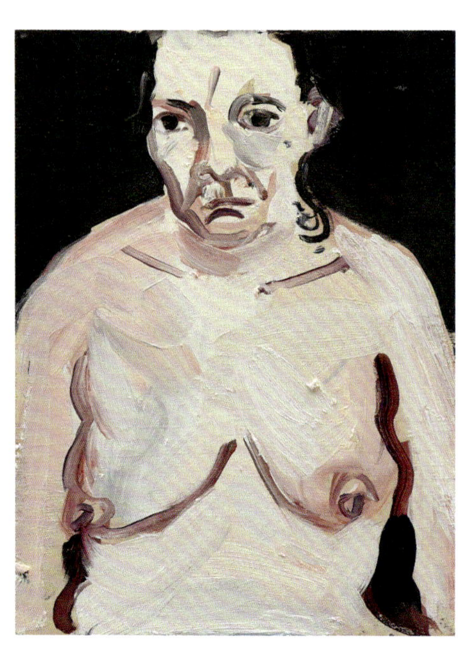

Hughie O'Donoghue RA
Yellow Man
Carborundum
79 × 107 cm

Stephen Chambers RA
Portrait of Agatha Roman
Oil
58 × 48 cm

Simon Burton
Fleet an' Candleleet
Oil
220 × 195 cm

Lisa Milroy RA
Dip
Oil and acrylic
217 × 276 cm

Allen Jones RA
Kind of Blue
Mixed media
H 244 cm

Conrad Shawcross RA
Fracture (R14C14)
Bronze
H 145 cm

Ann Christopher RA
Light Shadow
Bronze and neoprene
H 20 cm

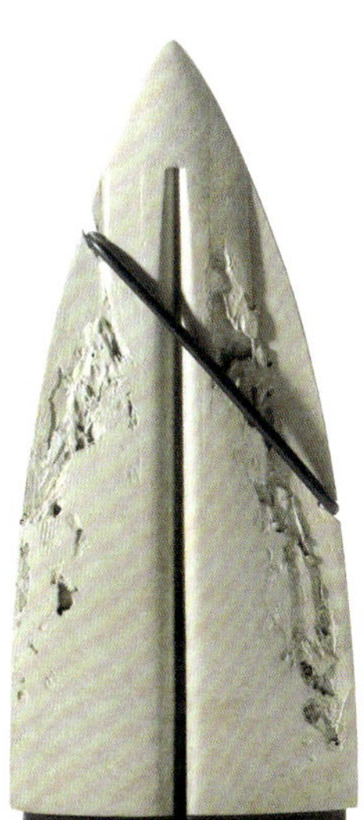

Simon Read
Wild Goose Chase, Waldringfield
Watercolour, ink and pencil
134 × 76 cm

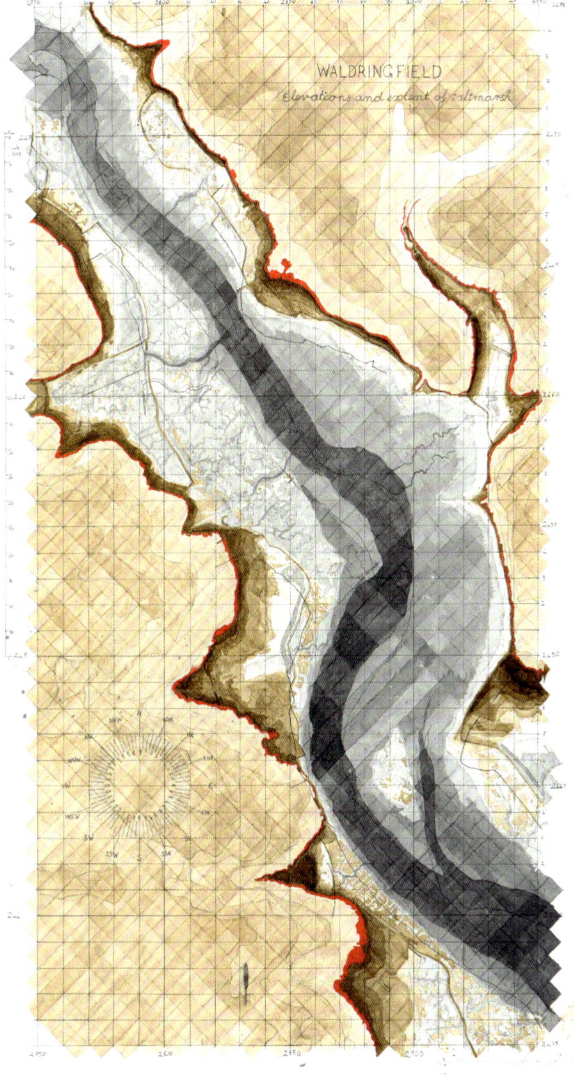

Neil Jeffries RA
The Green Lion
Aluminium
H 145 cm

Andrew Burton
Parrot
Ceramic
H 46 cm

Prof Dhruva Mistry CBE RA
Little B
Paint and stainless steel
H 44 cm

Robbie Fife
The Release
Acrylic and watercolour
33 × 25 cm

Mach Brothers
Easy Tiger
Resin and foil
H 115 cm

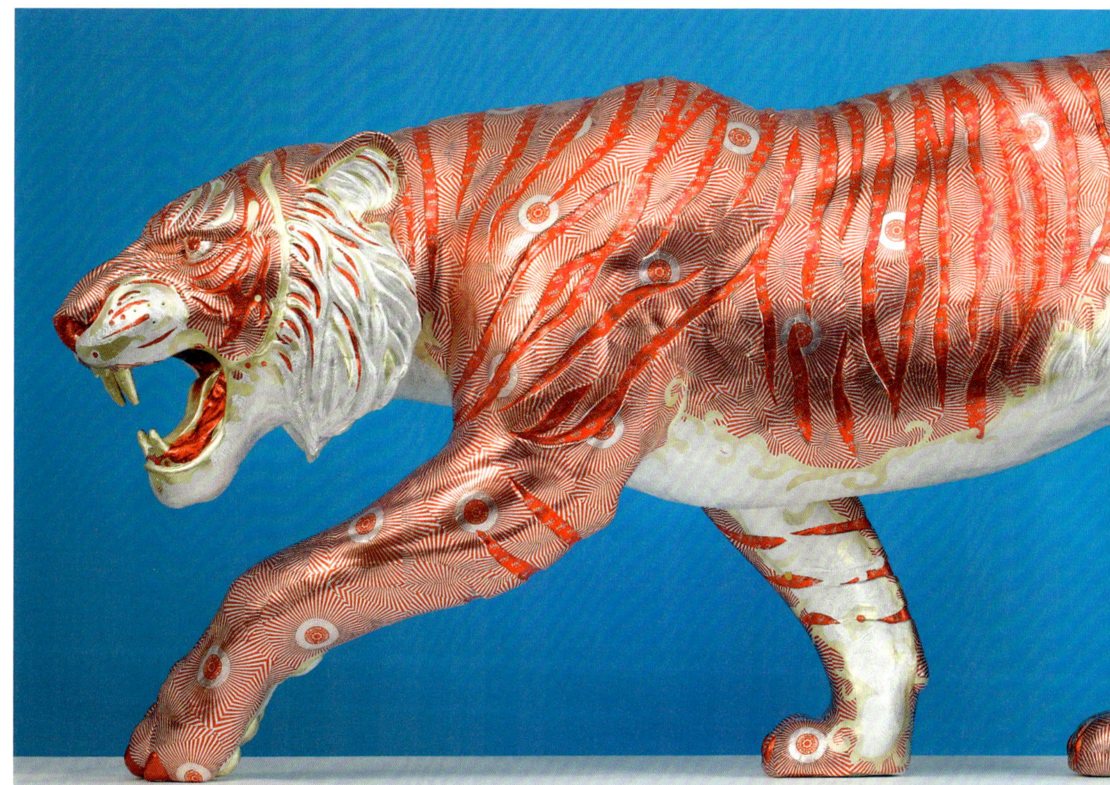

Timothy Blewitt
Sotar Rua
Mixed media
H 122 cm

Prof Stephen Farthing RA
The Miracle of Flight
Acrylic
171 × 201 cm

Georgia Peskett
Untitled (Commuter)
Oil
30 × 30 cm

Dame Paula Rego DBE RA
Death of the Virgin
Pastel
76 × 70 cm

Prof Phillip King CBE PPRA
Soh-Am-Moon
Mixed media
H 85 cm

John Carter RA
Tectonic Plates (For A. H.)
Acrylic and marble powder
90 × 80 cm

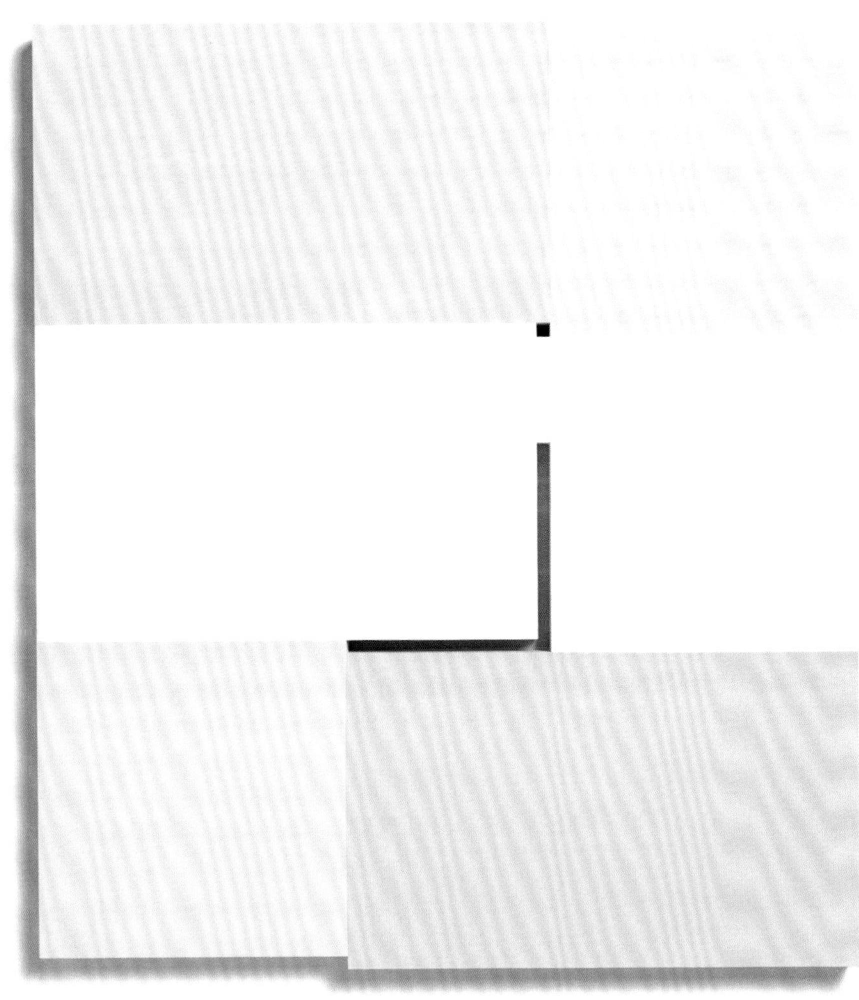

Georg Baselitz Hon RA
Elke VIII
Engraving, drypoint and aquatint
85 × 65 cm

Jayne Smith
Crosscurrent
Acrylic and oil
20 × 20 cm

Mimmo Paladino Hon RA
Untitled
Bronze
H 277 cm

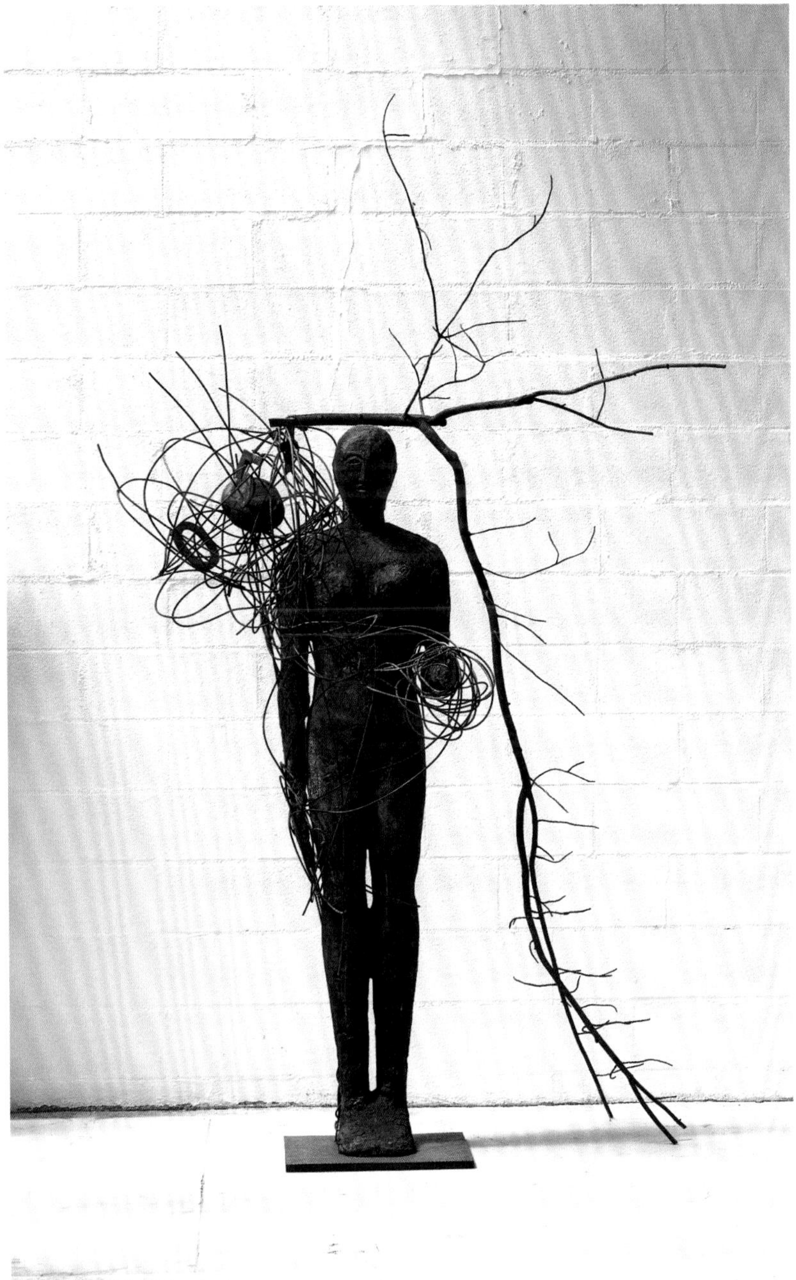

Index

Royal Academy of Arts in London, 2019

Registered charity number 1125383

Officers

President: Christopher Le Brun PRA
Keeper: Rebecca Salter RA
Treasurer: Chris Wilkinson OBE RA
Secretary and Chief Executive: Axel Rüger

Past Presidents

Sir Nicholas Grimshaw CBE PPRA
Prof Phillip King CBE PPRA

Senior Royal Academicians

Prof Norman Ackroyd CBE
Diana Armfield
Basil Beattie
Dame Elizabeth Blackadder DBE
Olwyn Bowey
Frank Bowling OBE
James Butler MBE
Jeffery Camp
John Carter
Prof Sir Peter Cook
Sir Michael Craig-Martin CBE
Edward Cullinan CBE
Frederick Cuming HON D LITT
Gus Cummins
Prof Trevor Dannatt OBE
Dr Jennifer Dickson
Jennifer Durrant
Anthony Eyton
Lord Foster of Thames Bank OM
Peter Freeth
Anthony Green
Sir Nicholas Grimshaw CBE PPRA
Nigel Hall
David Hockney OM CH
Sir Michael Hopkins CBE
Ken Howard OBE
Prof Paul Huxley
Bill Jacklin
Tess Jaray
Eva Jiricna CBE
Allen Jones
Prof Phillip King CBE PPRA
Prof Bryan Kneale MBE
Paul Koralek CBE
Sonia Lawson
John Maine
Mick Moon
Prof Chris Orr MBE
Tom Phillips CBE
Dame Paula Rego DBE
David Remfry MBE
Lord Rogers of Riverside CH
Prof Michael Sandle
Terry Setch
Philip Sutton
Joe Tilson
Dr David Tindle
William Tucker
Anthony Whishaw
John Wragg
Rose Wylie OBE

Academicians

Sir David Adjaye OBE
Ron Arad
Fiona Banner
Prof Phyllida Barlow CBE
Prof Gordon Benson OBE
Tony Bevan
Prof Sonia Boyce OBE
Adam Caruso and Peter St John
Prof Brian Catling
* Stephen Chambers
Sir David Chipperfield CBE
Ann Christopher
Eileen Cooper OBE
Stephen Cox
Sir Tony Cragg CBE
Richard Deacon CBE
Tacita Dean CBE
* Anne Desmet
Kenneth Draper
Tracey Emin CBE
Prof Stephen Farthing
Gilbert & George
Sir Antony Gormley OBE
Piers Gough CBE
* Spencer de Grey CBE
Thomas Heatherwick CBE
Lubaina Himid CBE
Gary Hume
Louisa Hutton OBE
* Timothy Hyman
Vanessa Jackson
Neil Jeffries
Prof Chantal Joffe
Isaac Julien CBE
Sir Anish Kapoor CBE
Michael Landy
* Christopher Le Brun PRA
Sir Richard Long CBE
* Jock McFadyen
Prof David Mach
Prof Ian McKeever
Lisa Milroy
Prof Dhruva Mistry CBE
Mali Morris
Prof Farshid Moussavi OBE
David Nash OBE
Mike Nelson
Prof Humphrey Ocean
* Hughie O'Donoghue
Cornelia Parker OBE
Eric Parry
Grayson Perry CBE
Prof Cathie Pilkington
* Dr Barbara Rae CBE
Fiona Rae
Peter Randall-Page
Prof Ian Ritchie CBE
Michael Rooney
Eva Rothschild
Rebecca Salter
Jenny Saville
Sean Scully
Tim Shaw
Conrad Shawcross
Yinka Shonibare CBE
* Bob and Roberta Smith OBE
Alan Stanton OBE
Emma Stibbon
Wolfgang Tillmans
Rebecca Warren
Gillian Wearing CBE
Prof Alison Wilding OBE
Prof Chris Wilkinson OBE
* Jane and Louise Wilson
* Richard Wilson
Bill Woodrow

* *Hanging Committee 2019*

Honorary Royal Academicians

Marina Abramović
Prof El Anatsui
Laurie Anderson
Prof Tadao Ando
Georg Baselitz
Jim Dine
Marlene Dumas
Olafur Eliasson
Frank O Gehry
Jenny Holzer
Prof Rebecca Horn
Prof Arata Isozaki
Jasper Johns
William Kentridge
Anselm Kiefer
Jeff Koons
Daniel Libeskind
Bruce Nauman
Mimmo Paladino
Senator Renzo Piano
Ed Ruscha
Julian Schnabel
Richard Serra
Cindy Sherman
Kiki Smith
Frank Stella
Rosemarie Trockel
James Turrell
Bill Viola
Ai Weiwei
Wim Wenders
Peter Zumthor

Supporting the Royal Academy

The Royal Academy of Arts has a unique position as an independent institution led by eminent artists and architects whose purpose is to promote the creation, enjoyment and appreciation of the visual arts through exhibitions, education and debate. The Royal Academy receives no annual funding via government, and is entirely reliant on self-generated income and charitable support.

You and/or your company can support the Royal Academy of Arts in a number of different ways:

- Donations from individuals, trusts, companies and foundations help support the Academy's internationally renowned exhibition programme, the conservation of the Collections and education projects for schools, families and people with special needs; as well as providing scholarships and bursaries for postgraduate art students in the Royal Academy Schools.
- As a company, you can invest in the Royal Academy through arts sponsorship, corporate membership and corporate entertaining, with specific opportunities that relate to your budgets and marketing or entertaining objectives. Upcoming sponsorship and entertaining opportunities for corporate partners include 'Antony Gormley', 'Lucian Freud: The Self-portraits' and 'Picasso on Paper'.
- By including a gift to the Royal Academy in your will, you could help to protect all that we stand for, and ensure we are there as a voice for art and for artists, whatever the future may hold. Your gift can be a sum of money, a specific item or a share of what is left after you have provided for your family and friends. Any gift, regardless of the size, can have an impact, and will allow art lovers to enjoy the Royal Academy in the years to come.

To find out ways in which individuals can support this work, or a specific aspect of it, please contact Karin Grundy, Head of Patrons, on 020 7300 5671.

To explore ways in which companies, trusts and foundations can become involved in the work of the Academy, please contact the Sponsorship and Partnership Team on 020 7300 5706/5813.

For more information on remembering the Academy in your will, please contact Frances Griffiths on 020 7300 5677, or email legacies@royalacademy.org.uk.

Friends of the RA membership

Redeem the cost of your exhibition tickets when you become a Friend today*

Enjoy free entry to every RA exhibition and much more…

There's never been a better time to become a Friend of the RA. Join today for unlimited free entry to all our world-class exhibitions including 'Antony Gormley' and 'Lucian Freud: The Self-portraits' as well as preview days, private views and extended hours just for Friends.

- Free entry to exhibitions for you, a family member and up to four children
- Previews to our exhibitions before they open to the public
- Private views, extended hours and exclusive Friends events
- Priority booking to all RA events
- All-day access to the Keeper's House
- RA Magazine and a weekly email newsletter
- 10% discount in RA shops

Why not join today?

- At the Friends Desk
- Online at roy.ac/friends
- By phone 020 7300 8090
- By email friends@royalacademy.org.uk

*Terms and conditions apply. Visit roy.ac/friendsterms

Head of Summer Exhibition and Curator (Contemporary Projects)
Edith Devaney

Summer Exhibition Organisers
Sinta Berry
Will Corner
Bronte Earl
Hayley Elnaugh
Florence Mytum
Katherine Oliver
Paul Sirr

Royal Academy Publications
Florence Dassonville, Production Co-ordinator
Rosie Hore, Project Editor
Carola Krueger, Production Manager
Peter Sawbridge, Managing Editor
Nick Tite, Publisher

Rights and Reproductions
Susana Vázquez Fernández

Editor's note:
All given dimensions are unframed, height before width (before depth).

Book design: Adam Brown_01.02
Colour reproduction: DawkinsColour
Printed in Wales by Gomer Press

British Library Cataloguing-in-publication Data
A catalogue record for this book is available in the British Library

ISBN 978-1-912520-02-2

Illustrations

Page 2: detail of *Hey Wayne on the Meath Estate* by David Hepher.
Page 4: detail of *Brief Encounter, Palazzina Cinese* by Karen Knorr.
Page 7: *Portrait of a Young Man Standing* by the late Dr Leonard McComb RA in the Robert Miller Vestibule.
Page 9: detail of *Poor Mother* by Jock McFadyen RA.
Page 10: Jock McFadyen RA selecting works in Gallery III.
Page 17: Jane Wilson RA with *Anthon Raimund* by William Marsden in Gallery I.
Pages 18–19: Anne Desmet RA in Gallery VII during the hang.
Page 20 (clockwise from top left): Timothy Hyman RA in Gallery VI; Hughie O'Donoghue RA in Gallery IX; Jock McFadyen RA and Christopher Le Brun PRA.
Page 21: Louise Wilson RA in Gallery I.
Page 22: Gallery VII during the hang.
Page 23: Richard Wilson RA in the Lecture Room. Behind him is *The Miracle of Flight* by Prof Stephen Farthing RA.
Pages 24–25: Jock McFadyen RA selecting works in Gallery III.
Pages 26–27: Bob and Roberta Smith RA selecting works in Gallery VIII.
Page 28: Dr Barbara Rae RA hanging works in Gallery V.
Page 29 (clockwise from top left): Spencer de Grey RA; Anne Desmet RA; Jane and Louise Wilson RA; Stephen Chambers RA.
Pages 30–31: Bob and Roberta Smith RA installing *Epicentre* by John Maine RA in Gallery VIII.
Pages 32–33: installing architectural works in the Large Weston Room.
Pages 40–41: the Wohl Central Hall. *Untitled (Duculi)* by Charles Avery is in the foreground.
Page 44: *The Victory* by Marcus Harvey in Gallery III. In front of the painting stand two sculptures by Harvey: *Full Nelson* and *Napoleon Invictus*. *Spiral Dub* by Oliver Marsden hangs above.
Pages 66–67: Gallery III on Sanctioning Day.
Pages 80–81: Gallery II. *Red Shells* by Richard Wilson RA is in the foreground. *Untitled* by Sir Richard Long RA hangs on the far wall.
Page 89: *Gut* by Jane and Louise Wilson RA in Gallery I. In the foreground are two sculptures by Amalia Pica.
Page 104: *Amorepacific Headquarters Performance Testing Model* by Sir David Chipperfield RA in the Large Weston Room.
Pages 112–13: Gallery IV. *Bear from Dump Circus* by Nicola Hicks is in the foreground.
Pages 122–23: Gallery V. *Riven Gemini* by Stephen Cox RA is on the left.
Pages 126–27: Gallery VI. *My Ghosts* by John Davies is in the centre.
Pages 150–51: Gallery VIII. The visible sculptures are, from left, *Epicentre* by John Maine RA, *Hatton Garden Heist Hole* by Richard Wilson RA, *For Michael* by Richard Deacon RA and *So-Am-Pots* by Prof Phillip King PPRA.
Pages 170–71: the Lecture Room. *Gravesend* by Hew Locke is in the foreground. Just behind is *Geometry of Desire IV* by Peter Randall-Page RA.
Pages 177–78: the Lecture Room. *Carrying the Hot Blur* by Denise de Cordova is centre right.

Photographic Acknowledgements

Unless otherwise stated: John Bodkin, DawkinsColour
Pages 10, 17, 18–19, 20, 21, 22, 23, 24–25, 26–27, 28, 29, 30–31, 32–33: photo Phil Sayer
Page 12: © Thomas Houseago, courtesy Gagosian. Photo Stefan Altenburger Photography, Zurich
Pages 12–13: courtesy Wim Wenders Foundation and Blain|Southern
Page 13: courtesy the artist
Pages 14–15: © Edward Burtynsky, courtesy Nicholas Metivier Gallery, Toronto / Flowers Gallery, London
Page 34: courtesy SPACER, Ramsgate, and Charles Avery Studio
Page 35: courtesy the artist (left); courtesy Mr Perou (right)
Page 36: courtesy the artist (left)
Page 46: © Anselm Kiefer. Photo © Georges Poncet. Courtesy White Cube
Page 49: photo © Lucid Plane (left)
Pages 50–51: courtesy the artist
Page 52: photo © Lucid Plane (right)
Page 53: photo Sam Roberts
Page 54: © David Tindle, courtesy The Redfern Gallery (left); courtesy Portland Gallery (right)
Page 60: courtesy Chris Beetles Gallery (left)
Page 61: photo Alice Wood
Page 62: courtesy the artist. Photo Alexander Brattell (left)
Page 63: © Bill Jacklin. Courtesy Marlborough (right)
Page 68: © the artist, courtesy White Cube
Page 70: courtesy the artist
Page 73: courtesy Pangolin London (left and right)
Page 75: courtesy Stoney Road Press (left); courtesy the artist (right)
Page 76: courtesy Michael Craig-Martin and Alan Cristea Gallery, London (left)
Page 79: © Phyllida Barlow. Courtesy the artist and Hauser & Wirth (right)
Page 83: photo Paul Dove (right)
Page 86: courtesy the artist and Maureen Paley, London
Page 90: courtesy Studio Libeskind © LUXIGON (left); courtesy the artist (right)
Page 92: © Aaron Hargreaves/Foster + Partners (left and right)
Page 93: CZWG Architects LLP (left); courtesy Cullinan studio (right)
Page 97: courtesy AI – DESIGN (left); courtesy Caruso St John Architects. Photo Philip Heckhausen (right)
Page 98: © Heatherwick Studio
Page 99: © Rogers Stirk Harbour + Partners (RSHP)
Page 100: courtesy the artist
Page 101: courtesy Sauerbruch Hutton (right)
Page 102: © RPBW (left); © Ahmad Angawi (right)
Page 105: © James Turrell. Courtesy Pace Gallery
Page 106: courtesy Mick Moon and Alan Cristea Gallery
Page 107: courtesy the artist (left); photo Steven Dunlop (right)
Page 108: courtesy the artist
Page 116: courtesy Jim Dine and Alan Cristea Gallery, London
Page 118: courtesy Richard Long and Alan Cristea Gallery, London
Page 119: courtesy Antony Gormley and Alan Cristea Gallery, London
Page 120: courtesy the artist and Frith Street Gallery, London
Pages 120–21: courtesy Emma Stibbon and Alan Cristea Gallery, London
Page 124: courtesy the artist
Page 125: courtesy Blackbird Pictures Ltd. Photo Lars Gundersen
Page 129: © Peter Darach
Page 132: courtesy the artist (left)
Page 133: courtesy Fosse Gallery (left); courtesy Chris Beetles Gallery (right)
Page 134: photo Strike-a-light (left)
Page 135: courtesy Glasgow Print Studio (right)
Page 136: courtesy the artist (left)
Page 141: photo Tom Willingham (right)
Page 144: courtesy the artist (right)
Page 145: courtesy the artist (left)
Page 146: courtesy the artist
Page 147: courtesy greengrassi (left); courtesy the artist (right)
Page 148: courtesy the artist (left); Ron Arad Associates (right)
Page 149: photo Colin Mills (left); courtesy the artist (right)
Page 152–53: image courtesy the artist and Hales Gallery. Photo Angus Mill. © Frank Bowling. All Rights Reserved, DACS 2019
Page 154: photo Colin Mills
Page 155: photo Justin Piperger (right)
Page 158: photo Nelson Huxley
Page 159: photo James Champion (right)
Page 160: courtesy the artist
Pages 160–61: © Rose Wylie. Courtesy the artist and David Zwirner
Pages 162–63: courtesy the artist
Page 164: courtesy Waddington Custot
Page 165: © Joe Tilson, Courtesy Marlborough
Page 166: © Chantal Joffe. Courtesy the artist and Victoria Miro, London/Venice (right)
Pages 166–67: © Hughie O'Donoghue. Courtesy Marlborough
Page 172: photo Thomas Jenkins
Page 174: image courtesy the artist, Victoria Miro, London/Venice. Photo Richard Ivey
Page 175: photo Steve Russell Studios (left)
Page 178: courtesy the artist (right)
Pages 180–81: courtesy the artists
Page 183: © Paula Rego (right)
Page 185: © John Carter. Courtesy The Redfern Gallery
Page 186: courtesy Georg Baselitz and Alan Cristea Gallery, London (left)
Page 187: courtesy the artist. Photo Pasquale Palmieri

Cognitive Politics

a Communications Workbook for Progressives

by Stephen Cataldo

Cross Partisan Press
First Edition
February 08, 2017

Additional materials online:
www.CognitivePolitics.org

Cognitive scientists are discovering the underlying differences between liberal and conservative mindsets. These differences are amplified by media and political messaging resounding through echo chambers, making it very difficult for us to have reasonable political conversations.

How can you have more effective and engaged political conversations?

Cognitive Politics reviews scientific discoveries, successful historical campaigns, and communication strategies. We'll integrate ideas that are rarely combined and explore the contradictions.

The second section puts these ideas into practice, applying them to different issues that are notorious for getting us into confusing and unproductive political arguments.

Please write me at www.CognitivePolitics.org/contact.

Developmental Editing by Andrea Barilla Editing and Writing Services:
www.andreabarilla.com

Exercise icon based on original *Designed by Freepik.*

Cross Partisan Press
First Edition, February 2017
4 3 2 1
Printed in the United States of America
ISBN 978-0-9985802-0-3

Additional materials online:
www.CognitivePolitics.org

Acknowledgements

I would never have been able to write this book alone, and so I want to express warmth and thanks to everyone who has helped bring *Cognitive Politics* to life.

Riana Good was my first thorough proofreader, followed by Rosalind Diaz, and then Lindsey Newbold and Emma Rudié. Bailee Sims has been standing by me and providing steady enthusiasm and encouragement on this long road.

More help came from Maria Sanders, Gene Chamson, Tucker Lieberman, Susan Calico, Alexa Razma, Bonnie Dixon, Jordan Kersten, and Mary Finlay-Sims. Rachel Kleinman listened. My book club provided a burst of enthusiasm and great ideas near the end: Maya Wolf, Erin Reeves, Alex Trahan, Lisa Trahan, and Annie L. Lin. And Sheila Meltzer, Katherine Brousseau, and the organizers and mentors at FinishUp Weekend in Oakland helped as well.

With publication approaching, Andrea Barilla provided developmental editing of *Cognitive Politics* and helped bring the book to completion.

With publication approaching, Andrea Barilla edited and helped bring the book to completion.

Dedicated to my grandmother Erna Schwartz.

Table of Contents

Section I: Theory, History, and Strategies

Review new theories exploring how liberals and conservatives think, and reexamine historically successful strategies in the light of those theories.

Section II: Issue-by-Issue Workbook

Each of the wedge issues below helps you practice some of the techniques introduced in the first section. When do you push your story, when do you listen, and when do you compromise?

Abortion politics keep good-hearted people at each other's throats. Explore how conservatives intertwine leadership and sanctity values. Even if we never agree, does abortion have to be a wedge issue?

People who find homosexuality uncomfortable are increasingly tolerating it, letting go of their need to impose their will on others.

Conservative politicians have created a closed community of people who feel that America should never apologize, with progressives left outside. Can we inspire a deeper and more open story of America?

Failure to engage conservative hesitations leaves us angrily repeating the points conservatives agree with while ignoring the real questions conservatives have — questions we *can* answer.

Appendices: Exercises and Techniques

Closure

Introduction to *Cognitive Politics*

Political conversations are often deeply difficult. In the last two decades, cognitive scientists have made rapid progress toward understanding why. They are finding the underlying values and psychology that divide us into left and right.

Yet so far, deeper scientific understanding is not leading to more effective political conversations. When we look back at historical figures like Martin Luther King Jr. and Mahatma Gandhi, we see campaigns that were much more alive, and effective, than anything progressives do today. *Cognitive Politics* integrates the new science with historical lessons — and adds in communication techniques developed for better relationships.

What makes our conversations so difficult? Can cognitive science explain why we divide into the teams we do? And why political conversations are taken so personally? Why is it so hard to understand each other's core points? This book seeks the psychology behind our political divisions and explores how to have better conversations across those divides. How can you express what really matters to you and be heard? How can you help the person you're talking with express their own values better?

The dream of this book is to prepare ordinary progressives to have better conversations with conservatives and moderates. The word "better" is intentionally vague; there are many ways politics could be improved. We might convince someone to agree with our points, and we might swing some swing voters; often we'll simply create space for both sides to focus more on fighting the corruption that thrives when politicians get good people angry at each other.

The scientific research has already been done, and history is full of vibrant and successful movements. What's been missing is a practical handbook that spans many different theories and communication practices. After introducing a wide variety of ideas, *Cognitive Politics* provides practical examples and exercises that weave them together, showing the best times to apply each approach. This book doesn't focus on proof: experiment with the ideas, pick and choose what improves your conversations, reject what doesn't work for you. *Cognitive Politics* provides a more mindful approach to politics that includes improvements in messaging but focuses on making your conversations more alive and connected.

Organization of the Book

The first section of *Cognitive Politics* reviews scientific theories, activist strategies, and historical examples. The second section applies these ideas to a variety of wedge issues where we struggle to communicate across ideological divides. The issues were chosen so that each implements a different set of techniques from the first half. It's a workbook: edit your own copy and pick techniques that work for you.

Organization of the Book

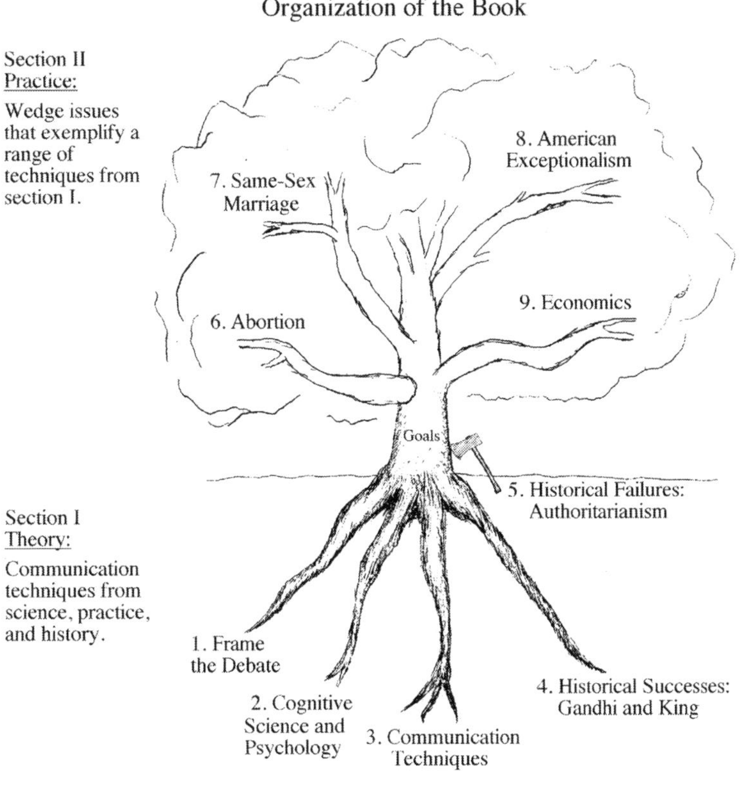

Section I starts at the roots, with a review of new cognitive-science research on the differences between liberals and conservatives. Cognitive linguist George Lakoff (*Don't Think of an Elephant! Know Your Values and Frame the Debate*) explores language choices that cascade into liberal and conservative ways of thinking. Jonathan Haidt (*The Righteous Mind: Why Good People Are Divided By Politics and Religion*) reduces different ideologies to their underlying moral foundations. These recent academic results are then integrated with a variety of communication techniques and

historical examples. Look for links between the theoretical chapters and the practice chapters in section II, making it easy to jump between them.

The wedge issues chosen for the second half are not necessarily the topics most in the news today. Instead, they are chosen to practice the full range of ideas from section I. For example, the chapter on abortion has its roots in values and active listening from chapters 2 and 3. American Exceptionalism calls for the framing techniques from the first chapter, plus understandings of group identity discussed in chapters 4 and 5.

Image Key

Exercises and **Questions.** *Cognitive Politics* is a workbook: take time to do the exercises and explore the questions. Or invite your community or book club to try them together.

Definitions. New terms will be introduced. Perhaps new vocabulary can help us escape well-rehearsed and entrenched political positions.

Weave Ideas. *Cognitive Politics* integrates ideas from a wide variety of fields. After you've read the book, come back and reread the weave sections to see how everything fits together.

It's Not Hopeless

Political conversations today are "bad" in every way imaginable. We live in a noisy world where we have messages near and dear to our hearts, and all sides are forced to reduce our hearts to shallow sound bites. We rarely unravel the motivations and values driving the other side. We typically assume they hold values opposite ours: if an issue draws out my compassion, I'll assume the other person is against compassion. When our values and priorities do differ, we have few tools to find healthy compromises that let us all meet our most desperate needs. At family dinners, politics is often used as a dominance ritual, like chickens fluffing their feathers and demanding their spot high in the pecking order.

It feels hopeless. The consequences, we all know, are enormous. Could you really convince a Trump supporter to vote for Hillary? We envision angry people at a rally, and try to imagine having a conversation. But really, we're getting lost in unnecessary

despair. While we envision core supporters, if just one in ten of Trump's grudging supporters were to have given up on him, the election would have been a rout. If you can't win an argument, can you instead inspire a relative who only watches Fox to explore other news sources? Or can you find a way to connect with an honest conservative, who may then stand up for decency within their circles?

Stop trying to imagine changing the most hard-core opponent into an ally, and the rules change.

Beyond electoral effectiveness, can we put heart back into political conversations? Find ways to disagree without wrecking friendships and family connections?

There's not one answer, and this book doesn't aim for one answer. We'll explore ways to improve messaging through a better understanding of your values and theirs, and seek ways to turn political arguments into healthy conversations.

In life, our difficulties often lead to growth. In yoga, we are encouraged to find our edge, to hold the poses that make us mildly uncomfortable, and we can learn about ourselves by engaging the challenge. In a relationship, conflicts are where we find out what is really going on; they are the place to look if we want to deepen our connections. Today, political conversations are not growth experiences for anyone — they are just painful.

> A key purpose of this workbook is to prepare you for more connected, calmer discussions with friends or at the Thanksgiving table. Explore how to adjust both goals and communication techniques to the reality that well-meaning conservatives see the world very differently than well-meaning liberals.

We can change that. Cognitive Politics provides ideas and exercises to transform difficult political conversations into practices where we learn about ourselves, develop new life skills, and connect more deeply.

Word Choices: Progressives, Liberals, Democrats

Research on political preferences most often uses the terms *LIBERAL* and *CONSERVATIVE*. These are often given modifiers: *SOCIAL* and *FISCAL* are the most common. This book adds a new modifier: *COGNITIVE*, defined as the typical psychological reasons for liberal or conservative preferences. The reasons for this new term are introduced in the section "An Age of Cognitive Politics." p.25

Dr. John Gray's *Men Are From Mars, Women Are From Venus* is full of massive overgeneralizations, of course, but it helped many women and men understand and negotiate rather than burn bridges over differences. I think something similar is

needed between cautious, protective *COGNITIVE CONSERVATIVES* and exploring, openhearted *COGNITIVE LIBERALS* — even if it's full of massive overgeneralizations.

DEMOCRAT and *REPUBLICAN* are used to indicate the current political organizations: What is each organization's position? How do its members vote?

According to linguist Geoffrey Nunberg, "The main difference between *LIBERALS* and *PROGRESSIVES* is that progressives insist there is one."[1] In this book, these terms are treated as synonyms.

Writing about demographic differences is always difficult. I could add caveats until the book was nothing but caveats. This is a workbook — a place to brainstorm, test ideas and experiment, not a place for final verdicts. Overgeneralizations can be helpful when looking for possible areas of misunderstandings between groups; don't expect them to apply consistently. Very often, demographic patterns do little to explain individuals but do match the large-scale echo chambers created by political campaigns and media.

Despite writing about the differences between conservatives and liberals, this book is really about the similarities: we're fighting at Thanksgiving not between good and evil but over different ways our brains are wired to see the world, with almost all of us oriented toward good. Understanding the patterns that separate us might be the first step to bridging them.

1. Geoffrey Nunberg, *"The Main Difference between Liberals and Progressives Is That Progressives Insist There Is One."* Twitter post. @GeoffNunberg, Aug 26, 2016, 5:34pm. https://twitter.com/geoffnunberg/status/769332247161810946.

Chapter 1

Frame the Debate: Language, Stories, and Metaphor

How can liberals communicate so that our values are clear? How can we draw moderates into a more liberal mindset? What language choices draw people toward compassionate politics?

George Lakoff's book *Don't Think of an Elephant!* gained fame for its critique of the Democratic Party's habit of saying "no" to one Republican initiative after another, rather than developing its own clear message.[2] This chapter is primarily inspired by his work as a linguist, exploring language, metaphor and framing. We'll begin with general messaging techniques and then move on to Lakoff's core finding: most people use family metaphors to understand government. Strict-father metaphors pair with conservative thinking, nurturing-parent metaphors with liberal thinking.

Lakoff's framing advice is openly partisan, aiming to help the progressive team win. This chapter follows his approach; other chapters take different perspectives. This workbook doesn't tell you what level of partisanship you should choose, but compares and contrasts different approaches.

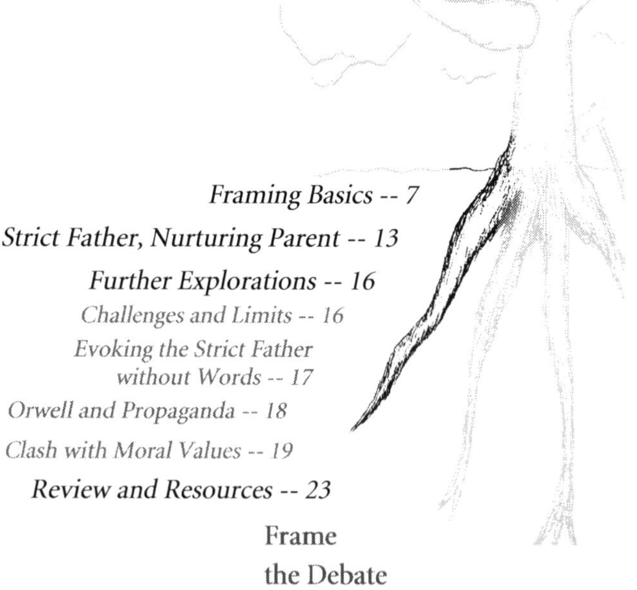

Chapter 1 starts where most of us start: We are partisan. We've been arguing. This is how to do it better, to get your point across. I've listened to Lakoff give presentations, and left the room with other progressives excited by his ideas but not ready to apply them to real conversations — the search for practical ways to apply Lakoff's ideas was the starting spark for this book. Upcoming chapters will blend these ideas with psychological explorations and communication techniques.

2. George Lakoff, *The ALL NEW Don't Think of an Elephant! Know Your Values and Frame the Debate.* (White River Junction, Vermont: Chelsea Green Publishing, 2012).

Framing Basics: Speak Your Truth So It Can Be Heard

Framing creates context for an issue. Framing is unavoidable. Even just one word, like "taxes," will evoke a frame. When you think of taxes, do you think of social programs, a strong defense, money coming out of your pocket? Do you imagine you would trust the people spending the taxes? Are taxes already too high, or inadequate? What emotions arise — do you feel bitter that you pay more than your share, or are you proud to help? Logical discussions about policy always evoke a context.

The frame of the word "framing" itself often includes assumptions of spin and dishonesty, but both lies and truth evoke frames. Gandhi and King built their frames very carefully, casting the membership of their movements as maltreated people with dignity and perseverance but neither powerless victims nor violent enemies.

If you describe logical policy choices and they don't form a memorable and convincing story, bad framing is a likely culprit.

> People supported acceptance for "gay men and lesbians" at a rate 15 percent higher than for "homosexuals."[3]

Framing is not subterfuge. You haven't confused anyone if you say "gay men and lesbians" instead of "homosexuals." The facts are the same and remain clear, but the emotional resonances differ based on the details of your word choices.

We tend to assume we live in a world of logical arguments. Explain the reasons for and against an issue, and if we are right, then logic will force people to change their perspective. But the frame, metaphors and messenger often predispose us to see an argument one way or another, well before logic kicks in.

Lakoff argues that every time you describe the world with a certain frame, you reinforce and strengthen that way of thinking. So, it might be important to say

> "For Democrats, we recommend sincerity and transparency. Understand your values, speak them out loud, repeat them, use the facts honestly, and link facts and policies overtly to values. Do this over and over… Do this not just as individuals, but together as a party."
> — George Lakoff, Elisabeth Wehling[4]

3. George Lakoff, "A Good Week for Science — and Insight into Politics," Daily Kos, Feb 21, 2010. CognitivePolitics.org/sacred.
4. George Lakoff and Elisabeth Wehling, *The Little Blue Book: The Essential Guide to Thinking and Talking Democratic* (New York: Simon & Schuster, 2012), 38.

"lesbians and gay men" every time you bring up the subject. Each time you talk, you might be slowly reinforcing swing voters' tendency to think about people as people, rather than mere projections of a sexual preference (i.e., homosexuals).

Our brains are not pure logic machines. When faced with complex or abstract topics, we often simplify using broad conceptual metaphors. For example, relationships are typically described as journeys, perhaps going somewhere or stuck in a rut. Political conversations are often thought of as competitive sports or wars: we score points, we win or lose, we collect arguments to use as ammunition and shoot down the other side's ideas. Metaphors matter: if you are unhappy with a political conversation and think you are not scoring enough points, that metaphor creates a frame of competition, and perhaps you will seek better ammunition for the next argument. If you think you and your conversation partner are stuck in a rut, you might focus instead on improving the relationship aspects. We are not logic machines, but live in a world of stories.

Imagining political conversations as relationships, rather than arguments, may help us get out of a rut.

How we think about an issue often cascades from the metaphors and language choices we use to describe that issue. Negatives won't change your frame: if you say "I am not a crook," your listeners' minds will cascade through the frame you create. Your audience will have to think about the idea that you are a crook before they can negate it. You have inadvertently reinforced those pathways.[5] Lakoff claims this is simply how our brains work, in politics and elsewhere. The Democratic Party often drops the ball on framing: Democrats practically forgot to frame the national health care plan, so the Republicans were able to name it Obamacare and make it about Obama instead of about health care.[6]

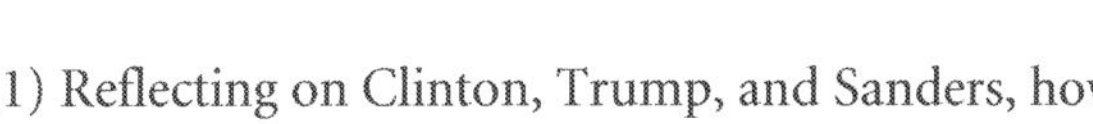

What Frames Were Used in the 2016 Election?

(1) Reflecting on Clinton, Trump, and Sanders, how did each candidate's message fit together in your mind?

(2) I associate Hillary with the word "qualified." Think of a typical sentence where you would use the word "qualified." Is it presidential? Have you ever called George Washington or FDR qualified?

Please see www.cognitivepolitics.org for current political discussions. Add your voice!

5. Lakoff, *Don't Think of an Elephant!*, 3.

6. Lakoff, *Don't Think of an Elephant!*, xv.

(3) Donald focused on his dealmaking skills, which included forcing Mexico to pay for a wall it didn't want. Who else makes deals you can't refuse? Trump was accused of inconsistency — but was his message inconsistent with that frame?

Evoke People's Stories; Don't Reduce People to One Issue

Lakoff's suggestions are easier in theory than in practice. Often, liberals want to evoke and expand on human stories, rather than reduce life to single issues. For example, the more you know about families pressured to migrate, the more empathy you will have for them. If you want to convince someone that taxes are worthwhile, they have to know about the people who are impacted by programs funded by those taxes. It's easier to develop a short and effective slogan like "illegals" or "tax relief" that reduces people's lives to single issues, more challenging to enrich an audience's understanding and compassion with just a word or two.

Example: Immigration Status

The one-word sound bite "illegals" evokes a powerful and problematic frame. In this frame,[7] a hardworking, churchgoing, underpaid mom who crossed a national border hasn't committed a petty, minor, nonviolent crime — nor even committed a major crime. Instead, she has *become the crime*: it is her noun, rather than just something she has done or an adjective that describes her.

If you travel to Thailand as a tourist and overstay your visa while goofing around, you do not become "an illegal," you likely pay a little fine while exchanging smiles with the immigration police. The same crime here, done to protect your children rather than goof around, is seen as a serious violation.

Often, progressive framing succeeds by making real the stories of complex human lives. It becomes easy to dislike a person when we name them with one characteristic. He is an illegal. She is a homosexual. They are liberals or conservatives. Compassionate politics is most successful when we are vigilant against reducing a person to a single characteristic, seeking richer stories instead.

The attack frame on people who immigrate illegally is to call them:[8]

7. Immigration does not have a clear "conservative" view. While many conservatives from Romney to the further right have used the "illegals" frame at times, many others including my conservative beta readers opposed this framing. I compared "illegals" vs. "undocumented immigrants" here to explore framing tactics, not assign blame to ideologies.

8. For examples, see: Jose Antonio Vargas, "Mitt Romney's 'Illegals' Rhetoric Alienates Latinos," *The Guardian*, October 3, 2012, sec. Opinion.

Illegals.

Liberals should break the habit of referring to people as a single action they've taken. In a conversation, we might instead choose:

People without green cards typically work hard to support their families, often doing jobs I don't want, and they are easily taken advantage of by employers.

This, unfortunately, doesn't fit on a bumper sticker.

Undocumented Immigrant >> is milder than *illegals*: Does it evoke a human story in your mind? Do you have ideas for a compassionate slogan-length frame?

Obama often uses "undocumented immigrant." If people hear the word "undocumented" in place of "illegal," that is obfuscation. Obfuscation is not the advice that Lakoff gives: it doesn't help in the long run, and it doesn't change people's minds. Obama has created clear frames when given a chance: "Americans in their heart, in their minds, in every single way but one: on paper."[9] This turns the message around, emphasizing the compassionate frame that is missing in "undocumented immigrant," admitting without obfuscating that they are not citizens according to paper or documents, and that is the problem. If this clarification were repeated over and over by a variety of Democrats, it might transform the phrase "undocumented immigrant" from being a way to obfuscate that a law has been broken into a morally clear frame.

Cardless Workers >> meaning those with no green card, is my current favorite term. The metaphor reminds listeners that they are here to work and contribute, and it implies an obvious solution — give them a card. A perfect match to policy isn't as important as the metaphors evoked: to have a short phrase that represents a longer conversation, so Democrats can add layers and layers of story to "cardless workers" until it does mean something. "Cardless workers" excludes children, but "undocumented immigrants" doesn't bring kids to mind either. So perhaps there needs to be two terms and two core stories for discussing immigration.

George Lakoff advises, "It took the conservatives a long time to get their conceptual system out there, to create the language, to find whom it resonated with, and to build on it over and over again."[10] For example, "Contract with America" is a meaningless

9. President Obama, "Remarks by the President on Immigration," June 15, 2012, whitehouse.gov.

10. Butler, Katy. "Why Liberals Lose: An Interview with George Lakoff." http://katybutler.com.

phrase until it is repeated over and over. To compete with Republicans, the Democratic Party would have to come together on messaging, agree to one or two imperfect phrases, and use them over and over, layering more complex and human stories onto the short phrases until they evoke the stories that represent our moral vision.

Resist Sound Bites at Home

Politicians have no choice but to communicate with sound bites and tune their message to the news cycle. They are stuck with slogans. But at home we should slow down. We want to weave many conversations into coherent larger stories. Use time to connect. Talk about real people. At home, it's our job to undo some of the shallowness of the media.

The very act of cutting an issue to a memorable slogan is itself political.

Not Just Sound Bites: Coherent Messaging with Vision

The Democratic Party has long struggled with messaging. Marketing slogans are often shallow and dishonest. They don't have to be. For compassionate politics, they shouldn't be. But we do need to work together until the stories we tell are coherent, building upon similar stories and underlying metaphors together.

Imagine you are writing a book along with many coauthors. We have to cooperate and choose a single title for the book and get the chapters to flow from one to the next. Sharing the title and thinking about marketing doesn't mean we have to be in lockstep or write a shallow book.

Examples of connecting stories into memorable frames include:

Tax relief >> "A conservative on TV uses two words … the progressive has to go into a paragraph-long discussion of his own view." — George Lakoff.[11]

Wall Street >> The Democratic Party never came up with a term for abusive bankers. The Occupy movement handed us "the 1%," along with its positive counterpoint of "the 99%." Yet again, mainstream Democrats are missing from the framing effort.

War on >> War on terror, war on drugs. *harm reduction* is the progressive approach to dealing with drugs — why don't liberal politicians and the supposedly liberal media use those words?

11. Lakoff, *Elephant*, 24.

Let's focus on *harm reduction*. Why doesn't Obama have a *Drug Harm-Reduction Campaign* to replace the *War on Drugs*? Harm reduction is an idea, but it's not repeated as a headline often enough to be a frame. It's not a term on the tip of everyone's tongue. If you took a poll today, it would do badly.

If this was a good frame for Republicans, what would they do? They would repeat it now, they would repeat it next week, you would hear it from many voices, and you would still be hearing it next year. Soon, you'd know the term and be familiar with their definition.

Democrats are failing to set the frame of important issues because we're failing to implement our own values: we're not cooperating on messaging nor planning for the future.

Quick Tips:

✓ Always focus on your values: don't start with your policy solutions, don't center on arguing against your opponent, and don't use their terminology.

✓ Make sure the metaphors behind your words invoke your story and your values.

✓ For each issue we can all tell our own stories, and we don't have to "dumb it down." But these stories should be connected with the same memorable term and reinforce the same metaphor.

Speaking Truth: Political Communication as a Mindfulness Practice

Lakoff's suggestions are reminiscent of simple meditation practices. He says to use words that evoke mental imagery like "forest, soil, water, air, and sky"[12] rather than "the environment."

In politics, this means talking about real people and using specific examples, attaching your stories to a repeated phrase or metaphor until that phrase accumulates a richer meaning.

Is your message mindful, real and present? When you meditate, you might focus on each breath. Not an abstraction like "the breath," but your breath, each one, in and out, paying attention continuously. You make life real, evoke presence. Contrast this with logical arguments like "everyone needs to breathe!" Framing calls for us to switch from "everyone needs atmospheric oxygen," followed by a long discourse on why we need to breathe and how stupid Republicans are that they don't know this, to

12. Lakoff and Wehling, *The Little Blue Book*, 42.

instead following and talking about each breath. I need this breath right now. And I feel gratitude for this next breath. And you need the breath you are taking now.

Imagine this approach on health care issues. The name of the set of policies I support is *Single Payer*. When this policy is used as the frame, we focus on who is paying, rather than the goal of providing health care for everyone. We should have heard stories of people, real or fictional but with names that we could all recite, who couldn't get insured because of a preexisting condition, who couldn't afford insurance, or who went to an emergency room because they didn't have insurance. Talk about the people who need health care, tell their stories, keep letting swing voters hear our values. Make the story one of real people with real problems — provide footnotes and data, but make sure you have stories for when that is all the attention you have.

Have you heard of *Joe the Plumber*, promoted by Republicans to represent lower taxes? Can you recite the name of someone promoted by the Democrats to represent improved health care?

Linguists find that we often use very basic concepts to understand more complex ones. English speakers, for example, often think of relationships as journeys.[13] And we understand abstractions like government and society using more personal metaphors from family experiences.

Government Evokes Family Metaphors: How to Frame Liberal and Conservative Perspectives

To win elections we need to repeat stories that consistently build upon a shared metaphor. This advice isn't new or unique, and it applies to almost anything from selling soap to politics.

Strict Father, Nurturing Parent

But Lakoff goes further than this, finding the specific metaphors most people use for government. We think about complex subjects using metaphors; with politics, we typically think using family metaphors. Each type of politics, each view of the nation, is built on a different view of a healthy family, led by either a strict father or nurturing parents.

Maybe you can sell soap with any marketing metaphor, but you can only advocate liberal ideals by reinforcing the nurturing-parent metaphor. Moderates — the people

13. George Lakoff, "Metaphor: The Language of the Unconscious: The Theory of Conceptual Metaphor Applied to Dream Analysis", June 24, 1992. CognitivePolitics.org/metaphor. The first few pages introduce Lakoff's concepts on metaphors for relationships, which are similar to his ideas for politics. Or for a longer introduction, read George Lakoff's *Metaphors We Live By*.

who might be swayed by a campaign — use both nurturing and strict metaphors to think about politics at different times. The more you use language and stories from a nurturing-parent frame, the more you strengthen those pathways.

Democrats win when we create, and repeat, stories with an underlying metaphor of nurturance. Evoke a strict father, even with the word "no" in front of your story, and Republicans win.

{We do / We don't} need a **strong military** to defend us against a/an {existential / nonexistent} **threat.**

I use the word "Democrats," rather than liberals, because this is best done in an organized way. Many stories need to riff on a shared theme.

Patterns in Politics

These two metaphors begin to explain the odd collections typical of liberal and conservative thinking: What do pro-life, the death penalty, lower taxes, a stronger military, and men with uniformly short haircuts have to do with each other?[14]

At heart, the difference is very simple: conservatives, liberals, and people in between all think about our leaders using the metaphors of parenthood. When your heart seeks a *nurturing parent*, you'll think liberal thoughts. When fear or mistrust lead you to seek a protective and just *strict father*, you wind up thinking conservative thoughts.

Suddenly, the odd collection of liberal and conservative views has a clear internal logic. A strict father in a scary world demands accountability. If you get pregnant, if you can't afford health care for your children, if you have trouble getting a job, it is required of you to deal with the consequences. No one is required to help you with your responsibilities. In many cases, help would make you weaker, dependent. And a disciplined father prepares you for a scary world: you need to support the group, be willing to join the army, fit in to a cohesive group — get a haircut that identifies you with your group members. It's all about your responsibilities.

"History teaches that wars begin when governments believe the price of aggression is cheap."
— Ronald Reagan[15]

Conservatives see a dangerous world: strength and discipline keep us safe, while gentleness and appeasement endanger us.

14. Lakoff, *Don't Think of an Elephant!*, idea introduced on page 5.

15. President Ronald Reagan, "Address to the Nation and Other Countries on United States-Soviet Relations," Jan. 16, 1984, ReaganLibrary.archives.gov.

Correspondingly, the nurturing parent wants us all to look out for each other and learn to thrive in a beautiful, abundant world where all our needs can be met if we cooperate. The ideal government provides support, acceptance, and protection from potential bullies while also shielding you from the worst consequences of your own failures.

Of course, individuals on either side will likely find this an annoying simplification, but it begins to explain why the parties and media divide the way they do.

A Metaphor on Metaphors

Imagine that you build thoughts with metaphors. And you build conservative thoughts with bricks, liberal thoughts with lumber. It is more effective to build the whole house with your metaphor, ignoring theirs. If you say "bricks are a bad choice," people will think about bricks and will build a conservative thought structure.

Swing Voters Think Using Both Frames; Reinforce the Nurturing Frame

Most people, especially swing voters, do not stick to one framework but jump back and forth between both strict and nurturing frameworks. Swing voters do not hold centrist views — rather, they use both frameworks. Liberal messages won't reach people by aiming for the center but by reinforcing the nurturing frame that almost everyone uses at least sometimes.[16] Metaphor choices influence politics whether you are focused on one issue or hoping to change society's general views.

When discussing a controversial issue, use a nurturing metaphor. For example, instead of being against the *War on Drugs*, you might support *Treatment for Addiction*. This changes the frame in two ways: the metaphor switches from war to care, and the main focus switches from the controversy of drugs to the needs of people.

In the long term, whichever metaphor is used more often will be reinforced. So the more you get people to think about compassion, abundance, and nurturing, the more they become progressive; the more they think about fear, scarcity, and anger, the more they become conservative. This reinforcement doesn't only happen in political conversations. If family gatherings are compassionate, if you watch movies where cooperation is effective, this can influence political thoughts later. Head-to-head arguments are not the only way to change your friends' and relatives' political views.

16. Zoe Williams, "George Lakoff: 'Conservatives Don't Follow the Polls, They Want to Change Them … Liberals Do Everything Wrong'," The Guardian, February 1, 2014, Books. CognitivePolitics.org/centrists.

Further Explorations on Framing

Framing a Compassionate World: Challenges and Limits

We've covered the basics of Lakoff's ideas, and the Democratic leadership is familiar with them. So why aren't these ideas being implemented well? Sometimes the Democrats fail to develop, share and repeat a message and story. But often there are underlying challenges when compassionate people try to develop sound bites and marketing campaigns.

Progressives Demand Rights Instead of Telling a True Story

Conservatives are constantly evoking a strict-father world, evoking a need for sternness in a rough and immoral world: crime, terrorists, illegal immigrants who are lazy, illegal immigrants who work too hard and take our jobs, runaway deficits. They talk about war, *ILLEGALS*, and criminal activities, which all evoke a need for a discipliner who keeps the troops in order.

Conservative politicians and think tanks implement the kind of advice that Lakoff gives.

Progressives often skip telling a story; we miss the opportunity to evoke a nurturing parent. Pro-life advocates claim abortion *"stops a beating heart"* — I can picture that. Meanwhile, pro-choice advocates call for choice as an abstract right — I have no sense of a story. Liberals have no story until some person is considering a particular choice. There is no progressive story — nothing is happening — until you picture a woman making the choice of an abortion. If you have a friend with an unplanned pregnancy, there are many ways to be supportive or nurturing, but this story is rarely used. We don't call ourselves pro-abortion, and our policy choices are not pro-abortion, but poor framing leaves that as our story. Rights are not stories, and we need to tell our stories rather than say no to theirs.

A PIG IS AS INTELLIGENT AS A DOG.
Ok, did that fact alone work? Did that fact cause you to stop eating pork yet? Why not? Blasting facts at people only rarely works: Can you fit facts within the stories they use to understand the world? Can you evoke the stories that would be most helpful?

Marketing Is Easy; Speak Your Truth

The world we want calls for attention to policy, but sound-bite framing has dehumanizing bias that works better for cynical *Fox News* politics than for liberal ideals — or for honest conservative ideals. My advice: keep winning policy debates and expect to lose the framing fight! Just try not to lose so badly.

The Democratic Party often ignores framing and marketing advice. When the Party does turn to marketing, it tends to overdo it. Those politicians ***follow*** the polls. Following polls merely squeezes out short-term electoral success, rather than **influencing** long-term thinking. Conservative think tanks use polls to look far forward and define the debate.

Framing does not mean repeating shallow platitudes and slogans nor eschewing logic. It does mean having memorable hooks and consistent metaphors, shared by many politicians and many nonpoliticians, that weave together policy specifics into a larger, memorable story of our values.

Evoking the Strict Father without Words: From Current Events to Angry Conversations

How do liberals accidentally evoke the strict-father metaphor and undermine nurturant views? Lakoff has a straightforward answer: you use the words that evoke the metaphor, whether you affirm them or negate them.

We should { intensify / say no to } the war on drugs.

Using war as the metaphor for drug use evokes the strict-father frame, whether or not we put the word "no" in front. What else moves people toward thinking in the conservative frame?

Lakoff says we think using metaphors. This would mean that situations of powerlessness or chaos will lead us to seek metaphors about power or evoke a wish for a strict-father protector, no matter what words are spoken. For example, when Iranians took hostages in 1979, and President Carter was unable to bring the situation under control, did anyone have to say anything? Or would each of us have thoughts that sought more power and control and security, evoking the strict-father frame without a word being spoken?

If this is the case, it puts another constraint on Lakoff's paradigm. Yes, a great communicator like Reagan was can push metaphors a bit, but the underlying reality

also generates metaphors. If we create more effective programs and take responsibility to fix them if they don't work, then no one will need to call in the strict father to clean up our mess. Liberals dominated American politics from the Great Depression through the 1960s. In that last decade, we built a welfare system that damaged many communities' work ethics, and our programs helped but far less than we promised. Reality trumped framing; reality defined a limit to what frames would be tolerated.

Compare and Contrast Orwellian Propaganda with Framing

Sometimes Lakoff and parallel language experts on the conservative side are seen as dishonest propagandists, as Orwellian. Careful attention to language is a part of both Orwellian manipulation but also poetry and therapy. Lakoff himself is very explicit in his advice to Democrats and their allies: tell the truth. A good way to dig deeper into Lakoff's framing advice is to compare and contrast it with Orwellian or dishonest propaganda.

> "The great enemy of clear language is insincerity."
> —George Orwell

Lakoff's perspective is that you are *always* framing. There are no complex thoughts that aren't built on simpler ones. For example, let's look at the "Affordable Care Act." Affordable might be true, a lie, a distraction, or your side's belief — if it were untrue or insincere, that would make it Orwellian. But for the moment putting truth or falsehood aside, it is a poor choice of metaphor: *affordable* evokes thoughts of consumer products, either affordable or expensive, like a TV is affordable or expensive. Both the *Affordable Care Act* and the *Expensive Care Act* use the same consumer goods metaphor. Only free-market health care advocates should be using a consumer goods metaphor. Democrats shouldn't draw attention primarily to whether care is affordable or expensive if they want you to think of health care as a right, nor if they want to evoke a nurturing mental framework. We might evoke "Health Care for All" or Lakoff's suggestion of "The American Plan."[17]

Orwellian Framing

Enhanced interrogation and *revenue enhancement* are examples of careful framing used to avoid the truth or, in Orwell's words, "to name things without calling up mental pictures of them."[18] Lakoff encourages us to tell the truth: if we believe our agenda is worth the taxes required to fund it, say so.

Honest Framing

Honest framing means taking pride in what you believe. For taxes, Lakoff suggests the metaphor of *membership fees:* this metaphor does not hide that you are paying, it only suggests that the payment is worth it, which is what Lakoff

17. Lakoff and Wehling, *The Little Blue Book*, 116.

18. George Orwell, "Politics and the English Language," 1946. http://www.orwell.ru/library/essays/politics/english/e_polit.

believes. *Tax relief* parallels the advice Lakoff is giving Democrats: it's an honest framing from a small-government perspective, casting taxes as an affliction. Evoking a metaphor either of membership or of affliction when discussing taxes are both non-Orwellian framings that emphasize what the speakers sincerely believe.

There are many approaches to political messaging. You can find examples of politicians trying every one of these: advocating a policy without careful messaging; choosing policies based on polls; pretending or lying that a policy does what polls say people want; attacking opponents; telling your story hoping that people will begin to see the world the way you see it. Lakoff advocates for the last approach.[19]

Backfire: When Metaphors Clash with Moral Values

Lakoff encourages us to have a set of progressive metaphors across a wide range of issues. I've met many grassroots Democrats who love his ideas, while politicians rarely implement them.

For example, George Lakoff and Elisabeth Wehling (coauthors of *The Little Blue Book* and various articles) encourage progressives to stop calling abortion "abortion" — the metaphor that you are aborting a mission that you began on purpose — and instead use "development prevention." [20]

What do you think would happen if Obama refused to use the word *abortion* and instead used *development prevention?* Imagine a Catholic churchgoer who gives to charity, volunteers at the food shelter, is against the death penalty, and does not understand how Iraq fit the requirements of a just war. If President Obama began calling the termination of a fertilized egg or fetus "development prevention" rather than "abortion," would she internalize the new frame and no longer think of development prevention as an important issue? Or would it not fit into her worldview, making liberals seem outside her community of shared moral values? Experts are in conflict. What do you think?

"Cognitive psychology has not shown that people absorb frames through sheer repetition. On the contrary, information is retained when it fits into a person's greater understanding of the subject matter."
— Steven Pinker (author of *The Blank Slate*) challenging Lakoff's ideas[21]

19. Lakoff, *Don't Think of an Elephant!*, 100-101.

20. George Lakoff and Elisabeth Wehling. "The Sacredness of Life and Liberty," The Huffington Post, July 16, 2012, TheHuffingtonPost.com. CognitivePolitics.org/abortion.

21. Steven Pinker, "Block That Metaphor!" New Republic, October 9, 2006, NewRepublic.com. CognitivePolitics.org/pinker.

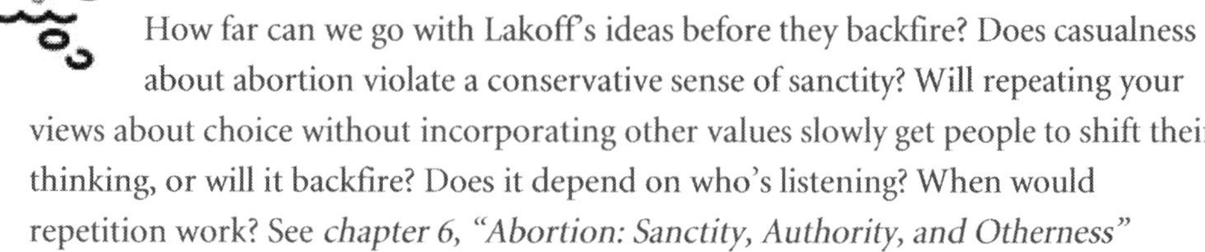

When Does Framing Backfire?

How far can we go with Lakoff's ideas before they backfire? Does casualness about abortion violate a conservative sense of sanctity? Will repeating your views about choice without incorporating other values slowly get people to shift their thinking, or will it backfire? Does it depend on who's listening? When would repetition work? See *chapter 6, "Abortion: Sanctity, Authority, and Otherness" (p.99).*

Real-World Example: Connection and Compromise Require a Shared Frame

Changing metaphors can be key. For example, after the Democratic primary in 2016, Hillary Clinton supporters were trying to rally Bernie Sanders voters. Many young Bernie voters saw Hillary Clinton as a powerful establishment authority who was unfair to them — the metaphors could be students describing a teacher or children describing a parent abusing authority. Hillary's supporters often described her as qualified, intelligent and committed — metaphors related to grading or job interviews, with voters as the judge while the politician is the applicant. This leads to broken arguments across two disconnected metaphors: "she doesn't deserve my vote" is answered with "she is more qualified." You can't meet in the middle of such different framing: piling on more and more evidence that she is incredibly qualified does not answer whether she deserves your vote.

Getting people to switch metaphors is often very tricky; you can't just insist that someone switch through repetition. Hillary Clinton supporters might try starting conversations that assess politicians point by point, making your conversation fit the job interview metaphor. You might start by saying that Sanders is more qualified to rally the youth vote. A Sanders supporter will be happy to agree with you, and now you are having a conversation within your preferred frame. Find every small way in which Sanders does well in your frame and focus on those. Leave out the most obvious ways in which your candidate does well in your frame, and let them think of those independently. [22]

If you successfully build a framework with your metaphor for a topic, people are likely to change their mind on their own. A previously resistant Sanders supporter who stops asking the yes-no question "does she deserve my vote" and starts asking

22. In this example, aiming to convince Sanders supporters within their frame is also an option — which would mean setting aside all your arguments about qualifications or whether other politicians deserve their vote less.

"in what way is each candidate qualified" won't need your help answering the new question.

Breaking the Frames Used in the 2016 Election?

An earlier question asked what frames you thought the presidential candidates used. I think Bernie Sanders followed the advice for liberals, consistently framing with the cooperative nurturing message "Not Me, Us." Hillary Clinton described herself as "qualified," a neutral and centrist frame. Her word choices brought to mind a qualified job applicant, someone ready to step into a role — not a leader, not someone who would break out of that role. Trump focused on his dealmaking, strength, and bluster. He made me think of a mob boss or gang leader — a dominant alpha male who would get things done for you, asking nothing of you but your loyalty. This is not a frame of discipline and guidance typical of the *STRICT-FATHER* campaigns run by Republicans in the past.

For each candidate, what would cause their frame to unravel? Consider the different ways you might finish these two sentences:

(1) The job applicant was qualified, but:
(2) The mafia boss tried to make deals you couldn't refuse, but:

- ☐ they cheated.
- ☐ they lied.
- ☐ they bought off a prosecutor.
- ☐ they were unfair to people who were not like them.
- ☐ they weren't loyal to people loyal to them.
- ☐ they ______________________.

Exercise: Differentiate Policy, Frame, and Types of Compromise

Framing connects many concepts: goals, truth, marketing, policy, polls, and compromises. The last exercise of this chapter is to deconstruct a single issue, looking at these concepts side by side. The example explores President Bill Clinton's approach to gay men and women serving in the military that led to "Don't Ask, Don't Tell." Pick an issue you care about and explore different approaches.

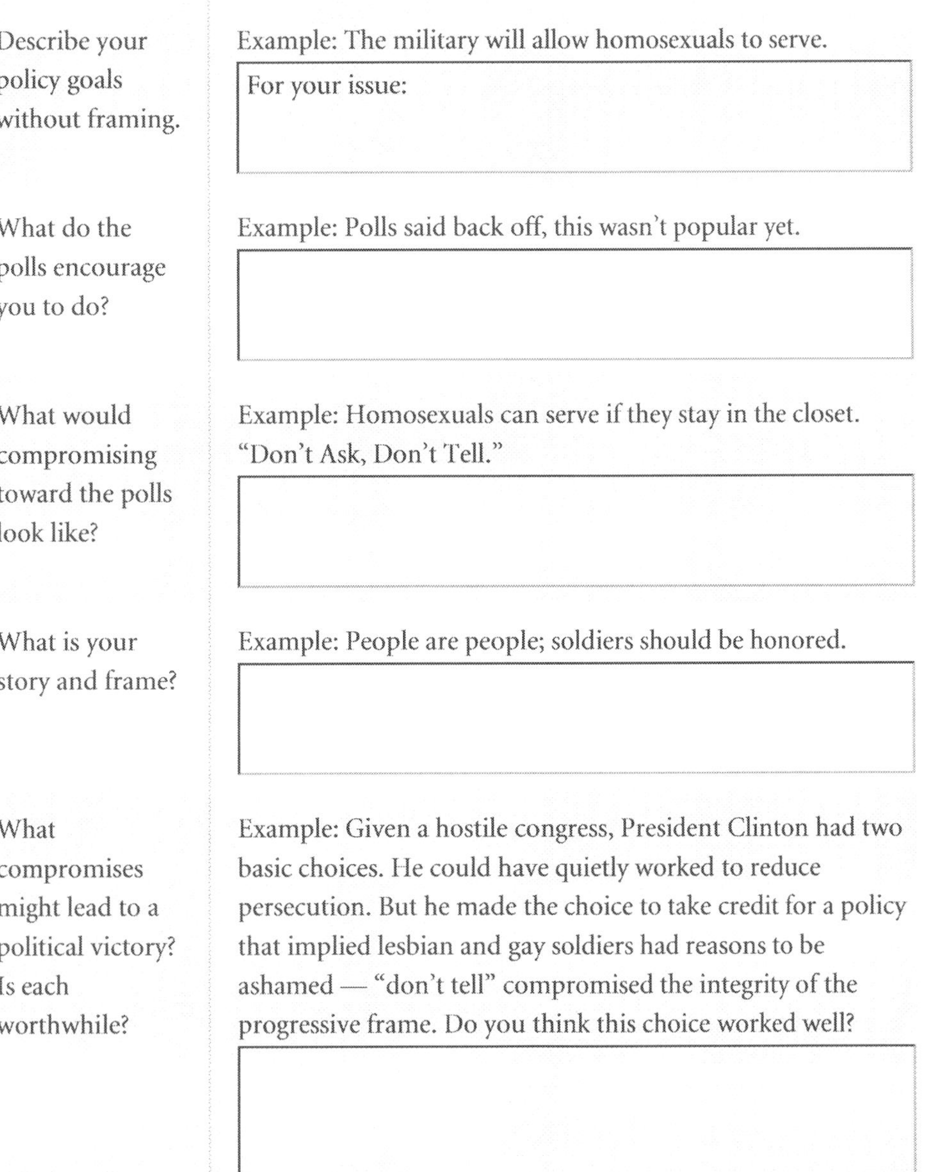

Describe your policy goals without framing.	Example: The military will allow homosexuals to serve. For your issue:
What do the polls encourage you to do?	Example: Polls said back off, this wasn't popular yet.
What would compromising toward the polls look like?	Example: Homosexuals can serve if they stay in the closet. "Don't Ask, Don't Tell."
What is your story and frame?	Example: People are people; soldiers should be honored.
What compromises might lead to a political victory? Is each worthwhile?	Example: Given a hostile congress, President Clinton had two basic choices. He could have quietly worked to reduce persecution. But he made the choice to take credit for a policy that implied lesbian and gay soldiers had reasons to be ashamed — "don't tell" compromised the integrity of the progressive frame. Do you think this choice worked well?

Review

Part II of this book will use many of Lakoff's ideas when discussing specific issues. It will also point out when other approaches are more powerful and when Lakoff's one-sided framing might throw fuel on the partisan fires. In my experience, Lakoff's framing techniques work much better to define new stories than to crush entrenched ones. For example, we might tell a story of America's history that focuses on egalitarian and democratic values shared by most moderates and conservatives, leaving the story of American Exceptionalism to fade. Or we might be able to frame trade policy. But we need to be cautious trying to reframe strongly held views on abortion or gun control.

Recommended Resources

George Lakoff's *Don't Think of an Elephant!* is a good foundation for political audiences, and *The Little Blue Book* is a very fast read that focuses on the issues. *Moral Politics* gives a more solid, academic foundation.

James Dobson's *Dare to Discipline* is a good primer for liberals to see the strict-father approach from a conservative's perspective.

Chapter 2

Cognitive Science and Psychology: The Roots of Conservatism and Liberalism

What psychological differences lead to our political differences? What are the fears, hopes and values that differ between liberals and conservatives? How can good people communicate when they have different ways of seeing the world?

Remember: Patterns are just patterns. They are clues that sometimes lead to interesting questions — using them for answers will lead to problems. Individuals break these patterns in countless ways.

Cognitive scientists studying liberals and conservatives are finding deep differences, differences that go well beyond politics. There are traits visible in childhood that predict our adult politics: future liberals are more excited by new experiences while future conservatives are more focused on safety and cleanliness. Conservative brains also seem attuned to a wider range of values: we all consider compassion and fairness, but conservatives also focus on community-building values. In the last two decades, studies of liberal and conservative psychology have seen an explosion of results using everything from simple surveys to MRI brain scans.

Cognitive Science and Psychology

Much of this research is used as useless ammunition in arguments no one can win, trying to prove which side is superior. Liberals often slightly twist the results to mock conservatives as more fearful. Jonathan Haidt's *The Righteous Mind*, introduced halfway through this chapter, is one of the main exceptions. He shows that when we're curious, we'll find that both approaches have insights worth understanding, and that curiosity can help us both build bridges and change minds.

The Psychology beneath Liberal and Conservative: New Research, New Perspectives

An Age of Cognitive Politics

Political views often come packaged together in superficially surprising patterns. We're not surprised to see pro-life and pro-gun on one side, standardized access to health care and a diversity of lifestyles welcomed by the other. Even if there are many individual exceptions, today these patterns dominate our government and our media.

Chapter 1 explored Lakoff's explanation: we think with metaphors, and each set makes sense depending on your metaphor for government, whether that is the strict-father or nurturing-parent metaphor. But these sets seem to have deeper roots than just politics. For example, the main conservative pattern also includes preference for cleanliness and order, a trait expressed in childhood long before someone thinks about government.[23] Psychological studies don't contradict the government-metaphor model but indicate that we can look deeper.

And these psychological differences seem to be driving our politics ever more since the Culture Wars of the 1960s — when Civil Rights, Vietnam, and social issues replaced economics as the loudest conflicts between the parties. In the middle of the twentieth century, labor unions played a major role in defining the divisions in politics. Working-class people with a wide range of psychological intuitions about politics would form one community and often vote their working-class interests together. Whatever your position on abortion, you would read your economic class's news source, whether that was a union newsletter or business paper. Today, psychological differences seem to dominate not just individual politicians but entire parties.[24] Whatever your economic class, you might read social media that echoes your thoughts on gun control and abortion.

US Speaker of the House Tip O'Neill said "All politics is local." There are times when the electorate is dominated by people paying attention to their local economic interests. In recent years we have shifted toward a politics of underlying values. We're no longer asking if politicians can help us but instead relying on how they feel to our intuitions.

23. Jack Block and Jeanne H. Block, "Nursery school personality and political orientation two decades later," Journal of Research in Personality, 2005. http://www.berkeley.edu/news/media/releases/2006/03/block.pdf

24. These summaries are based on many studies, some of which will be explored in the next section.

Definition: Cognitive Politics

Liberal and conservative are defined in many ways, each definition with imperfect overlap — for example, "fiscal conservative" or "social liberal." This book adds another: a person with the underlying values that *most* liberals share will be called a *COGNITIVE LIBERAL* and likewise for a *COGNITIVE CONSERVATIVE*.

Summary of Current Research

The last two decades have seen hundreds of studies exploring the differences between liberals and conservatives, and we're seeing some degree of consensus. An excellent and very readable cross-section of peer-reviewed studies spanning the field is "Differences in Conservative and Liberal Brains: 20 Peer-Reviewed Studies Show Liberals and Conservatives Physiologically Different"[25] at ProCon.org.

"The Secret Lives of Liberals and Conservatives" reviews the history of the psychological study of politics, all the way back to Freud. Just as liberals and conservatives follow patterns — guns, abortion, taxes and militarization lining up in the same way across many times and cultures — they seem to have consistent sets of psychological characteristics. "Resistance to change and support for inequality," for example, are different characteristics but are "very often found together." In other words, liberal and conservative are not arbitrary groups of characteristics but connected to deeper psychological patterns.[26] "The Secret Lives of Liberals and Conservatives" summarizes a wide range of research as follows:

"In general, liberals are more open-minded, creative, curious, and novelty seeking, whereas conservatives are more orderly, conventional, and better organized."[27]

These psychological patterns start early.

25. "Differences in Conservative and Liberal Brains," (Updated January 26, 2015). *http://2016election.procon.org/view.resource.php?resourceID=005927*

26. Dana R. Carney, John T. Jost, Samuel D. Gosling, Jeff Potter. "The Secret Lives of Liberals and Conservatives: Personality Profiles, Interaction Styles, and the Things They Leave Behind," (Political Psychology, Vol. 29, No. 6, 2008). psych.nyu.edu Entire article recommended reading. Freud, p811-812. Discussion of evidence that what underlies the political patterns tend to come as sets, not as independent characteristics, p814.

27. "The Secret Lives," p807-808.

"Nursery School Personality and Political Orientation Two Decades Later"[28] shows that there are psychological differences before we are old enough to have political views. For example, nursery school children whose teachers described them as relatively undercontrolled and preferring less structure were found to be more likely to become liberals as adults. This is strong evidence that if we think of liberals and conservatives as *also* having other characteristics, we are probably reversing causality. The psychology that drives many people toward a political ideology is in place very early in life, before real opinions on political issues are formed.

The rest of this chapter will generally use the results from the above three sources — though there are countless other papers that could be referenced instead.

Is Studying These Differences Useful?

Bias Leads to Error and Distraction

These studies show real differences between liberals and conservatives as demographics, appearing over and over in a wide variety of studies, but there is no path to judge these differences without bias. Even at the extremes the research seems to hold up — for example, right-wing Nazi psychologist Erich Jaensch extolled certain conservative traits as "stability" while left-leaning psychologists described the same traits as "rigidity," but they largely agreed on the underlying research and merely labeled the results with their opinion.[29]

It should surprise no one that left-leaning scientists use positive adjectives for left-leaning behavior while right-leaning scientists see the positive aspects of right-leaning behavior. What is striking is how much the patterns themselves are consistent across the research.

> "It is possible to generate either flattering or unflattering psychological portraits at either end of the political spectrum."[30]

In the partisan press these studies are often reduced to simple ideas and insults, such as claiming that conservatives are more fearful. The same survey answers can be called *healthy caution* or *unhealthy fear,* revealing more about the person summarizing a survey's results than about the people who answered the survey's questions. It is not subtle that conservatives more often believe you should prepare to deal with criminals or other nations by being well armed and prepared. Conservative values are adaptive when the threats are real. The psychological studies don't tell us,

28. Jack Block and Jeanne H. Block, "Nursery School Personality and Political Orientation Two Decades Later."

29. "The Secret Lives," 810.

30. "The Secret Lives," 809.

can't tell us, who is right or how cautious we should be. They might help us understand how we fear or hope in different ways and why good people might still disagree.

Marketing Segmentation

Opinions on what psychology says about politics have a tendency to go to extremes. Some people use these studies as "proof" that psychological shortcomings completely explain the other side, while others reject that there is anything to learn at all. Away from politics, market segmentation is similar but without the controversy. No one is surprised when an advertising campaign is more effective for trying to understand the audience, and no one is surprised when many individuals fall far outside the statistical average of their segment.

This book gives tools to break the feedback loop that comes from listening to media tuned toward your political marketing group's preferences. *Cognitive liberal* and *cognitive conservative* are best viewed as mere marketing terms: user personas for politics, or marketing demographic segmentation. These studies point at the places where we most often make mistakes when talking to people with different perspectives. They are fascinating as starting points for questions and terrible as ending points for assumptions.

The psychological studies tend to be more accurate for explaining how the media target their audiences and how politicians are advertising to us. Understand the divisions, so you can work on breaking down the usual feedback loops.

Another useful comparison is with personality tests such as Myers Briggs or the Enneagram. They never describe one personality type as better than another. At their best they focus on challenges and growth opportunities for each personality type, exploring ideas on how to handle conflict between them. *Cognitive Politics* is not aiming to make judgments nor to prove any particular theory, but to help you sift through ideas coming from psychology departments and keep the ones that improve your conversations.

Making Psychological Studies Useful: Tell New Stories

It's hard to do much with data points from surveys. What should we emphasize? What influences politics? We have come to see liberals and conservatives as pure political opponents; if one side wins, the other side loses. We know that liberal and conservative attitudes come from psychological frameworks much deeper

> "Early and provident fear is the mother of safety."[31]
> — Edmund Burke, often called the "father of modern English conservatism"

than politics, and that there are good people on all sides. Can we tell stories that are true, but don't describe us merely as opposites and opponents?

Some of the differences that start in early childhood take us right back to the basic definitions of conservative and liberal we learned in high school: that liberals wanted society to brazenly explore what is new and experiment wildly, while conservatives seek to hold on to established traditions and experiment more slowly. In broad demographic averages, kids who enjoy exploring and take risks are more likely to grow up to be liberal. Conservatives-to-be tend to like order, cleanliness and the familiar just a bit more, on average, than future liberals.

What story would let us be one community instead of warring factions? Let's explore new terms that might help us drop old baggage:

Cognitive Liberals as Risk-Taking Explorers

Even as children, typical future liberals like to explore, to meet and trust new people, to try new things. Life is better when you shake things up. Liberal brains are relatively tuned to notice hope and opportunities. We don't just take more risks — we enjoy risks. It's fun to be far from home, in a land where you don't speak the language, surrounded by people who don't look like you.

Cognitive Conservatives as Cautious Protectors

Prototypical conservatives enjoy a safe home: order, tight communities where everyone knows and supports each other. They focus on the smallest communities of family, church, or perhaps a band of brothers in the military. Life is better when things and people are all in their places. Conservative brains are tuned to watch out for danger and band together to create safety: it's a dangerous and dirty world out there, so look after the people in your immediate community, stay clean, and respect that your elders may have found some wisdom — taboos might be there for a reason.

31. The Project Gutenberg EBook of *The Works of the Right Honourable Edmund Burke, Vol. VII. (of 12)*. Speech on the Petition of the Unitarians. Gutenberg.org.

Reframing Left versus Right: We Function Better Together

On an evolutionary timescale, it's easy to imagine communities thriving with both defensive and exploratory members. In dealings with neighbors, the explorers might express excitement to trade, and the defenders might share their views of all the risks involved. These conversations would have happened around a campfire, a town hall, or when the US had three major networks watched by most voters.

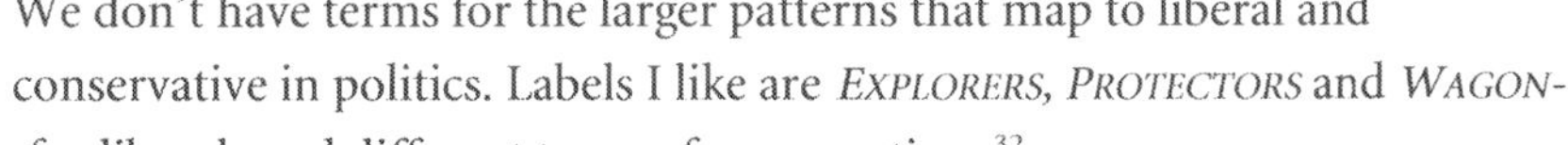

Explorers, Protectors, and Wagon-Circlers

We don't have terms for the larger patterns that map to liberal and conservative in politics. Labels I like are *Explorers, Protectors* and *Wagon-Circlers*, for liberals and different types of conservatives.[32]

Explorer describes people who are less fearful, more trusting of strangers, prefer equality, second-guess authority, and don't take taboos too seriously. They listen to John Lennon's "Imagine" and feel inspired.[33] Explorers express these values across their lives, and when these values intersect with politics, we label them liberals.

When protectors hear Lennon sing "imagine there's no countries," they imagine a world where we would let our guard down and soon have chaos and war. This attitude reminds them of Chamberlain declaring "peace for our time" while trying to appease Hitler, which led to disaster and war.[34] Instead the phrase "peace through strength" resonates for protectors — they want peace and are willing to work for it, not just daydream.

Both *protectors* and *wagon-circlers* are metaphors matching different flavors of conservative moral foundations. Protectors I imagine as hardworking good neighbors, rooted in their own communities but confident and caring to give a helping hand to strangers. Wagon-circlers are similarly rooted in their communities, but afraid of those outside their communities. Protectors and wagon-circlers might agree on deficit spending but diverge strongly on admitting Syrian refugees.

If you want to lower the heat of political arguments, it might be helpful to find words for the larger psychological frames that lead to our politics. There are many other psychological frameworks: many of us know our Myers Briggs scores or our

32. Note that both *explorers* and *protectors* are positive frames, while wagon-circling is a frame fewer people would choose for themselves. I've purposefully chosen words for the best and worst aspects of conservatism and separated them, intending to seek out positive ways for liberals to connect with and negotiate with conservatives. Chapter 5 covers wagon-circling politics.

33. *Righteous Mind*, 307.

34. Conservative British Prime Minister Neville Chamberlain spoke that phrase after signing the Munich Agreement, agreeing to Hitler's demands to annex territory in Czechoslovakia in the hopes of appeasing Hitler and preventing further aggression.

Enneagram number. People can talk about their psychological types at a party while enjoying themselves — these differences lead us to curiosity, not bitter fights. The Enneagram is a great example in focusing on how each type has common patterns of being psychologically healthy or unhealthy. The models don't have to be perfectly accurate for the advice on communication and self-improvement to be helpful. If we view the broader psychological patterns that lead to our politics with similar stories and models, it may help us shift from anger to curiosity.

Liberals and Conservatives Are Separating

In America today, the cautious and the explorers are talking to each other less. We are no longer mixing as much in the same unions, churches, or neighborhoods — large numbers of explorers are leaving family churches and home communities, moving toward each other in cities.[35] Today we don't just disagree about the news; partisans often get news from sources that don't even cover the same stories.

If ordinary people are not divided by greed or stupidity, but rather by two different worldviews that both make perfect sense from an evolutionary psychology perspective, what does that mean for politics? When we watch the same news as our neighbors and talk to each other about it, we might discuss our views and disagree with one another. But when we separate into groups watching entirely different media that don't even cover the same issues, we increasingly believe the views of other groups are alien. And with so many people deciding their votes based on ideology, fewer votes are cast to resist special interests and corrupting influences.

Historical Examples

Franklin D. Roosevelt, Churchill and Hitler were contemporaries with very different approaches to fear, discipline, abundance and change. These historical examples both fit the psychological research comparing liberals and conservatives, and show how easy it is to oversimplify those differences.

Faced with the Great Depression in the 1930s, Franklin D. Roosevelt exemplifies the liberal or explorer ideal, reminding us that "the only thing we have to fear is fear itself." He saw a world of abundance where "plenty is at our doorstep." He was immediately ready to move on, experimenting with program after program exploring new solutions. [36]

Hitler used the same Depression to increase fear. He manufactured conspiracies in order to convince some Germans that they were the real Germans, and to circle their wagons against everyone else. The Nazi movement built right-wing electoral success by systematically increasing fear and defining an in-group.

35. Bill Bishop, *The Big Sort : why the clustering of like-minded America is tearing us apart* (Boston: Houghton Mifflin, 2008).

36. President Franklin Delano Roosevelt, "Inaugural Address," March 4 1933.

Under attack during World War II, Churchill stepped up as Britain's protector. The electorate craved his invocation to "keep buggering on" — encouraging discipline in the face of real fears. He didn't manufacture paranoia like Hitler, nor imply that there was nothing to fear like FDR. He was militaristic, strict, and had built his career around reducing change in the British empire, while FDR was nurturing and explored change with abandon. Both those very different approaches were successful at leading their nations through dark times.

Many of the studies so far explore demographic patterns based on the assumption that you can draw a graph with an axis from liberal to conservative, or from nurturing to strict leaders. But it also mangles the truth to draw a single line from FDR to both Hitler and Churchill. The studies so far only begin to shine a light on the differences between liberals and conservatives, and it is important to look from many different angles.

Historical Failures: Distinctive Shortcomings of Different Moral Foundations

Authoritarian leaders have often induced fear among people who feel strongly about their communities, whipping up the majority against racial, religious, or other minorities. Left-wing victories play out differently, but have sometimes also led to disasters. While Hitler came to power riding on hate for outsiders, Stalin did not. The messages that ultimately brought Stalin to power were his predecessors' liberal messages of empathy and fairness, broad empowerment, and equality for all, along with anger aimed at actual overlords. But liberals should be very cautious when they gather power but *lack* fear of how it could ultimately be used. People who identified on the left have won a few tremendous victories — notably the Russian Revolution that led to the Soviet Union and Democratic President Lyndon B. Johnson's Great Society reforms in the 1960s — then lost power when their focus on compassion and idealism alone didn't sufficiently consider how authority and communities could become unrooted.

In both cases, people on the left overestimated the power of idealism against bureaucracy, self-interest and human nature. In the Soviet Union, they failed to constrain the lines of power. In the US, shortcomings of the Great Society programs brought a long period of Democratic dominance and ever increasing social welfare programs to an end. The key to the failure was very relevant to this book — projects such as public housing showed a failure to intuit community-building moral foundations, and poorly designed welfare programs simultaneously helped reduce poverty but also damaged many people's self-discipline.

Healthy politics doesn't come from one party rule, but from the interplay between healthy flavors of liberalism or conservatism. What can liberals do to challenge conservatives to be their best?

We Misinterpret Differing Priorities as Cross-Purposes

Politics plays out with left opposed to right. It's hard to compare the psychology of liberals and conservatives without making them sound like opposites. But is this really the case? In a community, seeking ways to explore and preparing to protect what you have are both healthy values.

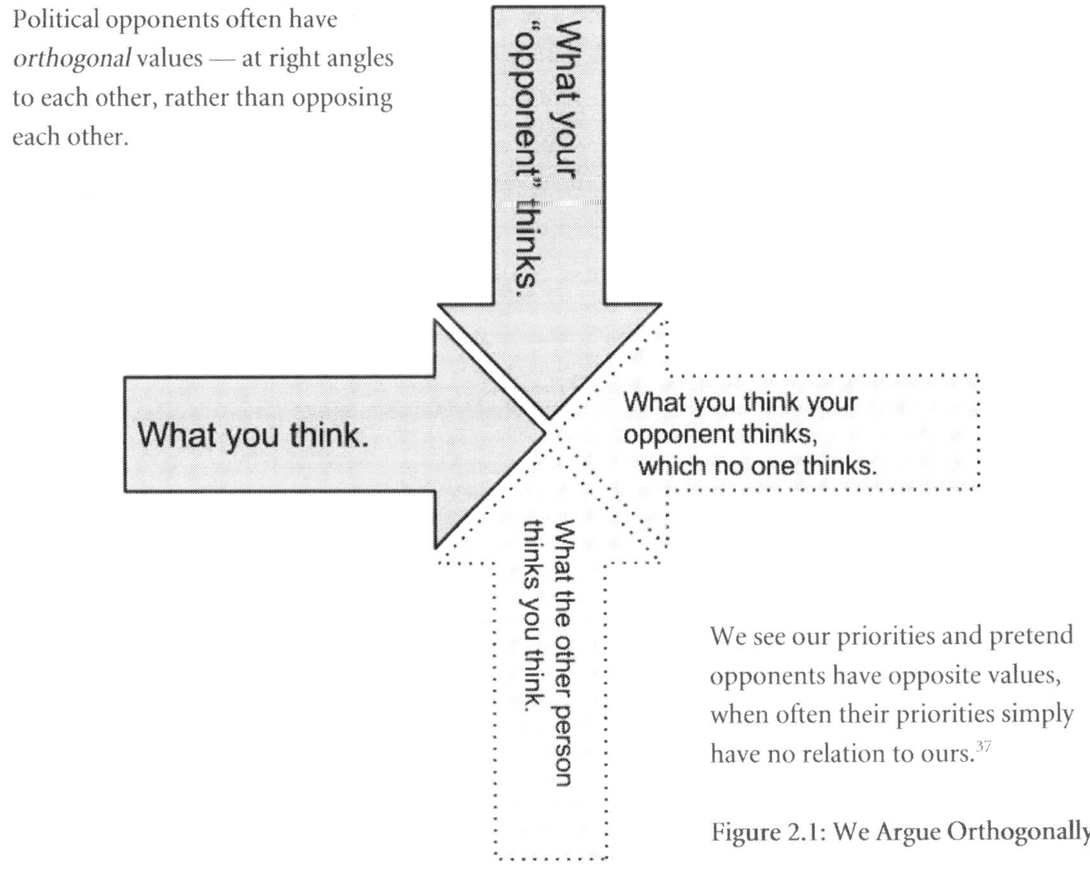

Political opponents often have *orthogonal* values — at right angles to each other, rather than opposing each other.

We see our priorities and pretend opponents have opposite values, when often their priorities simply have no relation to ours.[37]

Figure 2.1: We Argue Orthogonally

37. Russ Roberts, Interview with Arnold Kling. "Kling on the Three Languages of Politics," Library of Economics and Liberty, EconTalk.org. Kling shares his views on why libertarians, conservatives and liberals talk right past each other.

Asymmetries on Fear: Global Warming

Global warming is a huge threat — do we need a Churchill to protect us? Climate change is a particular challenge for liberals: we face real dangers, but fear nonetheless shifts people into conservative mindsets.

From the outside it might not be obvious, but if you get involved with environmental groups, their strategists advise to tone down the fear.[38] Of course, fear is sometimes used to drive the base, the true believers, to donate. Activists in private conversations are extremely afraid of how bad global warming will be, but find that fear of global warming crowds out hope and loses votes. Compare this with the color warnings for terrorism, where fear successfully wins votes toward the right.

What Would You Emphasize?

If you were to share news via social media about global warming, what would you emphasize: hope and solutions, scientific understanding, local preparations, or how bad things will be? Whom do you hope to influence? What do you want them to do?

Feedback Loops between Abundance and Hope, Scarcity and Fear

Compassion is not among the traits where psychologists find differences between liberals and conservatives. But at the political level, liberals are much more focused on caring for those in need. Why?

Improve the Status Quo

Liberal mindsets correlate to a feeling that we live in an abundant world where problems can be solved, where we can take care of everyone. We can all afford to live well.

Protect the Natural Order

Conservative mindsets correlate to seeing a world that we can damage. Finding a way to get health care to every child will have an important cost, a real trade-off with important consequences.

Causation seems to go back and forth: if someone is afraid and in a defensive mindset, they will assume the world is a zero-sum game with scarcity; convince someone that there is enough to go around, and some of that fear can go away. Both

38. Example: Climate Outreach, "Using scare tactics: does it work?" Available at ClimateOutreach.org.

the worst right-wing disasters and the best progressive expansions of compassion have happened in times of scarcity, pivoting on whether people overcame or drowned in fear: the Depression led to the New Deal *and* the Nazis.

What happens if we assume that cognitive conservatives who oppose government-provided prenatal care are not lacking compassion, but rather struggle with fear?

Our arguments would need to stop pounding the message that compassion is needed. Instead, we should engage the fears that block their compassion: engaging those fears on economic issues means having both the rhetoric and reality of *effective* compassion.

Exercise: Scarcity and Abundance Messages in Liberal Media

Review a liberal news source such as Huffington Post, Daily Kos, or MSNBC, ideally your favorite liberal news source. Find half a dozen articles about people in need and solutions, such as food stamps, welfare, or more school funding. For each article, ask the following:

1. Does it amplify how much need there is, or focus on possible solutions?
2. For someone who assumes we live in a world of scarcity, how will the amplification of needs feel?

Upon reflection, are you seeking out and sharing links to abundance-first and solution-first media, or scarcity and fear media?

Exercise: Countering Fear-Based Hate

Think of a time when someone in your circles was being racist, sexist or hateful.

If fear is at the root of racism, what do you do when people in your demographic are discriminating against others? Do you ostracize and attack them? Find a way to give them more hugs and support to get over their fears? Something else? How do you choose the right tactic at the right time? What did you do the last time you encountered hate politics within your social circles, and how well did your tactic work?

Moral Foundations Theory: Liberal and Conservative Core Values

Jonathan Haidt, social psychologist, has been asking detailed questions to identify what conservatives and liberals care about, finding patterns to the values underneath our political differences. He uses a metaphor to help us make sense of these patterns: comparing our moral senses to taste-bud receptors. Just as there are only a few types of taste-bud receptors — salty, sour, sweet, bitter and umami — most of us have just a few major "tastes" for moral values.[39]

If we see someone suffering, we desire to help. We get upset at unfair situations. This is true for nearly every human, and is sometimes even seen in other species. Moral Foundations Theory claims that nearly everyone can taste these two values:

---

1. Care — Harm
2. Fairness — Cheating

But there are more *moral taste buds* than these,[40] not shared by everyone. Being conservative is correlated to having three additional "moral tastes" that moderates hold less strongly and liberals hardly at all:

---

3. Authority — Subversion (Leadership and Followership)
4. Loyalty — Betrayal (Support Your In-Group)
5. Sanctity — Degradation (Cleanliness and Taboos)

Cognitive Politics focuses on Moral Foundations Theory amidst all the other studies because it provides useful tools to improve conversations. It avoids the counterproductive approaches such as wondering if liberals or conservatives are better or worse in some particular way. Instead, it helps us navigate key ways we

39. Jonathan Haidt, *The Righteous Mind: Why Good People Are Divided by Politics and Religion* (New York: Pantheon Books, 2012). "Moral Foundations Theory" introduced, 124-125; moral senses compared to tastes, 127. MFT was developed by more than one person based on multiple studies. More information — and the chance to participate by answering questions — is at YourMorals.org.

40. *LIBERTY* is often included in more recent formulations of the theory. Liberals and conservatives often see liberty differently, which makes the results less clear. This chapter focuses on the clearest results that are ready to be applied to politics.

misinterpret each other's motives and suggests ways to be curious abut each other's worldviews.

Below is a summary chart, showing how people answer survey questions about their values. Holding a value is more than perceiving it: we can all experience disgust, or recognize when someone leads well. But liberals and conservatives differ on whether they consider these important moral values. A person who is kind (care) but who is perceived to have a disgusting personal habit (violation of sanctity) remains morally acceptable to a cognitive liberal. In each case, having a value means noticing both positive and negative instances. In other words, a prototypical cognitive conservative does not automatically respect all authority. But an honest and caring politician who is seen as a bad leader will frustrate a cognitive conservative more than a liberal.

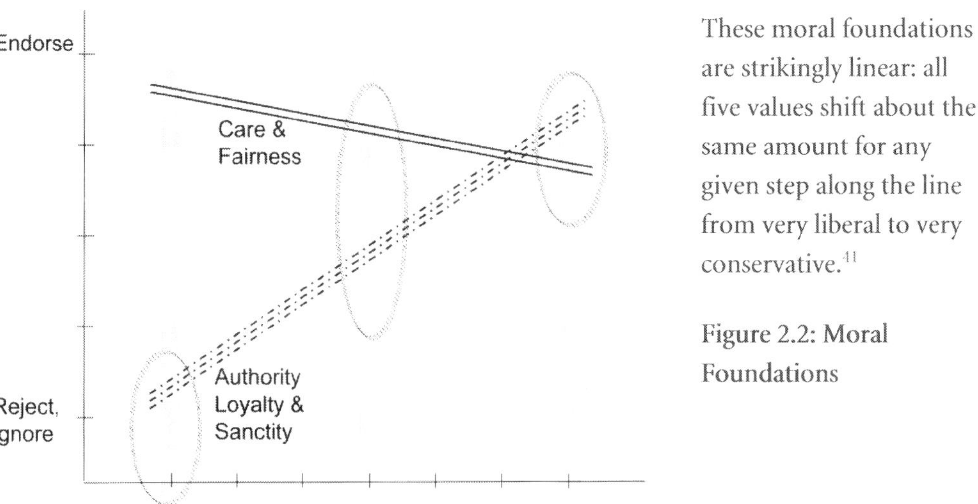

These moral foundations are strikingly linear: all five values shift about the same amount for any given step along the line from very liberal to very conservative.[41]

Figure 2.2: Moral Foundations

Notice the three circled areas:

1. Very liberal people ignore leadership, in-group loyalty and sanctity values. This often leaves liberal activists unable to engage in conversations based on these values.
2. For moderates — for swing voters — the most important values are the same as for liberals. But they also care about the community-binding values enough to want them addressed, which activist liberals rarely do.

41. This chart is based on answers to the Moral Foundations Questionnaire, with data from YourMorals.org, and Figure 8.2, p 161 of *The Righteous Mind*. It is slightly simplified here to focus on the key points. Without a careful reading of the questions chosen, slight differences in line angles are not significant and just a distraction — which is far beyond the scope of this book and available in the original data.

3. Conservatives value all these moral foundations nearly equally. The evidence goes against a common liberal perception that they lack compassion.

Liberals Don't Understand Conservatives

Haidt asked liberals and conservatives to fill out a questionnaire about their political values, then switch and say how the other side would answer. He found that conservatives accurately answer what liberals value, but we don't have a clue about them. This is one of those moments when we need to stop: I and pretty much every liberal friend assumed that Fox-watching conservatives were completely clueless,[42] and that they didn't listen to us while we did listen to them. Studies by mostly liberal and moderate scientists make it clear: we're wrong. We're like cooks who can taste sugar but not salt, trying to replicate a salty recipe. We often don't understand what's going on in conservative and moderate minds — but as the chart shows, conservatives do share and understand the values that most liberals hold.[43]

"People often move to right-wing churches, which become conduits to right-wing ideology, precisely because they hunger for a vision of a world based on love and caring and generosity ... while the Left meanwhile, seems to only identify with values of fairness and equality."
— Rabbi Michael Lerner [44]

Reading online conversations about the psychological differences between liberals and conservatives, I find that many conservatives see most of the academic theories as attacks. Moral Foundations Theory stands out as making sense to at least a reasonable proportion of conservatives. These differences are at the root of why we miscommunicate — especially for liberals trying to reach moderates or work with conservatives. It's worth digging in to the details: let's look at each of the conservative moral foundations in more detail.

42. There have been multiple surveys finding that Fox viewers are lost on basic facts — for example, Fox viewers were *18 percentage points less likely to know that Egyptians overthrew their government than those who watch no news at all (http://www.thestar.com/news/world/2011/11/22/fox_news_leaves_viewers_ignorant.html)*. But facts and Fox aside, conservatives are much better at intuiting liberals' values and motivations, at how we describe our own values, while liberals are more likely to misinterpret rather than just disagree with conservatives' motivations.

43. Haidt, *The Righteous Mind*, 287.

44. Rabbi Michael Lerner, *"The Psychodynamics of the Tea Party's Success in Closing the Government — and How to Beat It"* (Tikkun Magazine, October 1st, 2013), Tikkun.org.

Components of a Conservative Moral Foundation:
Authority and Leadership

A basic value for conservatives, not shared by liberals, is an expectation that authority should deserve respect. Communities can't function well without good leaders. For cognitive conservatives, some people having authority over others is not merely a necessary evil but the natural order.

This "moral taste" described by Haidt, along with the increased fears that conservatives tend to feel, clearly overlaps with Lakoff's work. Someone with the moral tastes of a conservative is more likely to turn to a strict-father authority figure to be their leader.

Cognitive conservatives will find someone trustworthy and capable, then trust and follow them. Leaders are with us or against us. If a leader is a good person, if their sense of the sacred is true, then you should line up behind them. This is not only about the leaders: there is honor in following well. You don't desert a leader for being human, for having an occasional moral lapse, nor desert them if you disagree on a few issues.

Liberals tend to look to ideals. We judge leaders perpetually: many of us have long lists of the things Obama has done that we agree with and long lists we disagree with. It's his job to get behind us: "if the people lead, the leaders will follow."

> "Strong people don't need strong leaders."
> — Ella Baker,
> US Civil Rights leader

To a cognitive conservative, the people would lead only when the leaders failed — leadership is part of the natural order. Instead, the liberal's *ideal* leader does a lot of listening and following the general will. For example, many conservatives are hoping for another Reagan. But at Occupy gatherings, people toward the further left didn't want another MLK or Gandhi; rather, they hoped the people would lead themselves and make leaders obsolete.

=> Example: Ineffectiveness of the Hypocrisy Message

To a conservative or moderate, a strong moral compass is an absolute requirement for leaders. You must know what is right and what is wrong. Knowing and saying the right thing about family values is a requirement, even if once or twice you sinned against those values. It's vital that leaders understand what is right, impossible for humans to be perfectly sinless.

This is one of the reasons why the religious right has many leaders who talk incessantly about family values, then commit particularly nasty versions of the sins they preach against, and yet are forgiven. Liberals need to understand that people who speak a conservative truth but have failings — for example, a divorced man who talks about family values and the need to stick it out in marriage — will not necessarily be seen as a hypocrite but merely as a mortal. Battering a hypocrisy message can make you seem merciless instead of just, and them seem merely human.

Cognitive-conservative voters are looking for the annunciation of clear values worth following. They are looking for leaders who know the path and can point it out, not students who will be graded on how well they walk that path. This is discussed further in *"Reviewing Violations of Sanctity" (p.131)*.

Components of a Conservative Moral Foundation: Loyalty to Your Community

Loyalty to your community and *IN-GROUP* is a very complex moral taste. You can find it at the root of racism — and also at the root of conservatives donating more to charity and to their communities than liberals do.[45] And so liberals need to learn both how to counter in-group loyalty gone wrong, and also learn what we might be missing when we don't hold these values.

Conservative thought imagines a rough world out there. Look after your family and your immediate community, put them first and trust them to put you first. *COMMUNITY LOYALTY* pairs well with *LEADERSHIP*; there is a natural order to life and we should discipline ourselves to follow it.

> "I am not a member of any *organized* party. I am a Democrat."
> — Will Rogers, 1935[46]

In politics, community loyalty means figuring out who is on your side, rather than how much each leader conforms to your policy preferences. "Either you're with us or against us" is a frame that normally seems unbalanced to liberal ears, but the conservative mindset may more readily seek to clarify *IN-GROUPS* and *OUT-GROUPS*. When President George W. Bush used that language, anyone who listened to him — not just conservatives — had to use his frame for a moment to process his words. This language reinforces the cognitive-conservative frame in many moderates who hold – however weakly – those values. Note that in 2016, we are at the far end of two decades since Newt Gingrich

45. Charitable giving is discussed in *chapter 9 -- p.153.*

46. Will Rogers, as quoted in P. J. O'Brien, *Ambassador of Good Will, Prince of Wit and Wisdom* (The John C. Winston Company, Philadelphia, 1935), p.162.

and others started heavily emphasizing this frame, accusing liberals of being outsiders and less patriotic in an ongoing assault — after twenty years of reinforcement, it is becoming a more widely shared frame.

=> Practical Example: Grouping Tactics

Liberals face an unfair conundrum: we're going to be accused of not being patriotic. While some may believe this accusation to be unworthy of an answer, it does require an answer for pragmatic reasons. But reversing the tactic and accusing Republicans of lower patriotism is not likely to rally our base: Republicans since the Southern Strategy[47] have been dividing Americans into us and them, solidifying their in-group loyalty to their party. More division is not a countertactic.

What can you do so that a moderate will feel frustrated and disconnected from a leader who draws divisions by demanding everyone be "with us or against us"? And what can you do to break down the barriers between groups that this rhetoric feeds on? *Scoring* points and *winning* arguments doesn't help here — successfully putting someone on the *defensive* only makes the feeling of separate teams strong. Most swingable voters are not very politically active, and their entire experience with politics is likely to be listening to others. Switch that experience: listen to them, help them feel heard. Keep the volume down whenever possible, use *active listening* *(p.56)* techniques, and ask questions that come at issues from angles not easily divided into left and right. Make sure people feel welcome to be part of your community, not like they fail to meet your admission standards while politicians like Trump welcome them. It's often as simple as this, especially with people who are turned off about politics: respect the person you're talking with and they'll feel respected, and no longer wonder if you are against them.

=> Countering Hate Politics: Own Your Culture's "Normal"

Humans at our worst are cowards. As a child first learning about Nazi Germany, I imagined a land completely full of hate, but the researchers have consistently found that thriving evil does not look quite like it does in fiction or imagination. Apathy and cowardice, not burning hatred, were the typical German's sufficient contribution to the Holocaust. The *COMMUNITY-LOYALTY* moral foundation aims for the middle of a

47. The Southern Strategy is the name of the Republican plan to use "the dividing line" ... "of the race issue" to "cut the Democratic Party and country in half," as described by by H. R. Haldeman, Oct 5, 1971 in his Nixon White House memo "Dividing the Democrats." White disapproval of the Civil Rights efforts by Democrats transformed the South from Democratic to Republican. Before the Southern Strategy, positions on civil rights and other social issues varied within both parties. See www.cognitivepolitics.org/southernstrategy for more info.

community. The prototypical authoritarian-minded German was looking to dislike Jews *as much as their neighbor did:* not more, not less.[48]

This means that marketing has a huge impact: the Nazi propaganda machine made hatred normal through repetition. In the other direction, lesbian and gay TV characters plus people coming out of the closet have made homosexuality vastly more normal than it was twenty years ago, and a losing fight for conservative politicians trying to mobilize against same-sex marriage.

> If we stay in community with authoritarian-minded people, not forming separate groups even as we voice our full opinions, we help create a tolerable, safer middle ground.

People want to belong. If belonging means being racist, many will be racist; if it means not being racist, many will stop. In politics, we must raise our voices against hateful views without separating from neighbors who hold those views, repeating in many ways that *we* are in the same boat, *we* are on the same team, and our team does not accept racism or sexism. If you are safely within an *in-group* while others are the targets of abuse, it is particularly important to stand up against hate consistently but *without* separating communities completely — *community loyalty* is one of the strongest tools to combat hate; don't give it up. Don't unfriend them, don't isolate them to define their normal only among others with same views, but do keep challenging them as a member of a shared community.

=> Loyalty in Politics: Asynchronous Preferences for Cooperation

---

> "Beyond Red vs. Blue: The Political Typology" looks at different groups of liberals and conservatives. They find "core GOP groups largely prefer elected officials who stick to their positions rather than those who compromise. Solid liberals overwhelmingly prefer officials who compromise, but the other two (less solidly liberal) Democratic groups do not.
> — Pew Research Center for the People & the Press, May 4, 2011

The most solid liberals prefer compromise, unlike the moderate liberals and conservatives. Haidt's theory is borne out by the research: various types of moderate liberals still hold values of *community loyalty* and want their team to win, while solid liberals (in normal political times) instead want us all to come together and compromise.

48. Bob Altemeyer, *The Authoritarians.* (Winnipeg: University of Manitoba, 2006), 28-29.

If Obama walks out of a meeting, if he shuts the government down rather than compromise, his core supporters are unhappy with him. This often makes for a very weak team, easily divided and beaten. Republicans don't pay the same price, and this imbalance gives them more reason to play aggressive politics — as they tell us, peace comes from strength, and the Democrats are weak.

What strategies and framings could help people who idealize cooperation to thrive in an environment where many people hold a core belief of loyalty to their group? How do we build resilient communities through conscious decisions without intuitions about community values? As churches and patriotism lose their hold on us, how do we hold together?

Components of a Conservative Moral Foundation: Sanctity and Cleanliness

We've explored a connection between fear (or caution) and community-building values. When we're afraid, we circle the wagons, rely on our team, and respect strong and strict leaders. But the conservative demographic often holds another set of values built on cleanliness, leading to a sense of sacredness and taboos. Respecting the natural order keeps you out of trouble in a dangerous world.

This is a young field with many unanswered questions, but I expect that cautiousness underlies a desire for a tight community and for order, driving Haidt's *authority* and *in-group* values and Lakoff's *strict-father* metaphors. Meanwhile, cleanliness is connected to sanctity — and perhaps not so clearly related to Lakoff's parental metaphors.

"Let the ruler be a ruler, minister be a minister, father be a father, son be a son."
— Confucius

Referencing something filthy, or perhaps even just placing a handwash station in view,[49] influences people to shift slightly more conservative. Some conservative political thinking tends to use the same part of the brain used to think about dirt and cleanliness.[50] A visual thinker might hear a description of a policy they dislike and say, "that looks bad." A person with a cognitive-conservative brain might curl their lip,

49. Erik G. Helzer and David A. Pizarro. "Dirty Liberals! : Reminders of Physical Cleanliness Influence Moral and Political Attitudes" (Psychological Science, Apr 1, 2011), http://pss.sagepub.com/content/22/4/517

50. Avoid overinterpreting these studies. These studies do not claim that either liberals or conservatives are more easily influenced or more rational. Some environments influence all demographics in one direction or the other. A painting class might lead students to momentarily be more visual thinkers, a singing or writing class might lead the same students to rely more on verbal thinking. We can likewise be guided toward cleanliness thinking, and cleanliness thinking is associated with conservative thoughts.

using the same pathways that would fire for anyone if they found dog poo in their shoe.

This research about cleanliness and disgust matches survey results indicating that conservatives emphasize a moral foundation of sanctity vs. disgust.

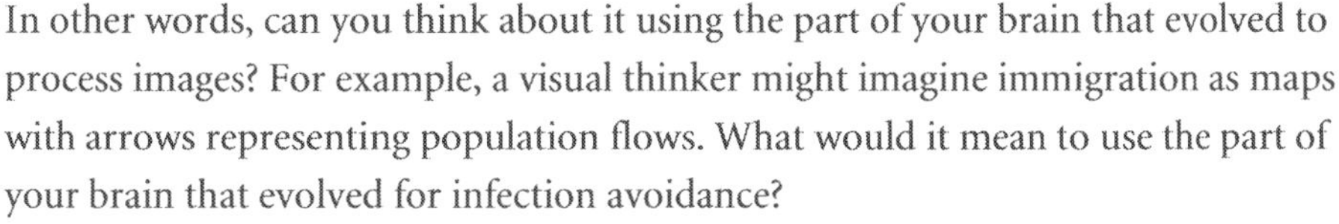

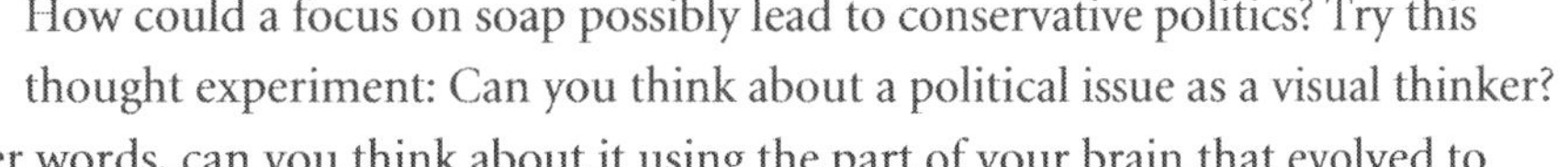

Exercise: Visual Thinking, Verbal Thinking, Disease-Avoidance Thinking

How could a focus on soap possibly lead to conservative politics? Try this thought experiment: Can you think about a political issue as a visual thinker? In other words, can you think about it using the part of your brain that evolved to process images? For example, a visual thinker might imagine immigration as maps with arrows representing population flows. What would it mean to use the part of your brain that evolved for infection avoidance?

Sanctity and Politics: Logic Is the Wrong Tool for Avoiding Disgust

Let's look at abortion from this lens. Imagine for a moment that abortion makes you react — fires the same neural pathways — as if a dog had pooped in your shoe. Your lip curls. You are disgusted.

Conservatives can listen to, and perhaps mildly agree with, the idea that women should have the option of choice, without that impacting this strong, visceral reaction. What liberals say about abortion simply isn't what *feels* important. No logic — and no simple linguistic reframing — will overcome a visceral response.

The Lesson for Liberals

The PRO-LIFE political machine is not centered on reducing the *number* of abortions, nor consciously on taking away women's rights. Women's rights just don't count for much when someone is thinking about abortion with the same part of their brain as if they stepped in dog poop. Countless pro-life activists have never even considered how long a woman would be locked behind bars if their laws pass. Yes, their votes will lead to women being imprisoned if they win just a couple more elections and Supreme Court seats; no, they can't be bothered to think about that now. This perspective is a liberal way of seeing the issue, as well as a true perspective, and a *good approach* to mobilizing anyone who *can* see this argument. But the people reacting viscerally won't recognize themselves as fighting a war on women, so accusations that are obviously true to you won't stick if they are your audience. This includes many moderates, who might agree about women's rights if they are in a logical mindset, and become pro-life in a visceral mindset.

Many pro-life people are seeking leaders and a government in tune with their sense of sanctity. If you want to reach across the partisan divide to people who are intuitively against abortion, neither logical arguments nor a willingness to compromise on policy are the right tools to reach across to heartfelt values. Instead, spend time listening and making clear that you see what they are talking about — you don't have to fully agree, nor agree at all on policy. This can be what *Difficult Conversations*[51] calls an "*AND*" conversation: I see why you care *AND* I believe empowering women is the right path. Get good enough at describing their views so that there isn't a place for an unending argument. Reach the point where moderates are no longer triggered by a visceral reaction and may be open to look at more abstract rights later. Or where you can say "I hear you" and move on — perhaps to issues where you agree, or to fighting corrupt politics, instead of being stuck where you viscerally disagree.

Abortion is perhaps the biggest Republican trap that influences people with even a few conservative moral foundations but who are also very compassionate to stop listening to liberals. *Chapter 5* covers abortion politics in more detail. *p.99*

Choosing Goals when Faced with Different Values

There are issues for which it will be very difficult to change people's minds when our values clash, especially when conservatives see a violation of the sacred. It's important to carefully consider *goals* in these cases. We all enjoy winning debates. But, we aren't setting policy around the Thanksgiving table or the watercooler. Very often, moneyed interests will try to focus good people on the most contentious issues to pull our attention away from corruption issues. We need sane politics to win elections; we don't need complete agreement at dinnertime. When you hit a subject where the other person will never change their mind, scoring points is not a helpful goal: talk about something more fruitful.

Surveys of moral frameworks find far-liberals unable to tune in to values such as respect for authority, while far-conservatives hold those values strongly. It's important to realize that the middle of the electorate holds key progressive values strongly, and holds the more conservative values only somewhat. Nonetheless, conservatives can speak with clarity to moderates who lightly hold those values, while liberals are left talking to ourselves.

51. Douglas Stone, Bruce Patton and Sheila Heen, *Difficult Conversations: How to Discuss What Matters Most.* (New York: Penguin Books, 2000), 39.

Contrasts between Lakoff's Metaphors and Haidt's Moral Foundations

How do we follow Lakoff's advice to emphasize stories and metaphors that work for liberals without violating the deeply held values Haidt described?

Haidt finds:	Lakoff instructs:
"Conservatives and many moderates are opposed to gay marriage in part due to moral intuitions related to ingroup, authority, and purity, and these concerns should be addressed, rather than dismissed contemptuously." [52]	"Reframe the debate, in everything we say and write, in terms of our moral principles."[53] In other words, dismiss the moral intuitions of conservatives and stick to your own.

Lakoff and Haidt are looking at much the same data, but coming to opposite practical conclusions: they encourage contradictory approaches whether for Democratic speechwriters or Thanksgiving table discussions. Should you create your own metaphors, or address theirs? *This is explored using same-sex marriage as an example* *on p.122.*

How much can you frame a world where compassion and fairness are emphasized, where people cross in-group boundaries fluidly, without triggering the conservative worldview? Lakoff wants to grab the metaphor by the horns and overpower it: he says to stop calling abortion "abortion" and instead call it "development prevention."[54] Haidt's research indicates that conservatives' strong sense of sanctity around a fetus is a core value, not something we can easily metaphor away. What works for you?

We've reached the central contradiction, a key reason for this manual: scientists exploring conservative and liberal mindsets are reaching almost the same consensus about what those mindsets are, while proposing diametrically opposed recommendations to speechwriters.

---

52. Jonathan Haidt and Jesse Graham, "When Morality Opposes Justice: Conservatives Have Moral Intuitions that Liberals may not Recognize," Soc Just Res (2007) 20: 98. doi:10.1007/s11211-007-0034-z, p13.

53. Lakoff, What's In a Word, Feb 17, 2004. http://www.alternet.org/story/17876/what%27s_in_a_word

54. George Lakoff and Elisabeth Wehling. "The Sacredness of Life and Liberty" (The Huffington Post, July 16, 2012), TheHuffingtonPost.com.

Outside of theory, what works? Are you more effective when you speak your own truth and repeat your own metaphors, or address theirs? There is no single answer: try both, keeping track of which works better for you, *and when.*

Example: Speak Your Truth to Their Moral Tastes

The political struggle for lesbian and gay marriage has been a stunning success for the left. Seattle's successful campaign won by balancing both techniques, sharing stories and listening at appropriate times.

> "When I'm honest with myself, I'm not comfortable with gay people …
> but it's not my job to judge."

This quote comes from a powerful video describing a political campaign to support gay marriage, well worth watching: *How to Move a Conflicted Loved One to Support LGBT Dignity (http://vimeo.com/51161395).*

This quote doesn't describe the "moral flavors" that I taste. This is a cognitive conservative who hasn't let go of the idea that homosexuals breach sanctity. The speaker believes in respecting authority, and people claiming authority are encouraging him to blame others. Yet, he's voting for a policy on the cutting edge of the progressive agenda.

We can get along much more easily, and transform American politics, if we can help conservative-minded people recalibrate their respect for authority away from "with-us-or-against-us" politicians. We have to be careful to listen patiently and understand where people are coming from, before we start asking them to listen to us.

We don't have to walk people through every step,
just help them past their triggers.

Framing considerations challenge us to change our language from "no, homosexuals should not be punished" and "don't ask, don't tell" to "love makes a family," pride, and simply repeating the stories of good people who love the same gender over and over. Understanding which moral values are triggered adds a twist to this campaign: you can seek ways that someone's existing values can agree to the policy you desire. For same-sex marriage, this often means putting aside frontal assaults on sanctity values, and reminding people of their beliefs on authority: "you can feel what you feel, but is it your job to judge?"

Once someone decides it's not their job to judge, once they stop feeling like they are on an opposing team, then they can look at news articles about gay couples getting married as observers rather than partisans. Then they can absorb the new frame, the repeated stories — and the work suggested by Lakoff can slowly grow roots.

Once a person has stopped expending their energy judging, how long until they can actually see the happiness in the smiling faces of newly married couples, and let go of their intolerance?

Sometimes you can reach the same policy end-goals through different moral values than the ones you hold dearest.

Quick Guide to Integrating the First Two Chapters

Tell your story with clarity — Lakoff's advice — far from politics, when people don't have an opinion yet, or when an uncommitted audience is listening. Both the media and many individuals coming out of the closet regularly reinforce that gay men and lesbians are regular, *in-group* people. When you have a chance to tell your story, tell it uncompromised and with pride — but recognize that telling a story is not a conversation.

But once people have strong opinions, listen first. Following Haidt's approach, find out where their values are coming from, and seek answers that pull them closer to their hearts and further from the Republican Party playbook. We all value fairness: give a point if you want them to give a point.

How Liberals and Conservatives Think Alike: Shared Cognitive Challenges and Biases

This chapter explored the differences that cognitive science is finding *between* liberals and conservatives. However, cognitive science is also finding patterns that apply *across* the political spectrum.

Jonathan Haidt describes our minds as a rider upon an elephant: the rider is our conscious mind with only a limited ability to influence the elephant of our unconscious and automatic desires. Away from politics, many of us make a conscious "rider" decision to follow a diet, and then ride the elephant to junk food. Similarly in politics, people across the political spectrum are consciously searching for the real and unbiased truth, but are subconsciously driven to agree with our friends or rationalize conclusions that support our interests or our egos.

> "Still a man hears what he wants to hear / And disregards the rest."
> — Simon and Garfunkel, "The Boxer," plus too many cognitive science studies to list

I have yet to hear any evidence that either liberals or conservatives do this significantly differently: the evidence is that we almost all do it much more than we think we do; it's simply how our brains work. For anyone having a political conversation, here are some key considerations.

Trusted Sources or Messengers

We tend to listen to trusted sources. This means if you want to convince someone, it's important to find, or become, a trusted messenger.

If you hit a conservative over the head with the fact that a military or religious person whom they respect supports your cause, they'll still feel hit over the head. But it's particularly powerful to amplify the voices of morally credible, unlikely messengers who have a story to tell, who start at the beginning and not at the conclusion. For example, when politician Al Gore stands as a leader on climate change, he further politicizes the issue. A religious leader who is a religious leader first and later comes to see the dangers of climate change will make a much better advocate.

Logic Can't Beat Down Rationalization

Human brains are designed to rationalize more than we reason. Our rational brains are like lawyers, defending our intuitions and desires. You can't convince an opposing lawyer to agree with you. When you disagree, instead of throwing facts and battling the opposing opinion, seek the roots of the rationalizations. Many people are both compassionate and afraid. If you can talk about the roots of their fears, this can give compassion room to grow. When expressing your own views, reinforce the roots of your own beliefs and talk about deeper needs, rather than your final strategies and policies.

Asking for Agreement Is Asking for a Favor

Changing your mind is work. If you want someone to listen to you and change their mind to match your ideas, you are asking for a favor. Cook them something. Listen to them. Do something in exchange. Don't try to defeat them into agreeing with you. An atmosphere of trust allows us to get past our instincts and move to reason: people don't use reason when

loyalty is in question. Reason is a key part of the equation, but it is the last step, after trust is built.

Be Alive — No Stale Anger

Most anger in politics is stale and impersonal. Whether you watch *Fox News* or read *Daily Kos*, most partisan news seeks and repeats the worst about the "other side." We get cranky at that other team. If you don't want to let go of your anger completely, consider this approach: if you must get angry with the person you are talking with, make sure it is personal and focused. Keep your feelings in the room, based on what they are doing, not something "their team" is doing. Continue to treat them as a person whom you would like in your community — emphasize the connection you want, not just the failure. Sometimes real relationships have anger; a goal is to make political conversations into real conversations, make them alive. Avoid getting angry at an amalgam of Republican leaders and the person you are talking with.

Exercise: Imagine an Apology

Don't get angry unless it's personal. In real life, when someone makes you angry, you hope for an apology. Next time you are angry in a political setting, imagine a fantasy in which the person you are talking with apologizes. What do you want them to apologize for?

Fantasy apology:

"I apologize for thinking that lower taxes would help the economy."

"I apologize for not listening to you."

Don't get angry that someone thinks Israel or Palestine is the more-just side. Listen to them; ask them for their stories. And *in turn* if they are unwilling to listen to stories of peace activists, dignity and safety, then express what you feel when they won't be fair in their conversation with you, when they won't explore both sides before coming to a conclusion. Express if you feel angry, discouraged or sad, because you'd like to feel connected, respected or treated with fairness — rather than angry that their side has a different conclusion.

Active listening (*chapter 3 -- p.56*) will review some tools that can work wonders.

The Limits of Logic

To learn more, I recommend reading Jonathan Haidt, especially the first few chapters of *The Righteous Mind*, which focuses on politics, or *The Happiness Hypothesis*.

I found new perspectives on politics by thinking about non-political paradoxes in my own brain: if it's so hard to convince myself to exercise and stay on my diet, no wonder it is hard to talk to other people about politics with logic alone. We know that convincing ourselves to eat right and exercise takes more than repeating logical points; so do political conversations.

Seek out paradoxes: if conservative working-class people aren't voting in a way that makes sense to you, notice that it doesn't make sense. Then, dig deeper and ask questions; don't just throw up your hands.

> "The only cure for the confirmation bias is other people. So if you bring people together who disagree, and they have a sense of friendship, family, having something in common, having an institution to preserve, they can challenge each other's reason."
> — Jonathan Haidt[55]

Exercise for Progressives: Examining Our Own Biases

Preparation: Pick a contentious economic issue, and write your first thoughts about how a typical conservative sees this issue.

Reconsider: On average, the typical conservative gives more to charity and to their communities than liberals do. Does your perspective on conservatives fit this data? If not, how would you rewrite your answer above?

Possible Future Research

Studying Groupings besides Liberal and Conservative

Grouping people into just two camps is very relevant at election time in a two-party political system. Obviously, many individuals don't fit the patterns, but perhaps

55. Haidt, Jonathan, "Jonathan Haidt Explains Our Contentious Culture." Interview by Bill Moyers, February 3, 2012, BillMoyers.com. CognitivePolitics.org/moyers.

entire groups don't fit and merely have their data overwhelmed and averaged by the larger groups. In my experience talking about this book, libertarian advocates of small-government fiscal conservatism balk at many of the descriptions of cognitive conservatives. They tend to vote as a subset of conservatives, but often for different reasons arising from different moral foundations.

There are many ways to subdivide conservative thinking patterns relevant to this book. Research is underway to explore libertarian values, which are likely to be very different from social-conservatives, even if they were lumped together in early research and are lumped together in elections. In addition, chapter 5 explores older research that divided conservatives into nonauthoritarian and authoritarian thinkers, and then divided authoritarians (wagon-circlers) into two separate patterns, leaders and followers, each with *very* different belief systems — authoritarian leaders are a small demographic that doesn't seem to share cognitive-conservative moral foundations at all.

- religious
- social
- fiscal
- libertarian
- neo-con
- cognitive

Keep in mind that these patterns are just patterns: see if they provide *clues* to better understanding people you're struggling to communicate with, but don't insist that they provide *answers*. Often, political marketing will break us down into demographics, just as commercial marketing does — and part of a citizen's work is to recognize marketing techniques so we can counter them. Recognize when we are being segmented, and aim to bridge the divisions when we talk with our neighbors.

In my experience, when liberals and libertarians disagree, it's more often a straightforward difference of values. For example, libertarians are often not willing to force the wealthy to pay more taxes to help the poor — everyone understands everyone else, and everyone simply disagrees.

Discussions between liberals and *social conservatives* or *cognitive conservatives* are different, and often involve misunderstandings rather than simple disagreement. The second half of this book explores many examples. One of the most common misunderstandings involves inequality: conservatives believe that inequality is driven by a lack of self-discipline that is often worsened by government programs, while liberals believe the government can help and so conservatives must lack compassion. Cognitive liberals and cognitive conservatives are big enough demographics to have their own media bubbles, big enough marketing demographics for politicians to craft targeted messages. With separate messaging, they more easily develop false understandings of each other, and so this book will focus on cognitive conservatives.

Addressing Roots and Causes

If we help kids grow up more confident, would they be open to everyone, not just their in-group? Is early childhood fear a cause of conservative viewpoints or just a correlation? Is a healthier, less fear-based conservatism possible?

Figure 2.3:
"Conservative" tangles many values:

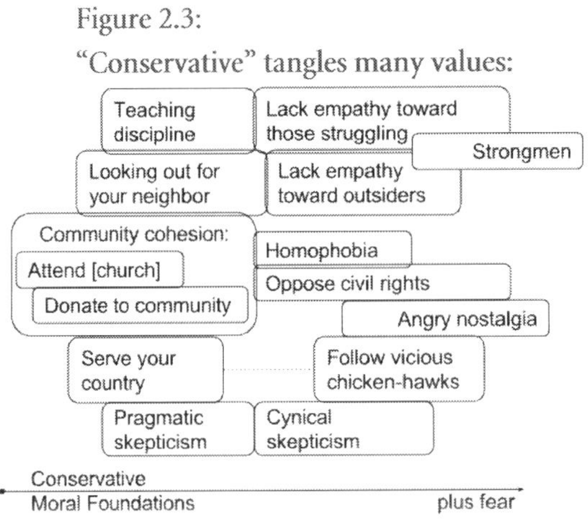

Haidt argues that neither conservatives nor liberals can be summarized as better or worse than the other. But within each group, both liberal and conservative values can go bad. If you can erase the fearfulness of a future-conservative child, are they more likely to grow up to be an agnostic liberal or a less fearful conservative who still goes to church every week?

Figure 2.4: "Liberal" values can be incomplete:

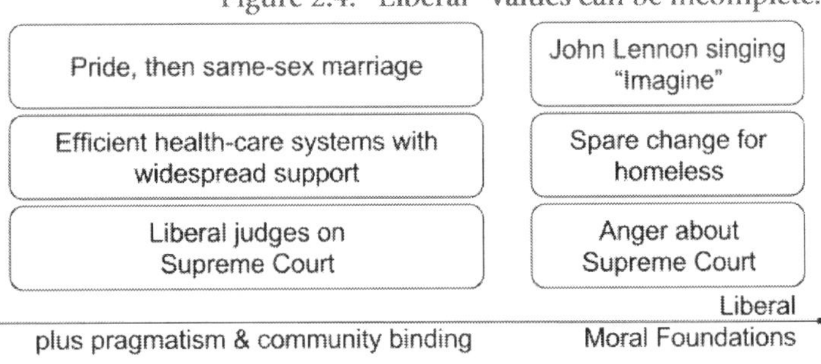

Review

So far we've covered new ideas. The remaining chapters in section I integrate these ideas with communication tools and historical examples. For example, did Gandhi and King ignore conservative metaphors and create their own? Did they engage conservative moral foundations?

From here this book will turn to conjecture: we're leaving the realm where theories have been tested, and exploring the next set of hypotheses that jump beyond those results. Often, there won't be solid, scientific answers but rather useful materials for you to explore and find what works *for you.* The second section of the book will put these ideas to the test with specific issues. Feel free to jump to the chapters that

interest you most; the order from here on matters less. Run your own experiments, sample the different techniques, see what works.

Recommended Resources

The Righteous Mind by Jonathan Haidt is a wide-ranging and fascinating exploration of politics and the human brain. It connects evolution, how we rationalize when we think we are reasoning, and differences between liberals and conservatives, including Moral Foundations Theory.

Political Conservatism as Motivated Social Cognition by John T. Jost, Jack Glaser, Arie W. Kruglanski, and Frank J. Sulloway. This academic paper reviews studies comparing liberal and conservative cognition. I particularly recommend looking at Figure 1: "An Integrative Model of Political Conservatism as Motivated Social Cognition." *Psychological Bulletin,* 2003, Vol. 129, No. 3, 339–375.

"Unconscious Reactions Separate Liberals and Conservatives" (http://www.scientificamerican.com/article.cfm?id=calling-truce-political-wars) is a quick introduction.

FIND LINKS ONLINE: WWW.COGNITIVEPOLITICS.ORG/RESOURCES

Chapter 3

Communication Techniques: Options Beyond *Fire with Fire* and *Give In*

US progressives have struggled to engage with aggressive tactics in recent years. We've switched unhappily between both of the obvious choices: jump in with raised voices, or cave in and get bullied. Therapists, mediators and the business community have all found ways to improve communication. It's time to bring those techniques to political conversations.

You often grow from difficult challenges. For many, talking politics has not been one of those *worthwhile* challenges, just a drain. Can that change?

There is a middle path between silencing ourselves and just shouting at each other.

Conservative ideals are adaptive in a threatening world: if we can't get along, if we have arguments in which neither side listens, if we divide into groups, then politics will shift toward caution and distrust. If your Thanksgiving dinner turns into an argument that evokes a need for a strict father to maintain order, then trust, hope and compassion have lost.

We can use politics as a chance to get to know ourselves better: What makes you angry? What silences you; when do you speak up? What opens your heart? Compassionate politics is in the doldrums in the US today, and many of us are waiting for big solutions from above. But grassroots answers exist already. Therapists, business leaders and mediators know how to handle difficult conversations. A more personal, connected, and compassionate approach to politics can be learned.

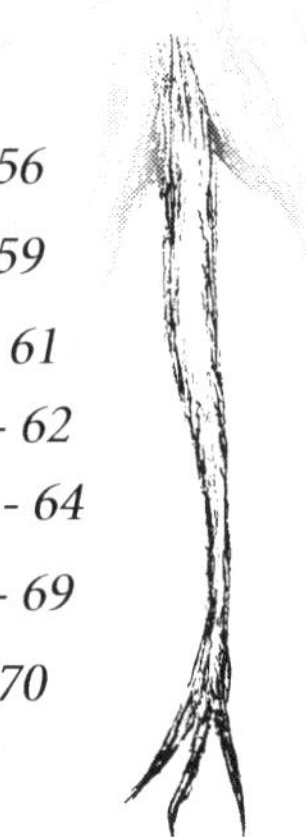

Communication Techniques

Active Listening and Building Connection

Wait to make your points until after you have fully heard, repeated back, and perhaps asked some honest questions. Begin conversations with the goal of more deeply understanding the other person's point of view.

Progressives believe in a world of compassion and hope. Do you practice compassion and hope when you converse with Republicans? Maybe you don't agree with a thing they say — do you listen attentively and let them know you've heard them?

"Without the cultural civil war, conservatives cannot win."
— George Lakoff[56]

If we turn the civil war into civil discussions, we win.

Ask yourself: Is my key question "is my anger justified?" or is my key question "what will work to change politics in America?"

1. Slowly build trust.
2. Focus on one point per conversation. Deluging a lifelong worldview won't work.

Cognitive science research finds that political perspectives are rarely changed by logical points but by whether we *trust the other person and see them as part of our community (p.49).* Before beginning a debate, step back and remember that the nature of your conversation is the most important part: What are your real goals? Do you want to verbally crush the other person and make them wish they had a powerful father figure to argue on their behalf — or do you want to create enough of a connection that just one of your ideas will sink in, maybe months from now?

Loyalty Moral Foundation: Be on the Same Team

If you are trying to score points, you've proven you're on the other team.

Cognitive liberals appreciate leaders who don't toe the party line, who look at all sides, and who discuss policy rather than repeat a sound bite. Meanwhile, *cognitive conservatives* value legitimate authority from their leaders. They seek a clear understanding of right and wrong, ideally led from the top, with a coherent message across their in-group.

Scoring points or crushing your opponent evokes a frame of conflict, an environment that needs a strong leader. That's great if you are Clinton trouncing Trump and claiming the role of strong leader. She would be showing who is fit to lead, and the

56. Lakoff, *Don't Think of an Elephant!*, p88.

two candidates are obviously not on the same team. Trump will never vote for Clinton, no matter how the debate goes. But if you are not running for office, just talking person-to-person, then claiming leadership separates you. It's better to evoke in-group loyalty with a very different kind of conversation.

Liberals, for instance, have great policy positions on reducing abortion: Scandinavia implements the liberal ideals and has very low abortion rates. So if you want fewer abortions, progressives already have the facts and policies on our side. **But being right alone doesn't work.** How are we going to convince swing voters who hold some conservative values that they want to trust us? We've supplied the facts; now we need to engage our neighbors and ensure they feel welcome.

Two keys:
1) Leaders beat opponents, but members of a community don't score points off each other.
2) Chaos evokes a need for a strict father.

What is the best possible outcome from assaulting a conservative-leaning swing voter with facts and logic? When my favorite politician is trying to convince mildly conservative swing voters that he or she is suitable to lead, then being strong and defeating the opponent politician is a positive outcome.

But in our personal lives, in one-to-one conversations, not many people are likely to feel that they themselves are truly wrong just because you outargue them. If they feel like they're losing an argument, this might increase their sense of fear and evoke a need for a strong, strict-father protector. There may be a few times, especially if you are reaching out toward an audience rather than the person you are talking to, when you can "win an argument." But in one-to-one conversations, you are trying to make a deal, to remind them you are a member of the same community, to let them know that you'll listen as earnestly as you want them to listen. Be sincere, learn something from the other person, and you open up the option for them to be sincere and learn something from you.

The *Drug Abuse Resistance Education* program, familiar for the slogan *D.A.R.E. to Keep Kids Off Drugs*, uses authority and facts to pressure kids against trying drugs. It's a fear-based, authority-based conservative strategy: studies have found it fails horribly.[57] Many political conversations at home use similar tactics: we crush the other's arguments, tell them what they have to do, overwhelm the person we're talking to with our knowledge-based authority. But no one is keeping score: crushing arguments when no audience is listening doesn't change any votes.

Republican politics today is based on creating an in-group of Republicans, instead of Americans. Breach that line, remind the people in your circle that you are part of their in-group, and you've done far more good than winning any single policy point in a debate.[58]

57. Lynam DR, Milich R, Zimmerman R, Novak SP, Logan TK, Martin C, Leukefeld C, Clayton R., "Project DARE: no effects at 10-year follow-up." J Consult Clin Psychol. 1999 Aug;67(4):590-3. Summary: "In no case did the DARE group have a more successful outcome than the comparison group."

Fairness Moral Foundation: Tit-for-Tat Listening

Conservatives and liberals disagree on many fundamental values, but we agree on *fairness*. This value doesn't just apply to policy; it applies to the conversation itself. If you are friendly, if you are part of their group of shared loyalty, then if you concede a few points, it's only fair that they concede one to you.

If one person does this, listening carefully for all the areas where you either already agree or pointing out merit or respect for the other's view, you will draw them to listen to you, to feel obliged to agree with you in turn. You can concede half a dozen points you already can agree with and push just one key, reasonable point. They can leave the conversation feeling proud, since you have conceded agreement on many points. They leave feeling aligned, that you are in the same loyalty group.

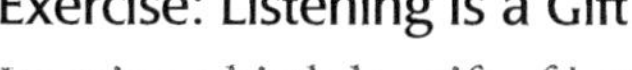

Exchange Listening

If both try the tactic, that creates a virtuous circle. If two people each try to concede points to get the other to feel obligated by fairness to concede points, soon everyone will be having an attentive and reasonable conversation even if they initially set out to merely "win."

Can you change the conversation from them defending against your logic and facts to a mutual sharing?

If you want to add a single communication tactic to your political conversations that will make the biggest difference, try *active listening.* Start each conversation by letting the other person talk, rephrase and confirm or ask real questions so they know you've heard them, and agree with everything you can. Note that agreeing when you can is not a normal part of active listening: normally, you listen and repeat back without editorial, focusing on them instead of your own views. Try it both ways for political conversations; see what works for you.

Exercise: Listening Is a Gift

Imagine a birthday gift of just listening to the recipient's views on the political world for twenty minutes, promising to neither agree nor disagree but just listen. What would it feel like to receive a gift like that? What would happen if you gave it? If both listening and agreeing take work and are a form of giving, giving your attention and giving your agreement to the speaker, what would make political conversations fair?

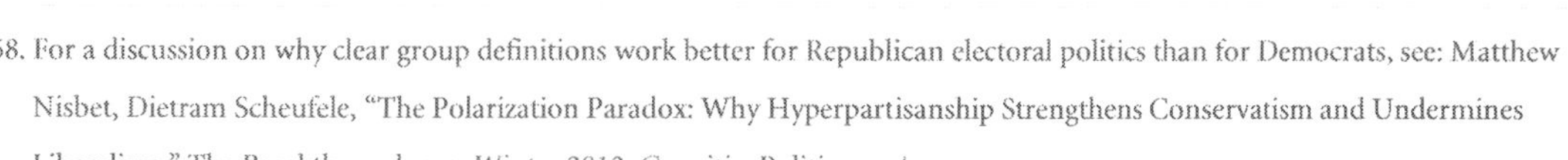

58. For a discussion on why clear group definitions work better for Republican electoral politics than for Democrats, see: Matthew Nisbet, Dietram Scheufele, "The Polarization Paradox: Why Hyperpartisanship Strengthens Conservatism and Undermines Liberalism," The Breakthrough.org, Winter 2013. CognitivePolitics.org/groups.

Compromise: Stubborn, Craven, or Heartful?

Lakoff and a few million other Democrats have lamented their leaders' craven compromising for many years now. We often hold the value "be reasonable" and are enthusiastic believers in compromise for our personal lives. But the Democratic leadership has made compromise seem weak instead of dignified, and shifty instead of constructive.

As politics in Washington have gotten more heated, Democrats have responded to bullying tactics in two ways:

The Old Plan: Make Nice.

Show up with a big compromise. See if giving them three-quarters of everything they want without a fight makes them change their tactics. Tell the world we *want* gays in the military to hide in the closet; we *want* the least inclusive health care system of any wealthy nation.

The New Plan: Become Like Them.

Fight fire with fire. Get angry. Pump up your base by building anger at the other side. Lie and exaggerate right back. Cognitive science research indicates that anger, us-vs.-them conflicts, and fear shift people to conservative thinking, though it does fire up the base.

Speaking Truth to Power

Step by step since the parties divided over social issues including Civil Rights in the 1960s, politics has become more divisive. Democratic insiders are chasing centrist polls, watching those polls shift slowly rightward. Today's Democratic Party is trying to fight half clean and half dirty: this loses all the benefits of fighting clean and leaves you second to opponents who fight dirty better than you could ever hope to. "Fire with fire" hurts Democrats more than Republicans, but there are alternatives.

The Republican base could tolerate Romney's disregard for the truth and stomached Trump's wild lies, while Hillary Clinton scored very well among fact-checkers but still not well enough for large sections of the liberal base. I believe — and hope that other liberals believe — that *IN-GROUP LOYALTY* won't carry dishonest liberal politicians as far with a liberal base as it has for Romney or Trump. Politically active liberals should demand our leaders stick to the truth and not fight fire with fire, not only for principled reasons but also because it doesn't work for us.[59]

Are you a conservative reader who thinks Democrats fight dirtier? Great! Join me! I'm working to clean up my side, and appreciate you challenging conservatives to win by being more honest.

Cognitive liberals have different advantages. Liberal leaders can admit to failures without causing their core to panic and lose faith. We can apologize. We can speak truth to power, while conservative leaders must claim to be the power or lose their base. We can admit areas of weakness. The natural order is not unbalanced when a leader apologizes. If a leader is strong but accepts that they made a mistake, they are evoking the nurturing-parent frame. In the Obama-vs.-Romney election, we saw how in-group thinking and an unwillingness to see problems or admit weakness left Republicans unable to admit or engage their difficulties when Romney fell behind.

Most Democratic politicians don't understand their advantage here, and still try to come across as always powerful: Obama refused to speak truth to power against the banks, which seem to have more power than he does. He refused to tell a story of ordinary people earning less because the banks are sucking up too much of our nation's wealth. It was a story that was true and popular with both liberals and conservatives, yet he never forcefully told it. He withheld his anger even when anything less than anger would be untruth.

Healthy Compromise:
"I've never been shy in talking about my belief in universal health care or fair Tax Code … The people of Connecticut might have disagreed with Joe Lieberman on specific issues, but they liked the fact — and they still like the fact — that he reaches out across the aisle to get stuff done. … Connecticut voters know exactly what side of the negotiating table I'm going to be on, but they want me to be at the negotiating table."
— Sen. Chris Murphy (D-Conn.) replacing Sen. Joe Lieberman[60]

Wait! Did the Sections on Active Listening and Compromise Contradict?

Do we listen attentively, or let more anger show about Wall Street?

Active listening techniques are most effective in one-to-one conversations. If you have an audience listening, it becomes more important to tell your own story with clarity.

Compromise requires being at a negotiating table, sitting across from someone ready to compromise in turn. Don't imitate politicians having a debate unless that is appropriate in the moment. Getting angry at a banking system or a politician benefiting from corruption is very different from getting angry at your powerless-except-one-vote uncle for his political views *(p.50)*. Listening and acknowledging another viewpoint is not the same as compromising your own views.

59. This is a book of partisan political advice telling *MY SIDE* that lying is bad for us. I would hope that conservatives similarly believe that Trump's habit of lying will damage both their party's integrity and long-term electability. My hope is that people across the spectrum will increasingly pressure politicians on "their side" to tell the truth.

60. Kate Nocera, "New Senate breed: Proudly liberal," Politico, Nov. 13, 2012, Politico.com.

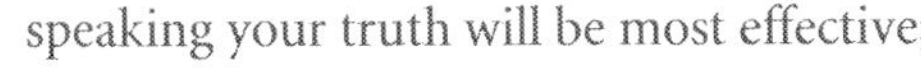

Exercise: Different Audiences and Targets

Pick a variety of conversations you have. Sort out some times when

- speaking your truth will be most effective;
- speaking your truth won't convince the other person but might open space for a policy compromise; and
- listening and strengthening community bonds will benefit more than any argument on the issues.

What differentiates times to speak or listen; to stay firm or compromise?

Triggers, Traps, and Wedge Issues

Many Americans care about politics too little to vote. But even many people who don't vote get upset. Thanksgiving dinners often involve liberal and conservative family members getting into arguments, with politics in distant Washington, DC setting off surprisingly deep reactions.

I'll use the term *triggered* when a person reacts so strongly to an idea that she or he gets upset instead of effective. As an example of a triggered reaction: "What do you mean my gay friends are destroying the country and you're going to tell them they can't see each other in the hospital? *Go to hell!*" This reaction might be merited, but you're not helping your friends if all you do is solidify another citizen to vote against them. Like it or not, if you're in the privileged position of *not* being the *target* of political hate, staying cool can often make you more effective.

I'll use the term *trap* when you trigger major conflict without knowing why. For example, the economics of contribution is full of traps. Liberals are often pointing out the differences in wealth between the rich and ordinary Americans. Every time we lead with this argument we tend to trigger conservatives, who then fly off the handle about fairness and who is contributing. As we'll explore in section II, there are strong arguments that fit within a cognitive-conservative moral framework in favor of a more balanced economy, but when we step on the *EQUALITY THAT IGNORES FAIRNESS* land mine, we lose the chance to have the real discussion.

Triggers keep us from connecting with people whom we do share interests with. They make us feel more different and more compartmentalized than we otherwise are.

What is a *wedge issue?* A wedge issue is a purposeful effort to introduce traps, to sensitize us so we do trigger each other. Abortion and gun control are issues that see little change over the years — decades of Democrats and Republicans taking turns in power merely tweak the edges of these issues. The people in power seem to care about economic issues once they are in power. Wedge issues are purposefully chosen by strategists to get ordinary, good-hearted people to trigger each other and reinforce divisions.

There are countless systems of communication besides active listening. If you have a favorite system for personal conflicts, try it in a political conversation, and let us know how it works at http://www.cognitivepolitics.org.

Business Negotiation Techniques in Politics

Books from the business world on sales or negotiations are a great choice for liberals to read before talking with conservatives. The ideas below are mostly inspired by *Difficult Conversations: How to Discuss What Matters Most* by Douglas Stone, Bruce Patton, and Sheila Heen.[61]

Go to a car dealer. They'll ask you questions. Seek your motivations. What blocks prevent us from being skillful when we have political conversations?

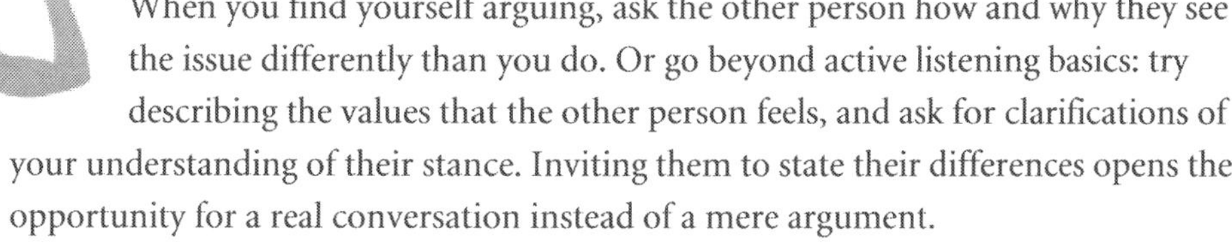

Exercise: Seek Their Values

When you find yourself arguing, ask the other person how and why they see the issue differently than you do. Or go beyond active listening basics: try describing the values that the other person feels, and ask for clarifications of your understanding of their stance. Inviting them to state their differences opens the opportunity for a real conversation instead of a mere argument.

Many liberal communication shortcomings come from our failure to understand the underlying cognitive-conservative values. We want a more compassionate world, so we assume the opposing side is against compassion. But they may believe real compassion calls for a different policy or that fairness prevents our solution, or perhaps their compassion is trumped by a fear we haven't answered. You can't progress in a discussion until you know where the other person is coming from. If you are not onstage in a debate, make your goal understanding rather than

Say, and mean, "Please correct me if I'm wrong" as you explore their values.[62] Open questions keep conversations hopeful and connected, instead of competitive.

61. Stone, Patton and Heen, *Difficult Conversations* (New York: Penguin Books, 2000).

victory: aim to figure out which cognitive-conservative moral-framework values are important to them.

Getting Big Disagreements Back on Track[63]

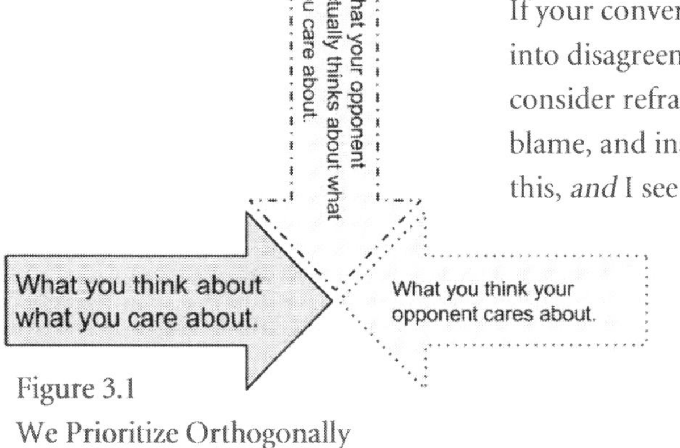

Figure 3.1
We Prioritize Orthogonally

If your conversations are being derailed because you run into disagreements too large to find common ground, consider reframing. Change from discussing truth and blame, and instead tell stories with contributions: you see this, *and* I see that.

Describe the problem you care about first. Then, aim to reach the policy conclusion together. Starting with policy maximizes partisanship while it minimizes creativity and connection.

Difficult Conversations recommends that we "name the trouble: make the problem explicit."[64] Political conversations are often heated because we're talking about different things. For example, we might be arguing about a *specific* US foreign-policy choice, and voices are being raised because underneath the argument one party or both sees the other as not having healthy pride in the US. Or in an argument about welfare, the liberal person is troubled by a lack of compassion while the conservative is troubled by a lack of common sense.

Yes, Make It Personal[65]

Should a political conversation be personal, or cool and rational?

Start each conversation fresh. Create an expectation of fairness. Listen first. Then, if the other person won't listen and won't treat you with decency, you might want to walk away. Make it gently clear that *they* have violated the terms of fairness by refusing to have a fair conversation with you. Don't let it be conservatives vs. liberals. Don't accuse all Fox viewers of being unwilling to listen. Don't accept and reinforce the definitions of different *IN-GROUPS* and *OUT-GROUPS*. Instead, call that person out —

62. Roger Fisher, William Ury, and Bruce Patton, *Getting to Yes: Negotiating Agreement without Giving In* (New York: Penguin Books, 1983), 123.

63. Stone, Patton and Heen, *Difficult Conversations*. Based loosely on chapter 11.

64. Stone, Patton and Heen, *Difficult Conversations*, 209.

65. Stone, Patton and Heen, *Difficult Conversations*. Based loosely on chapter 10.

as an individual — on his or her own behavior. When it becomes personal, stop talking politics and deal only with the relationship challenge. If it gets too heated and you're upset, then take a breather, only talk politics when and if you can come back fresh.

Treat the other person as if you are in the same *IN-GROUP* — Americans, humanity, your family — and request the respect accorded to people on the same side. Think twice before continuing in a heated conversation. Big fights gain nothing.

Nonviolent Communication (NVC)

Marshall Rosenberg's *Nonviolent Communication* starts with active listening but goes far beyond, providing techniques to create connections where previously there was anger and confusion.

NVC is a process of communicating that helps us explore deeper needs underneath conflicts — both our own needs and those of others. It aims to teach practitioners deep listening skills, releasing our conversations from patterns of blame, judgment and domination.[66]

When it is your turn to express yourself, the process begins with making observations free of evaluation, followed by expressing authentic feelings, and then exploring underlying human needs. Only at the end do you make requests — not demands. Deep listening involves asking questions to explore the feelings and needs, not just the requests, of the person you are potentially in conflict with. The technique aims to avoid blaming another person for your feelings — no one "makes you feel" a certain way. It focuses on broad human needs — for example, connection, love, and safety are needs, while asking someone to clean their dirty dishes is a request.

The introduction above is based on the Center for Nonviolent Communication's website at www.cnvc.org, where you can dig deeper and access many videos and training programs. This short section does not review the entire process but instead applies a few NVC techniques and lessons to political conversations.

Exercise: Notice Human Connections among Policy Arguments

Think of a political conversation that became heated, one which people left feeling unhappy.

66. "What Is NVC?" Accessed December 16, 2016. http://www.cnvc.org/about/what-is-nvc.html.

Policy aside, how did you respond to each other's feelings?

More than Policy and Strategy: Explore Underlying Needs

Policy arguments often **start at the end**: all your beliefs, desires, and pragmatic thinking about what works are piled together as assumptions. These assumptions ultimately lead to a policy choice, and you can argue that policy against someone with a different mix of starting assumptions. These arguments are battles with no way to pick who's winning. These arguments just turn up the heat.

Start by asking people what they need.

Political movements that favor laws against abortion rarely consider what has worked to lower abortion rates in different countries around the world. In general, conservatives don't *feel an emotional need* to lower the *total number* of abortions; their feelings and specific numbers are not connected.[67]

They do, however, feel a need to declare right from wrong. They do *feel a need* to have *AUTHORITY* define its legitimacy by recognizing *SANCTITY*, to have their truth spoken and heard. Your very act of listening and empathizing partly satisfies this need, without giving a millimeter on policy. Compassionate listening may mean that you convince a compassionate, family-oriented, antiwar conservative to change none of their opinions but vote for candidates who share their nurturing values instead of candidates who lead through anger about abortion.

We tend to focus on the strategies: making abortion legal or illegal. First, back up and look at the underlying needs. For many moderates and conservatives, the need is having a government led by people who express a basic understanding of sanctity, of right and wrong. There are no numbers or specific policies in this need. Focusing here creates room for more interesting conversations, or for exploring numbers and policies together after trust is built.

> A few years ago, surveys asked people if they opposed civil unions for gay and lesbian couples. They found that more people would accept civil unions if they were allowed to express their disapproval of gay marriage first. If you give people a way to voice their desire to see less abortion, they might not need to oppose abortion specifically by taking rights from women.

In conversations, conservatives often express this need to have the government say the right thing rather than to

67. Antipoverty conversations are similar, with liberals ignoring conservative criticisms that programs might not work.

take steps to objectively lower the number of abortions and prenatal deaths. It makes sense given the underlying moral "tastes," but it contradicts conservatives' conscious views of themselves as pragmatists. Compassionate listening, combined with the right questions, might eventually, slowly help them realize for themselves that they are expressing a need for a sacred government — even though they also don't believe government can be a sacred institution — instead of taking steps to effectively reduce the total number of abortions.

Jonathan Haidt describes our analytic minds as a rider trying to guide the elephant of our automatic desires: traditional political arguments, fear, and anger increase the power of the elephant and team loyalties; compassionate listening techniques empower your listener's rider.

Putting NVC into Action: Connection First, Strategies Last

NVC encourages practitioners to connect as people before making requests. For political conversations, this usually means postponing discussions of policy choices.

> The best questions are real questions: asked from curiosity, not to manipulate. You have to decide to be curious and begin a new conversation with respect; if you just want to manipulate someone, they'll know.

Begin by seeking connection. Spend much more time listening and letting your conversation partner know you are listening. Explore what their needs really are — liberals often struggle to see the conservative moral foundations described in chapter 2.

Listen. Then, ask questions that probe at their moral values. When their view is not automatically clear to you, look in particular toward the leadership, community, and sanctity values. What makes them afraid? What metaphor are they using? Turn debates into real conversations. If you want to convince someone, let them talk more than you.

Example: I hear that you believe federal assistance to people who are poor breaks down their discipline and hurts them in the end. It makes me wonder if all programs are the same, or do some programs encourage people and others discourage people? Maybe we can look at some real programs and talk about this further.

Example: You want a law against abortion. What did you experience that made you decide to focus on this issue? Do you feel that a government ban on abortions would change people's feelings about abortion, that the law would make abortion less socially acceptable? What else works to reduce the abortion rate? Imagine pro-choice and pro-life politicians got together and developed a program that reduced abortions by as much as reversing Roe v. Wade, would that feel like a success? Or would the

government still be failing in its primary role if it lowered the numbers but didn't declare abortion wrong?

Evoke What Is Alive in You: Values Before Policy

When it is your turn to talk, skip the policy and describe your needs. On abortion, don't *start* with opposing their position: don't start with saying when life begins, setting out to oppose their position instead of focusing on the heart of yours. Start with a story of the woman you are thinking of who does not need a man or government forcing its will upon her, perhaps avoiding the whole abortion topic for a good few minutes. If pro-choice is about empowering women — if that is your key issue — don't make it about women having abortions until you've described the values that *inspire you.*

When we combine the cognitive scientists' new discoveries with practices from Nonviolent Communication (NVC), our goals for Thanksgiving table interactions become clear: create a sense of connected community across progressive and conservative populations. Breach the in-group and out-group boundaries being drawn by Republican politicians. Show that you have an understanding of sanctity and values that meshes more often than it clashes. Anger politics won't be defeated by policy suggestions. Politicians may need specific policies, but in political conversations with friends and family, we need to restore democracy.

Choosing between Strategies and Connection at Thanksgiving

Sometimes talking with people who identify as conservative, I've been surprised at how few differences we actually have.

One friend desires to vote for fiscally conservative, responsible, fair-competition, pro-family *compassionate conservatives,* but her votes are going to reactionaries fracturing the country and tipping our economy ever toward crony capitalism. While my vote goes to liberals with the same crony-capitalist Wall Street advisors. The heat in America's political conversations is often misdirected.

If you're the one initiating political conversations, ask if they want to talk. Accept "no" graciously. If you're not ready to do that, you're not the messenger that person needs to hear from.

The nature of our conversations is fundamental to cleaning up politics. In particular, the worst of the authoritarian leaders and media are hyping up the conflict, creating a new *IN-GROUP BOUNDARY* around conservatives and stepping into the leadership roles they are creating. We can make that *IN-GROUP LEADERSHIP* role

disappear by getting liberal-minded people and conservative-minded people talking, back in the same community.

Fuel Solutions: Find Areas of Agreement

Finding areas of agreement is far more important than working your way through the areas of disagreement.

Listening to Marshall Rosenberg, who developed Nonviolent Communication, I find that he spends most of his time on conflict resolution, but his words indicate that finding ways to express gratitude may be more important.[68] Positive, gentle points don't make interesting reading, so I'm guilty of focusing on conflict too. But finding areas of agreement is a powerful way to get people thinking, *feeling,* that they live in a world where nurturing politics and hope can come out on top, where we don't need to live in fear all the time.

Rosenberg encourages us be present, to be personal, to get specific, to notice how we feel — don't blame someone else for your feelings, but do share what you feel, and be curious how they feel. This parallels the advice from chapter 1 to switch from describing policy to sharing stories: describe a real person, how government choices change her or his life, and how you feel about it.

Rosenberg also says that gratitude is the fuel for positive change. This is something left almost entirely out of politics. Political organizations on both the left and right focus on fear. We hate the idea that women will lose choice or are disgusted that Head Start won't be funded, rather than feeling that politics is primarily empowering and moving the world ahead. There is much less fanfare when things go well.

Politicians are likely to have a difficult time mixing gratitude into debates and elections. But we can do it: go to a soup kitchen with people who have different politics. Share stories that you know the other person will appreciate. Put hope back into politics: even when justified, anger and arguments are not the best fuel to move compassionate politics forward.

Just for Nonviolent Communication (NVC) Practitioners: Don't Use NVC-Style without Consent

There are many good ideas in NVC. But be warned, it very much matches the cognitive-liberal style of thought. When you make it clear that you are doing NVC, and they don't practice it, it's a bit like arranging the meeting-room furniture the way

68. Marshall Rosenberg, "Nonviolent Communication - San Francisco Workshop," CNVC.org. CognitivePolitics.org/nvc.

you like it — a way to make someone else feel that you are in charge of the negotiation. This is the opposite of the goals of NVC but very easy to slip into, and politics is already supercharged. So yes: observe without evaluating, avoid blaming them for your feelings, ask questions, share gratitude. But don't use catchphrases, and especially don't try to force the conversation into the standard NCV format. Or to give voice to conservative thoughts in the NVC style:

> When you phrase every sentence like this,
> I feel disconnected from you and a bit angry,
> because I am trying to talk to you like I talk to people, and you are doing some superior, smug exercise you know I won't like, yet you do it anyway.

Merging Advice from Past Chapters with Communication Strategies

Chapter 1, Framing:	Chapter 2, Values:	Mainstream Democratic Politics:
Repeat stories that reinforce your metaphor.	Listen until you understand their values.	Follow polls to craft a compromise story with centrist values. Don't sound extreme — but don't admit the Republicans are right about anything.

Merging Approaches:
Listen first, then tell your story with clarity. Build a story around your metaphor that includes both the values they have been expressing and your own. Admit the shortcomings in your ideas and the best parts of their ideas — build trust and indicate you are on the same team. Express their position so well they like your way of saying it. Once they feel heard, then tell your truth uncompromised.

Review: Integrate Communication Techniques with Cognitive Science Findings

Some of the most contentious issues seem aimed at triggering progressives into saying things that will separate us from good people on the "other" side. Rush Limbaugh is aiming to get you pissed so that you'll either be angry and help him separate your demographic from his, or else you'll quit talking politics and leave him unchallenged. We win with open, compassionate listening and strong, hopeful, and true voices.

Checklist for Effective Communication

☐ Review a recent political conversation you had. What question underlies your tactics: "Is my anger justified?" or "What will work to improve politics?"

☐ What is their metaphor? Will you stick with their metaphor or propose another? If you propose another, what questions would draw their mind into your new frame?

☐ What moral values are they expressing? Can you respect their underlying values without agreeing with them and without agreeing to their right to impose their views?

☐ Focus on listening and agreement first. Spend time agreeing to all the things you can agree with until they feel heard, and only then move forward into areas of disagreement. Remember: people who profit from divisive politics encourage ordinary people to believe we disagree about everything, so it's not necessary to list everything we disagree about!

☐ What are your goals: To get them to change their underlying values, to change which values they apply to this situation, or to get them to draw a different policy conclusion from their current values? Have them spend more time or less time focused on a particular issue? For example, on immigration, widespread conservative Christian values call on us to welcome strangers and also to obey laws. Do you confront their belief that everyone should obey the law, hammer at that belief, or hear it and then move on to a longer conversation about shared values? For example, someone opposed to homosexual sex could be challenged to give up their deep beliefs and intuitions about sanctity and agree that gay marriage is absolutely fine — or merely asked to leave this as a free choice that they suspect God may judge, for it is not their job to judge.

☐ If you are having a discussion, for example at the Thanksgiving table, would everyone else at the table appreciate it if a strict father came and told you both to shut up? If so, back off! Reassess your goals: What would let you both "win" this conversation?

Recommended Resources

Video: *"For Argument's Sake" by Daniel H. Cohen (http://www.ted.com/talks/daniel_h_cohen_for_argument_s_sake.html)* explores the problems created by seeking victory instead of understanding.

Books: *Difficult Conversations* by Douglas Stone, Bruce Patton, and Sheila Heen or *Taking the War Out of Our Words* by Sharon Strand Ellison are approaches to better conversations that can easily be extended to politics.

Nonviolent Communication can be learned from many sources, from books to videos to trainings. *CNVC.org*, for example, has resources including a video of Marshall Rosenberg's *Nonviolent Communication - San Francisco Workshop.*

For a good example of anger handled well, listen to *Michelle Obama's October 13, 2016, speech in Manchester, New Hampshire. (http://www.npr.org/2016/10/13/497846667/transcript-michelle-obamas-speech-on-donald-trumps-alleged-treatment-of-women)*
As she describes Trump's indecency, notice how she talks about her personal feelings, experiences and needs — and she talks as a person not just as a politician. This is *more hard-hitting* than just fighting fire with fire, tossing impersonal insults back and forth.

Find links online: www.cognitivepolitics.org/resources

Chapter 4

Historical Successes: Gandhi and King

Leadership That Engaged Cognitive Conservatives

My peers too young to remember Vietnam or the fight for Civil Rights often feel overwhelmed by dangerous and unethical conservatives. Mahatma Gandhi and Martin Luther King Jr. faced opponents who wanted to keep their peoples under foot, by law dominated as subhumans. They faced overt armed threats, and their followers suffered regular deaths. They struggled incredibly cleanly, played very fair, and overwhelmed their opposition. They understood something we don't. How do their tactics relate to frames and moral values?

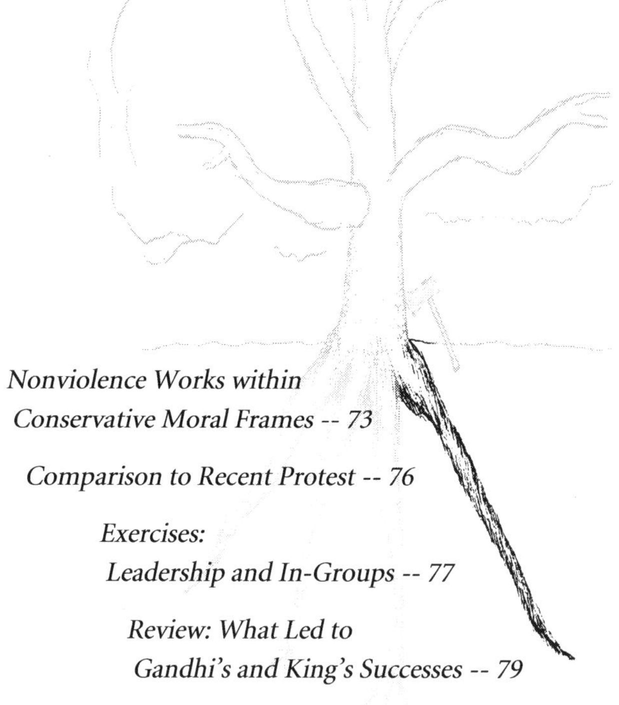

Historical Successes

Plenty has been written on Gandhi and King, and I'm going to assume readers already know the basics. This section will focus on their intersection with cognitive politics: How did they deal with moral foundations and higher levels of fear among *COGNITIVE CONSERVATIVES?* How does nonviolent resistance deal with leadership, in-group vs. out-group formation, and sanctity? Can we more systematically implement what the most effective leaders pioneered?

Nonviolent Campaigns Work within Conservative Moral Frames

Gandhi believed that even the Axis powers of World War II could have been stopped by a sufficiently brave and disciplined peace force.[69] Japanese and German leaders could maintain armies that were suffering tremendous casualties fighting an armed resistance; their armies would fall apart if all they did was murder a dignified resistance, out in the sunlight where they were forced to face it.[70] This extreme version of nonviolent resistance was never tested, but it highlights how Gandhi saw the moral values of war-making nations.

Let's translate this to a Moral Foundations perspective: nonviolent resistance breaks down the sanctity of the aggressor's cause and reduces the fear, and thus diminishes their leader's authority to lead. Forcing the armies to make eye contact and murder in cold blood would evoke the *compassion* "moral taste" while it erased the *respect for authority*.

You can see the other side of this coin in Nazi leaders' struggle to get ordinary Germans to commit mass-murder. The Nazi state employed euphemisms that only partly disguised their real activities — "Final Solution," "transfer," or "special treatment." Leaders provided flimsy excuses for ordinary Germans that let them rationalize away what they suspected or even knew.[71]

Even within the worst authoritarian or racist regimes, ordinary people are attempting to do right. They are propagandized to see their nation, their cause, or their leaders as sacred. No one tested Gandhi's theory with the Axis: no one found a way to break down that sanctity besides defeating them on the battlefield. But Gandhi did grapple with and threaten the British Empire using nonviolent resistance rather than armed rebellion, targeting the politicians' hold on their power instead of defeating armies.

69. *The Collected Works of Mahatma Gandhi* (Electronic Book), New Delhi, Publications Division Government of India, 1999, volume 82 of 98, p. 286.

70. Whether Gandhi was correct that a massive nonviolent peace force could have transformed and ultimately stopped World War II, we'll never know. But it's irrelevant to this discussion: this extreme example shines a light on beliefs that underlie all his work, much of which was tremendously successful.

71. Larry L. Ping, "Culture of Murder, Culture of Complicity: Anti-Semitism and the Origins of the Holocaust," Southern Utah University, SUU.edu. CognitivePolitics.org/ping.

Gandhi spoiled the British sense that their Empire was sacred, that they had appropriate authority. And he did it without triggering a sense of the British in-group: he didn't make the British feel like they were under attack.

> "My ambition is no less than to convert the British people through nonviolence, and thus make them see the wrong they have done to India."
> —Mahatma Gandhi[72]

King did something similar: he broke white America's feeling that their use of authority was appropriate, broke their sense that the way things were followed a sacred, natural order. He didn't place himself as a rebel attacking the natural order from outside but as a leader calling for a more sacred order.

> "I have a dream that one day on the red hills of Georgia, the sons of former slaves and the sons of former slave owners will be able to sit together at the table of brotherhood."
> —Martin Luther King Jr.[73]

Neither Gandhi nor King used a metaphor of creating sides. There was no "us and them." It was not white against black. Instead, they simply stood on the side of Truth waiting to welcome people not standing on that side to come over.

They neither diminished their truth nor attacked the other side.

Neither Gandhi nor King said their opponents were evil. It would be easy to make the case that the oppressors were evil: British imperialists sticking around in the mid-twentieth century, or American racists telling children what water fountain to drink from, did not have a legitimate excuse for their actions. But revolutionary movements set out to create large but achievable changes, not merely to be right. That meant **not strengthening the *in-group* feelings** of people who currently opposed their goals. We need to learn to do this.

> Gandhi and King both welcomed their political opponents as members of the same *in-group* of human beings with dignity, so even their opponents understood the sanctity of their goals. Meanwhile, *separate* movements expanded the "window of options" so the pacifists would be moderates.

Gandhi and King did not classify or judge people as good or bad based on their current actions, but were simply uncompromising in holding up truth. They fit a functional *nurturing-parent (p.13)* model: in charge, taking control, setting things right, but not here to punish.

A central metaphor of both Gandhi and King was that life has dignity. They didn't engage their opponents' metaphors; they told their own stories. And they went deep. They looked at the dignity of what it meant to be a human being, instead of fighting for a 2 percent change in a tax rate. England could choose dignity, India would act

72. "Mahatma Gandhi: a Short Biography." Accessed January 31, 2017. http://www.ppu.org.uk/learn/infodocs/people/pst_gandhi.html.

73. Martin Luther King Jr., "I Have a Dream" (speech, Washington, DC, August 28, 1963), American Rhetoric, http://www.americanrhetoric.com/speeches/mlkihaveadream.htm.

with dignity no matter what force was used; whites could choose dignity, African Americans would act with dignity no matter what force was used against them.

"Justice is love correcting that which revolts against love."
—Martin Luther King Jr.

Think back to Lakoff's metaphors. When King talked about justice "correcting," was he evoking nurturance or discipline? Both Gandhi and King created their own vision rather than saying "no" to an opponent, but neither adhered to Lakoff's later advice to avoid strict- or disciplining-father metaphors. Instead, they both invaded what is usually conservative cognitive space: they were leaders, religious leaders, evoking strict nonrelative morality. They claimed that the natural order, which is built on moral foundations conservatives visualize more clearly than liberals, calls for equality and justice.

Historically Successful Strategies

✓ Stick to your truth.

✓ Demand action rather than make judgments. Create clear options for moving forward, avoiding shame for the past.

✓ Make simple and small demands that are implicitly revolutionary. The Salt March and Bus Boycott asked for very little,[74] but forced the oppressors to expose themselves.

✓ Claim leadership under shared moral values. Welcome — don't attack — people currently following leaders who oppose you.

"The world is changed by your example, not your opinion."
— Paulo Coelho

---

74. During the Salt March (1930), Gandhi and others walked hundreds of miles to the sea to collect salt — an act of civil disobedience against a British tax on salt. The Montgomery Bus Boycott (1955-56) was initiated when Rosa Parks was arrested for refusing to give up her seat to a white person.

Comparison to Recent Protest: The Occupy Movement

How would the Salt March for India's Independence and the Bus Boycott of the Civil Rights Movement compare to Occupy?

Emphasizing or erasing boundaries between sides >> The Tea Party and Occupy Wall Street were founded in part to oppose government giveaways to Wall Street. In my experience with the Occupy movement, we propagandized the most racist and ignorant members of the Tea Party, rather than seeking people we might work with or pulling good people away from bad leaders. Gandhi's and King's tactics disengaged opponents' sense of being an in-group, calmed their fears, and reversed their sense of sanctity, leaving their leaders dangling.

Expressing sanctity and exposing authority >> Culture-transforming protests began with the Salt March or Bus Boycott — merely drying your own salt from the sea, or refusing to ride in the back of a bus. The overreaction to these gentle actions exposed *abuses of authority*. Occupy directly challenged *authority*, encouraging everyone to take sides. Occupy locked horns with authority; King and Gandhi got authority to expose itself. The one exception I saw in the Occupy movement was civil disobedience toward bank foreclosures: we were there to keep people in their homes, and it was the authorities who had to choose whether to clash or not.

Challenging, replacing, or invoking a strict-father metaphor >> Occupy built a movement designed for cognitive liberals — not just by the youthful and chaotic nature of living in tents but also by challenging authority by default rather than only exposing abusive authority. Cognitive conservatives who work to end poverty and oppose crony capitalism would likely not feel welcome. King and Gandhi both built strong, disciplined movements: they did not trigger the desire for a strong father through lack of discipline. Studies find that much of the population has a desire for order as early as first grade; that won't be easily changed. We can't successfully reduce the power of Wall Street elites without some allies who are cognitively conservatives.

Gandhi and King did not allow their movements to become chaotic and undisciplined — they did not invoke the need for a strict father to clean up chaos. Note that they did not spend their time arguing with people on "their side" who disagreed, and angrier opposition may arguably have enlarged the window within which they could maneuver, but they separated their movements from it.

Gandhi and King very much called for radical changes while inviting, welcoming, and challenging centrists to participate.

∞

Another way of looking at this workbook: we don't have a progressive Gandhi or King active today. Gandhi and King understood Lakoff's framing and the moral tastes of conservatives intuitively. They understood how to use stories and actions to share their visions beyond their base. But I don't want to wait for charisma, miracles, or heroes. This manual attempts to take what geniuses have done, look at what the scientists have theorized about it, and create some simple practices and exercises so that you and I can speak our truths and be heard.

Exercises

Leadership and In-Groups

Connect Actions with Intended Audiences

List different actions, protests, or viral internet articles you've encountered — for example, blocking a street, feeding homeless people, barricading to prevent a foreclosure, or interrupting a speaker. Then, for each, how are different demographics impacted?

How do you transcend your demographic niche?

- ☐ Fire up and empower everyone who agrees with you.
- ☐ Fire up and empower angry people who already agree with you.
- ☐ Extract donations from your base.
- ☐ Attract moderates and inactive liberals to actively join you.
- ☐ Attract moderates and slight conservatives to agree with you.
- ☐ Fire up your opponents. Many right-wing escapades cause a big increase in liberal donations; which of our tactics increase activism by conservatives?

☐ Create connection. ☐ Increase separation.

Turning Argument into Connection

Think of someone with whom your political conversations are difficult. What values do you hold in common?

✓ ______________________ ✓ ______________________

✓ ______________________ ✓ ______________________

✓ ______________________ ✓ ______________________

How could these areas of overlap lead to shared political strategies? To a feeling of connection?

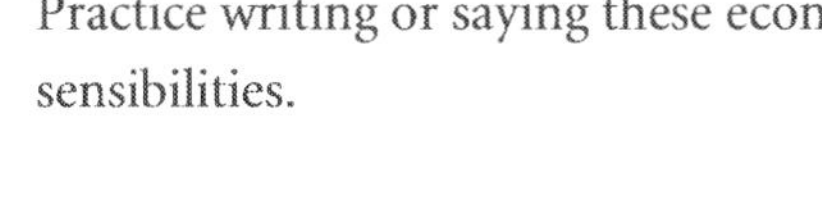

Describe Your Goals Using Their Frame

Explore your economic ideas, and sort out the ideas that a cognitive conservative would likely agree with. Which ideas will reward hard work, encourage competition, and break down barriers to a free and fair market? Practice writing or saying these economic ideas in ways that fit conservative sensibilities.

Listen to Critiques as if You Are on the Same Side

Find an area of agreement between yourself and a conservative you know, perhaps opposing government waste. Invite them to work with you to find and fight local pork spending. Sports stadiums are often being funded by liberal city governments in a way that shows how corruptible governments are, needing some conservative-minded waste-fighting to step in. Show that you've been listening to conservative critiques; be willing to clean up after "our" side.[75] The very act of working together breaks down the separation between groups: being on the same team is key to having real conversations. *Green Scissors (http://greenscissors.com)* is a great source of ideas: an effort by both environmentalists and antitax activists to find and reduce antienvironmental wastes of government money.

75. Democratic politicians chase business and lawyer money nearly as corruptly as Republicans. I expect much of the current weakness in the Democratic Party comes from dependence on money interests. It is bad enough when a pro-business party is corrupted by business interests; those contributions especially neutralize the power of people who should be speaking truth to power.

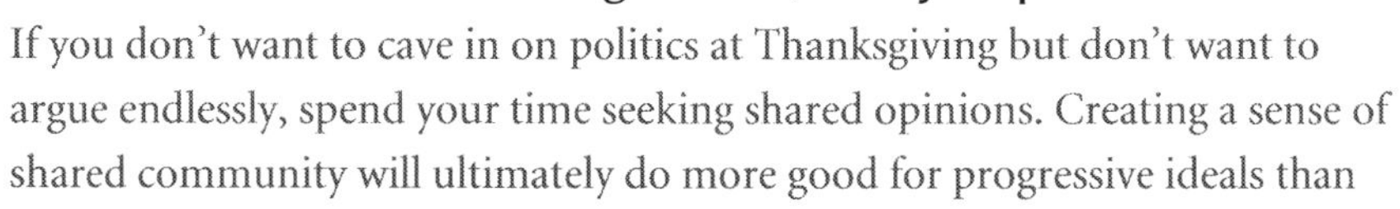

De-escalation Exercise: Seek Agreement, Clarify Requests

If you don't want to cave in on politics at Thanksgiving but don't want to argue endlessly, spend your time seeking shared opinions. Creating a sense of shared community will ultimately do more good for progressive ideals than trying to win through head-on confrontation, and you won't have to fight with family. Can you imagine six opinions you might share with a family member whom you usually just argue with? This pairs well with having a single request: Do you want them to watch a particular documentary? Spend twenty minutes researching a particular issue or history? What one thing can you ask?

Review: What Led to Gandhi's and King's Successes?

Gandhi and King both created their own stories, avoided the strict-father metaphor, and spoke to the moral foundations of conservative values:

✓ They framed their stories with strong truths that focused on their dreams rather than the oppressors.

✓ They did not separate the oppressed and oppressors into in-groups and out-groups, into us and them.

✓ They did not argue against the sanctity values of the oppressors but claimed and trumped those values. King was a Christian minister who quoted from the Bible and the Declaration of Independence; Gandhi stood for independence and integrity to many British voters.

✓ By claiming those values, they took on the role of "sacred" leadership, showing a better understanding of sanctity even from a conservative viewpoint. Large parts of the electorate of the oppressors saw them as true leaders, creating leadership crises for politicians who opposed them.

✓ They did not maximize shame, especially broad or historical shame, even when diatribes against centuries of oppression must have been tempting. Rather, all they asked past oppressors to do was the right thing, right now. They chose achievable goals.

✓ The goals they spoke of were vast dreams of universal love and decency. The goals they demanded or protested for were tiny first steps, like sitting at the front of a bus, that were very reasonable and maneuvered their opponents to expose themselves.

Chapter 5

Historical Failures: Authoritarianism

Shame and Blame Empower Unethical Leaders

We've just reviewed liberal leadership at its best. This section looks at conservative values gone wrong: What turns conservatism into authoritarianism or fascism, what are the warning signs, and how can we counter it?[76]

Authoritarianism

During the Great Depression, fascism spread like wildfire through much of Europe. During those years, the left had its usual factions, but the right transformed. Demographics who normally voted most strongly for the establishment suddenly overthrew it. I wrote the first draft of this chapter when fascist strongman approaches to politics were mostly a history lesson, and never an American history lesson. But American politics has overthrown itself to match the chapter. For two centuries American politics has swung like a pendulum, back and forth between left and right. Can we get the right back on track? If it chooses politics of hate and blame instead of pragmatism, how do we crush it?

76. These two chapters are not intended to be balanced against each other: one is successes from liberal history, the other is conservative movements at their very worst. This makes sense for a workbook for liberals trying their best to stop the worst of conservatism, and obviously is not useful for *comparing* liberals and conservatives. There is a need for the corresponding chapters written for conservatives: What do liberals get most wrong when they do have power? How can conservatives not merely defeat liberals but pressure us to be better liberals? Much of the cognitive science does seem to be coming from liberal scientists who focus on conservatives' fear and shame responses rather than liberals' shortcomings. We're not necessarily wrong when we find shortcomings with the "other side," but we should be conscious that we're not as good at seeing our own shortcomings.

A Closer Look: Subdividing Conservative Demographics

Are conservatives more fearful than liberals? Broad studies show that to be the case, but research intended to understand fascism has found a more nuanced answer. Personally, I have troubles imagining Arnold Schwarzenegger or Ronald Reagan as fearful people. But I find it easy to imagine Rush Limbaugh, Donald Trump, or their followers covering their fears or shames with anger. What differences are hidden by surveying conservatives as a single large group?

In the wake of World War II, there were many studies of the fascist right. One I find most illuminating is *The Authoritarians* by Bob Altemeyer.[77]

In this book, he explores the right wing at its worst — which is not the only option for conservatism, nor even a common result of conservative political victories, rather the worst-case disaster. Altemeyer writes in a blunt style and is often insulting toward demographics he considers the leaders and followers who create fascism, but he has a more tuned focus on the problems of the right than more recent cognitive science that lumps all conservatives together. Altemeyer's bluntness and Haidt's neutrality make excellent companions to read side by side.

Altemeyer is focused only on two subsets of conservatives. He has two scales: one for right-wing authoritarians (RWA) that loosely parallels Haidt's moral values of leadership, in-group support, and tradition along with tendencies to be fearful. The second test he calls "Exploitive-MAD" (Exploitive Manipulative Amoral Dishonesty), but it has little overlap with Haidt's moral values.

Do authoritarians want a strong leader? What is the history of American conservatives and presidential power?

Here is how Altemeyer groups people with authoritarian characteristics:

Right-Wing Authoritarian followers (RWA followers) >> take their team very seriously, don't interact much with outsiders, and follow their leaders. They "are highly submissive to established authority, aggressive in the name of that authority, and conventional to the point of insisting everyone should behave as their authorities decide." They tend to be fearful and self-righteous. They also give to charity and believe in their religion. They don't want to start wars — they prefer to ignore outsiders — but will follow their leaders enthusiastically into wars.[78]

77. Bob Altemeyer, *The Authoritarians* (Winnipeg: University of Manitoba, 2006). This is available as a *free pdf* via CognitivePolitics.org/authoritarians.

78. Altemeyer, *The Authoritarians*, 186. The RWA and Exploitive-MAD scales are based on answers to surveys.

Social Dominators >> are very different than high-RWA followers. They are not particularly afraid. They want to be in charge. They don't score high on the RWA scale; rather, they score high on the Exploitive-MAD scale.[80] A sample question on the Exploitive-MAD scale: "There's a sucker born every minute, and smart people learn how to take advantage of them."[81] They don't seem to fit Haidt's research at all: they are not *cognitive conservatives* as we have defined the term, they don't show a sense of the sacred, and they want to manipulate and lead their in-group rather than support it.[82]

Note that this is a small group while RWA followers are a much larger population, and so Haidt's statistical analysis of typical conservative characteristics will show the traits of *followers* much more than *dominators*. Social dominators are important politically, but their characteristics are masked when studying larger populations.

"Of course, the people don't want war… All you have to do is tell them they are being attacked, and denounce the pacifists for lack of patriotism, and exposing the country to greater danger."
— Hermann Göring, while imprisoned during his Nuremberg Trial[79]

Altemeyer's research would clarify that Göring's "the people" includes most conservatives, even the more authoritarian-minded.

Double Highs >> are people who score high as both social dominators and as RWA followers, feeling shame and fear but also desiring to lead others. Although a relatively rare group, Altemeyer considers them the biggest threat,[83] the most likely to appeal to RWA followers for being like them and the most likely to lead in fascist ways.

Altemeyer only discusses *right-wing authoritarians*, and his research is a response to the rise of twentieth-century European fascism. It's worth repeating that his research finds many conservatives are nonauthoritarian. Also, the lack of research doesn't mean that "left-wing authoritarians" don't exist. Though a cognitive liberal is here partly defined as not valuing authority, when the "left" takes power it attracts people with authoritarian mindsets, as was obvious in the Soviet Union. Nearly by

79. Gilbert, G.M. *Nuremberg Diary* (New York: Farrar, Straus and Company, 1947), 278-279.

80. Altemeyer, *The Authoritarians*, 166-167.

81. Altemeyer, *The Authoritarians*, 167.

82. Matthew Kugler, John T. Jost, Sharareh Noorbaloochi, "Another Look at Moral Foundations Theory: Do Authoritarianism and Social Dominance Orientation Explain Liberal-Conservative Differences in "Moral" Intuitions?" Springer Science+Business Media New York, 2014, Fig 1. The above paragraph was originally written based on reading the different questions asked in tests related to social dominance and moral foundations — Fig 1. confirms the weak connections between those tendencies. This section was written before the 2016 primary season. If it is reminding you of current politics, I would strongly recommend reading Altemeyer's work.

83. Hitler and Goebbels are the obvious examples of "double high" authoritarian dominators: suffering heavily from fear and shame, and tuned to the fears and shames of potential followers.

definition, authoritarians are attracted to and follow those in power, whether of a nation or sometimes a faction. In the US today, the center of the Democratic Party is socially, economically, and cognitively liberal, but these don't always line up so neatly, and there have been demagogues on the left elsewhere. Also, we shouldn't be surprised if small pockets of power dominated by the left within capitalist economies attract authoritarian-minded people whose politics line up with the left but who are not cognitively liberal.

Altemeyer is clear that not all conservatives show authoritarian values. In my opinion, one of the most valuable things that comes from studying the most frightening patterns on the right is not merely defeating conservatives in elections but rather influencing the dominant right-wing party to reject authoritarian tendencies. If liberals stop painting all conservatives with the same brush and instead reach out to nonauthoritarian-minded cognitive conservatives, then conservative parties will have to clean up their hate politics to stay competitive.

Moral Foundations Vary among Conservatives: Leaders and Voters Often Differ

In general, authoritarian leaders make up their own rules and can be vicious to those outside the group they hope to lead. Authoritarian followers follow the rules and take sanctity and taboos very seriously.

> It's important to remember that RWAs are a fraction of cognitive conservatives. Large portions of the conservative base do not test as right-wing authoritarians. Without bringing along these COGNITIVE CONSERVATIVES as allies, authoritarian leaders lose elections.

Progressives often focus on the highly visible *social dominator* politicians as if they represent conservatives. We look at Social Darwinists who seem to be nasty people treating even their own voters as suckers. They have a lot of power within the current Republican leadership, and have guided that party to an anger-fueled style of politics that is now turning on itself. However, these are the leaders, the politicians, and only a small slice of the followers — the electorate. This can be a big problem for liberals, leading us to craft our conversations around the morals of leaders rather than typical voters. We build our political campaigns as if we want to get Dick Cheney or Donald Trump to vote for hope and compassion, instead of focusing on a more ideal American conservative, who — unlike Cheney or Trump — would never dodge the draft, took the gun safety class, and donates 10 percent of his or her income. Good, fearful people who cover their fear with aggression and submissiveness are still at root good, fearful people. There is more to work with, much more, when you consider the average conservative voter instead of party leaders.

The research shows that different subgroups of conservatives hold different moral foundations. When surveyed, the average conservative respects a "natural" or God-ordained order more than liberals. Social dominators do not fit this pattern: they vote with but are not otherwise similar to cognitive conservatives; they use but do not hold themselves to taboos or sanctity.[84]

Empirical Studies on the Effectiveness of Activism

Altemeyer's work is fascinating in its direct applicability: by using an empirical right-wing authoritarianism (RWA) survey, he can test historical and activist events to see how they influence moral foundations.

> The only situation I found in which a crisis lowered RWA scores involved a repressive government that assaulted nonviolent protestors (which I have termed "the Gandhi trap"). Otherwise, when there's trouble, people generally look to the authorities to fix things.
> — Bob Altemeyer[85]

This might help explain why the amazing strength of angry, protesting leftists in 1968 happened at the same time as Nixon gained power. Cognitive liberals may love a wild political-protest parade, but much of the middle of the electorate will shift to the right, relying on authority or relying on a strict father, during chaos. Compare King's disciplined, well-dressed protests against the chaotic protests at the Democratic National Convention in Chicago — one of the great flare-ups of youth activism that the 1960s are remembered for. King's movement was successful, while the chaos was a step toward Nixon winning the election.

Who Is Your Audience?

Consider if your outreach efforts or social media posts

- ☐ speak to your base, or
- ☐ to a potential electoral majority.

Healthy campaigns find ways to do both.

84. Many conservatives fundamentally believe in an ordered universe. This universe mirrors chimpanzee or wolf pack order: leaders above, pack below. You can't effectively tell this to a conservative once you are talking about social order, but you can make sure that high school students study pack animals, and you can teach people to identify and perhaps overcome the instinct to defer to power outside of political conversations.

85. Altemeyer, *The Authoritarians*, 58.

Using Shame and Fear to Fuel a Rise to Power

Leadership Pattern: Shlumpy Superman

Political leaders using shame have consistent patterns. They target people with low self-esteem, telling them they are superior but their problems are all someone else's fault. A distinct marker is that the leader won't be very imposing and won't be an example of the superior, ideal man he describes. Hitler was not the blond Aryan ideal, nor did he have an unusually successful business or military career, nor was he physically imposing.[86] People who felt like failures listened to him talk about the superman Aryan and felt ok about it because he was fantasizing just as much as they. In US politics, Arnold Schwarzenegger is a good counterexample: he told conservatives to work hard, and he was a good example of what he talked about. Rush Limbaugh fits the shame-into-blame leader role perfectly: honest, self-aware cognitive conservatives realize he is damaging conservative political movements.

Contrast with Healthy Conservatism

Reading about European fascism or resistance to civil rights can be depressing. Conservative movements have created deeply hateful policies — not just when they lose control the way leftists in the Soviet Union centralized power and then lost control to Stalin, but as purposefully chosen policy. Now, research is finding that many of us are protectors, on our way to being conservatives, since first grade, long before we are responsible for our choices.

> "Every gun that is made, every warship launched, every rocket fired signifies, in the final sense, a theft from those who hunger and are not fed, those who are cold and are not clothed … The cost of one modern heavy bomber is this: a modern brick school in more than 30 cities."
> — President Dwight Eisenhower, Republican[87]

But Altemeyer's research of demographics inclined to fascism shows that many conservatives are not part of this demographic. And Haidt's explorations of conservative moral values points out positive conservative traits that are easy for frustrated liberals to miss. Conservative movements are led by different demographics at different times. There is value to the protector's instinct, if we can keep the purely power-hungry from leadership. America desperately needs a sane conservative party:

86. "Adolf Hitler and World War I: 1913–1919", *Holocaust Encyclopedia*. Hitler struggled as an artist, was brave but unexceptional as a soldier, and struggled again after demobilization until he found politics.

87. Robert Schlesinger, "The Origins of That Eisenhower 'Every Gun That Is Made…' Quote," US News & World Report, Sept. 30, 2011, USnews.com. Includes interesting back-story of the quote.

looking for wasteful spending, finding affordable ways to keep us safe, challenging us to be our best, to be self-reliant. I don't see that party today. I hope that learning to engage ordinary conservatives in a more constructive manner might help, especially if we can restore the sense that the USA is one *IN-GROUP* or community where we disagree but don't separate based on political opinions.

Liberals crossing the ideological divide may find that our most important long-term role is not turning conservatives into liberals but getting conservatives to be better conservatives. We need to build a political system where decency and honesty win: where hoping that America has an economic failure so that President Obama loses is seen as treasonous across the political spectrum. To do that, we do need to crush anger-and-shame elements of the Tea Party in elections until a sane conservative party rises from the ashes.

On the theme of healthier conservatism, a great gift for cognitive conservatives in your life might be *Crunchy Cons* by Rod Dreher, which describes how "countercultural conservatives plan to save America (or at least the Republican Party)."[88]

What Do Conservatives Fear About Liberals, Parallel to Our Fear of Fascism?

Many conservatives believe Stalin is a parallel to Hitler. The left concentrated power under idealistic slogans, and then lost control of that power to a monster. The left in the US slowly, eventually repudiated Stalin — long before I was watching politics. But many on the left think of the problem as mere random chance of a bad man taking power. Conservatives believe that concentrating enough power to regulate and redistribute invites the corrupt to grab power. What is the framing counterargument?

Personally, I don't think there is a good counterframe: conservatives are right about this, and I think liberals should be opposing concentrations of power in both corporations and government. One reason I'm personally allied with liberals at this juncture in history in the US is that we seem at least as reliably opposed to concentrations of power as today's deficit-spending, war-starting Republicans.

That hasn't been the case at every point in history. Before Nixon, when Democrats dominated national politics, they paid less attention to the growth of bureaucracies.

American politics today is mired, but in my opinion, if either party gets better at creating cleaner, more efficient government — whether more environmental and

88. Rod Dreher, *Crunchy Cons* (New York: Crown Forum, Random House, 2006). Quote on the cover.

compassionate or more disciplined and with lower taxes — they are likely to dominate elections. Liberals very often blame Reagan for the end of the liberal dominance, instead of blaming the failures of our poorly designed liberal welfare-state.

A Strong Presidency: More Complex than Left and Right

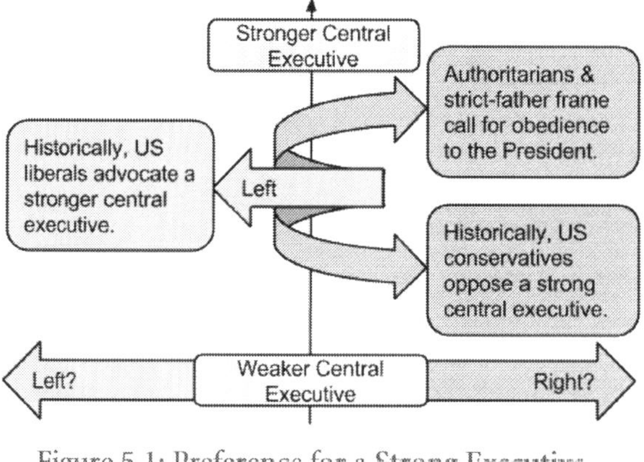

Figure 5.1: Preference for a Strong Executive

Traditional conservatives in the US have fought against a powerful presidency, while liberals have often wanted a president capable of pushing change. This contradicts Lakoff's "strict-father" theories, at least for the US. Meanwhile, fascists crave a single man in charge. This makes it clear that you can't call conservatives authoritarian indiscriminately; there are very important divisions within conservatism.

History exposes at least two very different flavors of conservatism still lumped together by the recent cognitive science research: let's call them *cautious conservatism* and *fearful conservatism*. Cautious conservatism believes in discipline and preparation — self-reliance, not reliance on a leader — preparing for actual danger. Fearful conservatism sees danger even where none exists, and is ready to hand over power to a protector. These different flavors can dominate a country's conservative politics at different times, though modern US conservatives have never turned to a strongman presidency before Trump. What does this mean for healthy politics? What alliances can liberals make? What role do liberals have in influencing the demographics who had conservative psychological traits as children to become defenders and not wagon-circlers as adults?

Exercise: Punching Up, Punching Down

A good way to separate cautious conservatism and fearful conservatism is whether they challenge people who have more power than they do ("punching up") or target those with less.

Often, conflicts come when one side sees power where the other side sees helplessness. Is a white male who watched their manufacturing job disappear, who is paid half what they used to earn, and who watched their brother commit suicide by drug overuse, a "punching up" target? He would often be treated as such by the center-left.

Put Out Brushfires of Fascism

Hitler rose to power in what had been one of the world's most liberal countries. What are the steps to put out early brushfires of fascism and authoritarianism?

Definition: Inoculation

In medicine, we create vaccines by introducing some aspect of a pathogen to create immunity — before someone is sick. In politics, it's much easier for us all to agree on general rules and principles before we know which team will be impacted by that consensus. Inoculation means reinforcing concepts that we tend to agree on — before they are the partisan fight of the moment.

Inoculate against the patterns that show up again and again:

✓ Draft dodgers who like wars.

✓ People born on golden elevators who demand others pull themselves up by their bootstraps.

✓ People who have failed at everything besides politics yet mock failure in others.

✓ People with power, or subservient to the powerful, who think the worst threats are the least powerful and minorities. From the Roman Empire through the Nazis, circuses and scapegoats have kept the oppressed targeting each other: repeat and reinforce this idea. When you look at history books not connected to current, active efforts to make excuses for those in power, it is obvious and uncontroversial to nearly everyone that the strong dominate the weak.

All of these are points where healthy conservatives and all liberals should be on the same side, working together.

Shared Humor

A powerful inoculation technique is to *share* jokes in nonpartisan settings, long before opposing a specific policy. If liberals want to frame

as successfully as conservatives do, planning for years ahead, then we should be joking about draft dodgers who love war, *now.*

Get a new term for draft-dodging war lovers into the language, or use chicken-hawk (someone who avoided service but likes war) more often. Make broad jokes about how pathetic chicken-hawks are, not related to any current politics. Or point out that Senator McCain is not a chicken-hawk and has the decency to have faced the risks he asks of others, separating those conservatives who actually believe in their values from those who are just manipulators. Have the term already at the tip of people's tongues when you need to use it.

> "I will do anything in my power to support our military, short of enlisting."
> —Stephen Colbert (in character)[89]

Humor lets you attack a behavior that no one feels loyal to, rather than a politician who already has a loyal following. Inoculation is one of the ways to create a culture outside of political campaigns that will constrain the worst behaviors of politicians.

Education

Liberals would also do well to make the study of authoritarian leaders part of high school education.

If we wait until hate-politics techniques are being used, it's too late. If we tell Trump's supporters that Trump is purposefully redirecting their fears into blame targeted at innocent people, and pointing out that Hitler used similar techniques, they'll just hear us comparing someone they like to Hitler — it's heard as mere name-calling.

Teach kids the details about how the Nazis used hatred to gain votes. Focus on how shame was turned into blame. Once those histories are familiar, it will be easier to help people notice it on their own as it begins to happen again.

In-Groups That Turn Against Out-Groups

Groupthink Must Include Antiracist Voices

Lakoff often encourages us to repeat our message. And Altemeyer's research indicates that this is far more key for authoritarian-minded followers than any other group explored. They seek the middle, to be securely inside the fences of their in-group norms.

89. Stephen Colbert, "The Colbert Report," Oct. 25, 2013.

We need to both expand the pro-empathy edge of the fence and emphasize a middle that is more compassionate than what we have today. If this demographic self-identifies as American including both liberals and conservatives, they will lean center-right. If this demographic identifies as conservatives and not part of an America framed on the left by liberals, they will center themselves only amongst conservatives, and we will have a powerful, angry far-right.

> "If you look at the high RWAs who do know someone gay or lesbian, they are much less hostile toward homosexuals in general than most authoritarians are."
> — Bob Altemeyer.[90]

> "The reality is that unfriending racists might protect YOU, but it doesn't protect me and my family. Unfriending all the racists creates an echo chamber of comfort for you."
> —Jasmine Banks Brown[91]

Whenever a demographic is targeted by hate, it's vital that good people who are not targets of that hate loudly declare themselves. Authoritarians are afraid and seeking the safety of the center: make sure your voice helps claim the center.

Disinfect Festering Racism

In 2016, people who previously voted for Obama and Republicans who chose Ben Carson above all other contenders ultimately voted for a man who left the KKK cheering. Martin Luther King Jr. campaigned against people who stood in school doorways and in front of cameras proclaiming their racist intentions. We now live in an era when few people claim to be racist, but from police statistics to the 2016 election, it's clearly still festering — sometimes in private and sometimes truly below the level of consciousness.

> "As moral, religious and law-abiding citizens, we feel that we are unprejudiced and undiscriminating in our wish to keep our community a closed community."
> — Neighbors in Levittown, Pa, 1957. Sign at pro-segregation protest.[92]

The above quote is from "The Good, Racist People" by Ta-Nehisi Coates, an op-ed piece about African Americans still facing perpetual low-level harassment. If you have an easy answer for this phenomenon — racism by people who don't think they're racist — you're probably not looking close enough. Political liberals have had a tendency to "call them on it" when we witness unintended racism. But when people

90. Altemeyer, *The Authoritarians*, 67.

91. Jasmine Banks Brown, "Do Not Unfriend the Racists," JustJasmineBlog.com, June 23, 2015.

92. Ta-Nehisi Coates, "The Good, Racist People", *The New York Times,* March 6, 2013, NYTimes.com.

are only subconsciously racist and then hear themselves labeled racist, they hear it as an insult rather than a call to change. Thus, the strategy of labeling them as "racists" backfires and makes the situation worse.

The above quote matches Altemeyer's surveys: authoritarian-minded people desire to be in the center of their in-group: they don't want to be particularly bigoted; at worst they hedge their bigotry and want to be average members of their group. And yet decades after Civil Rights and the end of openly acceptable racism, these struggles continue and politicians continue using racism.[93]

These tendencies go beyond the basic moral foundations that Haidt described. How do we challenge mindsets that people don't realize they have? There are many answers, but there is a pattern relevant to a book on framing: big changes start small. Educating people who don't know they are racist with examples of overt and nasty racism does not seem to help reduce milder implicit racism, but sharing studies of the subtlety of implicit racism does help people introspectively find those patterns within themselves and work on improving. [94]

Share what is alive in you; welcome political opponents to be part of your community sharing what is alive in them. When does shame lead to positive change?

A big caveat: speaking your truth trumps framing. This book aims to give general framing advice, especially for those impersonal political conversations that so often devolve into squabbles. When it is personal, don't frame; speak your experience. But when you find yourself in the same demographic as someone who is bigoted, then (1) silence, (2) fighting-words or insults, and (3) separating from them — such as unfriending them on Facebook so you don't have to hear it — are all acts of privilege and not helpful to the demographic they target. When you can, find ways to engage in actual conversation without creating separation.

Erasing Prejudice: Cleaning the Bathroom

People disgusted by racism, I'd include myself here, might daydream that if we lived during the 1960s we would march with Martin Luther King Jr. or perhaps with the first Pride parade when the risks were higher than today. It's easy and fun to daydream of being a knight in shining armor. But a large amount of the work is more like cleaning neglected bathrooms than galloping to the rescue. People around us grew up with too little love and too much fear in their own lives and only rarely can be forced, usually have to be convinced, to widen their circle of compassion. In conversations and social media, over and over we need to make

93. Curtis D. Hardin and Mahzarin R. Banaji, "The Nature of Implicit Prejudice: Implications for Personal and Public Policy," fas.harvard.edu. Provides a broad overview of implicit (unconscious) racism.

94. Dr. Sam Gaertner, "Prejudice among the Well-Intentioned." Lecture, University of Delaware, Newark, Purnell Hall, April 24, 2013.

nonconflictual statements of what we believe in. Nonviolent Communication describes many of the keys: stay connected to your feelings and deeper needs, avoid blame, and make (or imply) positive requests: "I see the refugees as human beings." "If it was my family, I'd pray that people let us flee the terrorists," "Two generations ago, America opened its doors to my grandparents who were refugees. I feel gratitude for that; that's the America I feel patriotic toward." "I believe the people who planted and harvested the food I ate deserve a home and health care." When people in your circles are publicly spewing hate or anger online, keep your voice in the conversations: cut and paste the same sentences each time if you need to. Don't expect fast miracles but don't let hate go unanswered.

How Do We Deal with Bullies?

Long Term: Teach Children to Stand Up for Each Other

Make sure children face no more bullying than they are capable of dealing with. Teach kids how to stand up for each other. Create a society where people grow up both supported and able to stand up for themselves and others.

When bullies have grown up with authoritarian leadership traits, it's beyond the scope of a book on framing to change them, and our main goal may be to keep them and their potential followers apart.

Short Term: Pull Authoritarian Followers from Leaders

There are few tools to attack or push followers away from leaders; you have to draw and invite them toward your community and your values. You have to *remain within their peer group* to apply pressure: once they would define you as *OTHER*, you have no more leverage. The military has been very successful at breaking down racism because it successfully creates a sense of being a single community or in-group — so that a rule for enlistees that racism will not be tolerated becomes internalized as part of group membership. Liberals often mock conservatives who, for example, can't find the nations they want to invade on the map. But yelling and mockery will merely solidify that you are an outsider attacking their group, thus solidifying their loyalty to their group's leaders.[95] Remind people of shared values and ideals. High RWAs want to be normal: invite them, welcome them, challenge them to be normal instead of racist or homophobic. It is particularly important to stand up for other religions, races or genders when you are potentially within the *IN-GROUP* of the authoritarian-minded.

95. When talking about a policy that impacts you directly, parts of this are reversed. Don't frame (what this book is primarily about), speak your truth and your feelings. From a framing perspective, as you feel safe and that you have leverage, demand that a group stop harming you so you can be a full member.

Exercise: Push or Pull; Mock or Connect

The Tea Party has mixed racism and blind privilege with a widespread desire to oppose government giveaways to Wall Street. Trump has reached an overlapping demographic that lashes out at both an establishment that has sold them out and minorities. Both groups hold events where liberals see striking amounts of ignorance.

☐ When is it effective to mock misspelled protest signs and policy misunderstandings; when does that backfire?

☐ What approaches could pull family members to feel more connected to your views and less connected to anger politics?

> Some youth antismoking campaigns attack the self-esteem of smokers, putting down the kids who smoke. You can see this approach in older "antismoking" materials designed by the tobacco industry, designed to backfire.[96] Kids tend to smoke in part because of low self-esteem: making them feel bad for smoking easily backfires. Getting authoritarian followers away from the authoritarian leaders has similar difficulties: insulting them or their leaders is an attack on them, a reason for them to feel shame and circle their wagons.

Questions: Politics and Disassociation from Reality

EASY QUESTIONS (FOR THOSE ANYWHERE ON THE LEFT) >> In the last few years, I've heard more and more conservative voices claim that Hitler and the Nazis were on the left. Somewhat similarly, in my experience, the "Southern Strategy" has gone down a conservative memory hole despite being the defining moment of the modern US political map. When you encounter historical blind spots among people you disagree with, how does this make you feel? Do conservative blind spots work or backfire, if their goal is to attract centrists or weaken the liberal base?

REAL QUESTIONS (FOR THOSE ANYWHERE ON THE LEFT) >> Are you willing to admit that the movements to overthrow the French monarchy and Tzarist Russia were, in broadest terms, started on the left? That these left movements led eventually to the guillotine and vast Napoleonic wars, and to Stalin? I don't mean that we have to accept childish baiting, or a claim that every liberal is a Stalinist with a guillotine, just like I don't think every conservative is a Nazi. Rather, can you admit that "our side" has made terrible mistakes, and discuss your own perspective on how "our side" will avoid these in the future?

HOLD THE CENTER >> If you want to win votes for sanity and hope, or a liberal version of sanity and hope, it's powerful to let the right wing be crazy and not jump in after them. If conservatives are implying that Hitler was a liberal, how do you think people would respond to a comment like this?

96. "Study: Teen Antismoking Ads Backfiring," Reviewed by Louise Chang, MD. WebMD Health News, WebMD.com.

> Look, right wingers gave us Nazism, left wingers gave us Lenin then Stalin. The liberals and conservatives you should trust are the ones who admit that their side isn't perfect, and learn from it. Liberals who pretend the USSR wasn't a horror of the left and conservatives who pretend Nazi Germany wasn't a horror of the right are wingnuts. (If you're not sure, get off the web and read a history book. This was never controversial.)

If an online conversation was started by a claim that Nazis were leftists, how would a teenager who hasn't yet studied twentieth-century history respond to a left-vs.-right shouting match between you and the author? Or to a comment like the one above? In general, I think the best way to deal with wingnuts is to reclaim the center, not validate them with shouting matches from the left nor silently leave public conversations to them. See "Reclaim Common Spaces" (p.180) for techniques on dealing with trolls and extremists. Separating honest conservatives from the wingnuts is much more powerful than trying to paint them all with the same brush. Invite honest conservatives to join you.

Review: Values Weave, Fear Unravels

Moral Foundations Theory shows us a world where liberals and conservatives are merely different, not better or worse. We also live in a world where some politics are clearly "worse," from fascism to hate politics and opposition to civil rights. At the individual level, we watch many politicians who seem uncaring, who don't match the positive community-building values ascribed to cognitive conservatives. My conservative neighbor may be described by Moral Foundations Theory — the leaders he follows are more varied, and some are very different from him.

Barack Obama and Hillary Clinton appear to have values typical of centrist Democrats. Liberals make a key mistake when they assume the Republican Party works the same way and design their messages based on the leadership. Liberals keep arguing that Republican policies create a merciless world where only the privileged and lucky thrive — but many Republican voters have underlying values very different from Cheney or Trump, even if they vote for those leaders.

Conservatives today are dividing. Some conservative individuals continue to believe that people need challenges to thrive. Others are feeling isolated and lost, and looking for someone to provide strength for them. The first group votes for politicians who are often merciless, but the voters don't desire to be merciless, nor do they see themselves that way. The second is attracted to leaders like Trump who display strength and anger. Many liberals want to stand up to Trump as a bully. Sometimes this might make sense, but we also need to be careful because his followers are often feeling disempowered, and shows of strength might cause them to increase their reliance on him.

I've often read liberal media that seeks inconsistencies to argue that conservatives don't believe in their religion, but the evidence is strong that most do. Inconsistencies are just inconsistencies.

You don't have to convince the leaders; you have to convince their electorate.

There are two competing explanations for the rise of fascism: Did all the hate grow from loneliness, fear, and apathy? Or from a consciously chosen path to power? Altemeyer's theories show that both were interwoven. Most voters rallied into an authoritarian movement are feeling isolated and fearful, while a few leaders are using that fear as a path to power. Resistance to authoritarian-minded politics calls for being conscious of whether you are dealing with isolated and fearful people — or manipulators — at each step.

Countering the Politics of Hate

Candidate Trump targeted hate at immigrants. Are you able to still feel compassion for people who have been betrayed by their politicians, their country, and their employers; who are now feeling lost and afraid; and who are being baited to turn on immigrants? How do you create an alternative community they can feel part of; how do you cost the Republican Party votes if they continue to welcome hate speech? How do you inoculate them against Trump's hate-filled speech?

Recommended Resources

Bob Altemeyer, The Authoritarians (Winnipeg: University of Manitoba, 2006). See the section (p.182) comparing global simulation games as played by groups of RWA followers on their own compared with mixed groups of RWA followers plus a few social dominators. Available for free online: *http://members.shaw.ca/jeanaltemeyer/drbob/TheAuthoritarians.pdf.*

Transition >> Choosing Your Goals

What Does Winning Look Like?

Political conversations at the Thanksgiving table are notorious for being simply bad conversations. Conservative ideals thrive in a scary world: if we can't get along, if we have arguments in which neither side listens, politics will shift toward fear, and people will metaphorically seek strict fathers to maintain order.

If people who desire compassionate and nurturing government want to win elections, we need to live our values: actively listening even when we disagree; modeling anti-fundamentalist behaviors by respecting people despite differences; and expressing our values with clarity, neither raising our voices to "win a point" nor losing strength as soon as someone else raises their voice. Living those values, showing up to each conversation as a new experience, will put moderates into a more liberal frame of mind.

Choosing Goals for a Conversation

The first half of the book reviews many possible strategies, but before you pick one, you need to decide your goals. What is it possible to accomplish in any given conversation?

Different techniques from the first section apply at different times. For the 2016 election, I wanted to see Clinton kick Trump's ass, maybe get in a zinger that made him look bad. But with a conservative friend, I want real conversations that get to the heart, so my approach might be active listening and Nonviolent Communication (NVC).

"Winning" is not a real goal. Winning what?

In any particular argument, "winning" can be complex. Is your goal to feel vindicated whether you convince anyone or not? Shore up your own base? Convince smart people on the other side? Convince people to agree with you on one particular issue? Convince people that your side should lead, whether they agree with you on one particular issue or not? Undo a "trap" or "trigger" issue that gets good people squabbling?

The sections ahead will vary the goals for each issue — for example, aiming to get moderate-conservatives to see the facts of the economy differently, change their

underlying values on gay marriage, or loosen their distrust for pro-choice candidates whom they otherwise agree with.

Progressive Values Thrive on Hope

It's easy to see the kind of world that pulls people to vote right wing. Angry voices, chaos, and confusion leave many people wanting a strong, strict father figure.

From Gandhi to the Black Panthers, on-the-ground community work amplifies more radical politics. Some of the best examples of transformation I've seen were vegetarian education efforts that were open-minded and welcoming — with actual cooking and real communities instead of just rhetoric. After the hosts and activists created enjoyable, welcoming potlucks that focused on healthy food and community, people were more open to considering challenging ideas regarding animal rights. Don't just frame: put work into building healthy communities that exemplify your values, and people will feel safe enough to believe in a nurturing world.

Consider Your Audience

> Republican politicians mock Democrats as intellectual and academic. I personally prefer academic-style debates, digging in to each point and checking footnotes. Occasionally, this communication style is effective. It has worked to bring a huge majority of scientists toward the left in the US today.[97] You don't need to remove academic debates from your toolkit, but only use this communication style when the person you're talking with appreciates it.

Are you trying to convince, to calm, or to connect with the person you are talking to? Or to convince other listeners? If your goal is to get them to one day vote for your candidate, tripping someone up and making them look stupid is worse than pointless.

- The scientific process is similar to a debate, defining a hypothesis and then examining evidence for and against it, but it allows all participants to collect evidence in each direction instead of defining sides.
- Laying out a problem and looking for solutions in partnership can draw people together, while a debate pushes people apart.
- Or take a step back, and explore an issue without seeking solutions.
- If you angrily disagree about one or two issues, focus on something else; seek shared values.

97. "Public Praises Science; Scientists Fault Public, Media," Pew Research Center, July 9, 2009. 6% of scientists are Republicans.

Section II: Issue-by-Issue Workbook

So far we've explored theory and history. Now we're switching to application, exploring four sample issues that use different concepts from the first section. These sections include speculation and brainstorming, ideas to try rather than well-tested theories.

Abortion Abortion keeps good-hearted people at each other's throats. It provides politicians who have sold out to military and financial interests with one life-affirming position they can use as a distraction during elections. Today, the sense that liberal politicians are violating the basic value of *SANCTITY* is leveraged into mistrust of their *AUTHORITY* to lead. Even if we never agree on the sacredness of a fetus, does abortion have to be a wedge issue?

Same-Sex Marriage Even many conservatives are now recognizing the legal right and even acceptability of people in love to get married. Like abortion, this issue is centered on *SANCTITY*. Unlike abortion, liberals have been reframing this issue and changing minds, reminding the whole country that we are one community with shared rights and values. What worked? What techniques can we apply to other issues?

American Exceptionalism People who believe that America should never apologize form an *IN-GROUP* of shared loyalties. Exceptionalism is a frame understood by both moderates and conservatives, with liberals often left baffled. This creates a disconnect in which progressives are left out of the conversation and out of the patriotic in-group. Can liberals tell a healthier story of America in a way that will erase those divisions?

Economics Progressives rage against policies but misinterpret the conservative values behind those policies. Progressives shout ever louder for more *CARE* and compassion, while many churchgoing conservatives donate out of compassion but see the current system as reasonably *FAIR*. Since the market is fair, they see competition as strength-building and healthy. Failure to engage conservative hesitations leads us to angrily repeat points about compassion we mostly agree on and ignore the real questions about *FAIRNESS* conservatives have — questions we *can* answer if we engage them.

These four issues were chosen because they each call for different concepts from the first half. To join framing discussions about current controversies, visit *CognitivePolitics.org*.

Chapter 6

Abortion: Sanctity, Authority, and Otherness

Abortion is a key wedge issue dividing good people who give money to charity or time to volunteer. We wind up calling each other evil or crazy over honestly held differences of opinion.

Abortion is the first issue in this workbook because it's at the crux: people who all want a better world are wedged against each other. How do *you* talk to someone who believes that life begins at conception? You probably can't change their religious values, but can you deflate the anger politics that feeds on our differences?

Have we fallen into the conservative frame by talking about when life starts? Are we reactively saying "NO!" to the conservative story instead of telling our own story? Liberal policymakers have often treated conception and the beginnings of life with at least as much sanctity as conservative politicians: in fact rather than in rhetoric. Seen from an anti-abortion perspective, liberal leaders lower the rates of abortion at least as effectively as conservatives. Yet we've bungled the communications and misunderstood the conservative "sense of smell" around this moral question, leaving good people divided.

The abortion issue breaks apart an otherwise widely shared framework of compassion held by most Americans — does it have to?

Abortion: Today's Frames, Values, and Goals

Conservative Framing: **Respect for Sanctity as a Leadership Requirement**

For Ordinary People

For many good people whose politics are based on their honest beliefs, abortion is a heartrending cause. A fetus is a defenseless human baby, and the sacred values are unlimited: this issue overwhelms any day-to-day politics or mere theories about rights. When people don't respect the idea that babies' lives are

sacred, they become other, outsiders from the society of good people. In a world where defenseless human babies are treated callously, there is an opening for a stern, powerful father figure to step in and restore sanity.

For Politicians

Abortion is not only something ordinary people care about but also a major political battleground. To understand why restricting abortion and improving prenatal care are on opposite sides of the political spectrum, start with this question: Imagine you represent the interests of the wealthiest .1 percent — how do you get 51 percent of the population to vote for you anyway?

Political parties that represent elite interests tend to seek issues of honest controversy but little budget impact, like abortion and gun control, and rally people around these ideological wedge issues far from the budget issues and giveaways to lobbyists. Note that there is something strange about these wedge issues: they dominate debates, but as Republicans and Democrats each take turns in power, nothing much happens quickly, just minor laws at the edges. When establishment Republicans take power, they rush to lower taxes on the wealthy. It's been a successful strategy: many cognitive conservatives ignore their own self-interest and use this issue alone to define their political loyalties.

Money interests support Pro-Life because it helps define us into two camps. Remove abortion's value as a wedge, even without changing anyone's mind, and you ruin the value of Pro-Life to the money players. Remain one community, disagreeing but not separating, and you ruin the wedge.

Conservative Story and Frame Summary: Women are making bad choices, violating the sacred, and we need a strict leader to step in and make things right. People who don't understand how bad abortion is aren't morally fit to lead.

Implications for Liberals: If we're going to keep abortion safe and legal, we have to win elections, but we don't have to convince *everyone* that abortion isn't a *sin*. We merely have to convince swing voters that we are sane, honest, and capable of leading even though we disagree on this one issue. Progressives can give women choice within the world of force and politics, while letting Pro-Life advocates preach their views on when life begins outside of politics. As long as we keep this from being a useful wedge, it won't attract right-wing funding.

Exploring Liberal Framing Failures: Don't Think of an Abortion

If you can't trust me with a choice, how can you trust me with a child?

I've seen this bumper sticker on many cars. Linguistically, it's hard to imagine a worse-framed slogan. The words will be

heard to twice slander your own side as untrustworthy, both with choices and children.

To a conservative or moderate ear, this framing evokes a need to summon a strict father to straighten out the mess created by "untrustworthy" liberals. This helps explain why politicians who want to cut funding for maternal health care are so often loud advocates of Pro-Life rhetoric. It's an issue that helps politicians who support elite economic interests to convince good-hearted people that liberals, and especially liberal leaders, cannot be trusted. They want to reinforce that some women "can't be trusted with a choice." The goal of conservative strategists is to mix together progressives, untrustworthiness, irresponsibility, and mistakes: exactly as this liberal bumper sticker says.

Countries with pro-women policies find that paid maternity leave, day care, and health care lead to more women being empowered to choose not to have abortions.[98] So why isn't our frame:

Respecting women is pro-life.

A frame isn't the same as a policy goal or wish list like "empower women with the option to control their own bodies and make their own choices, and stop making this an issue." The above frame creates real unanswerables for conservative pragmatists, rather than just defining which team we are on.

Against abortion? Don't have one.

This implies two factions, two societies with different values. This slogan's core message is that we are separate and shouldn't listen to each other, not that we should respect women. The quote aims to score points in an abstract debate about abortion, rather than win elections and thus get progressives on the Supreme Court.

This slogan also reinforces the conservative frame that the issue is abortion. We are merely saying *No* to their idea, rather than mindfully speaking our own values: the issue is women's control of their own bodies. "Respecting women is pro-life" breaks the conservative frame while aiming to avoid conservative triggers. It both expresses

98. Abortion statistics are incredibly complex, and people tend to find statistics that support their existing beliefs. Moving the conversation into looking at what works is a very positive step — ask your conversation partner to join you in looking at the mess of research to find out which pieces of legislation actually lower abortion. Finding proof in statistics is neither possible nor required — simply making it clear that you want to work together seeking answers is the goal.

our core value of respecting women (imposing our ideas about abortion is not what we're here for) and — if you gently follow it with the facts about low abortion rates in Scandinavia or the failure to reduce abortion in pro-life Latin America[99] — it helps us answer some of their fears.

Don't win points in debates; win elections!

It's important to review goals: many of us desire to tell uterus-centric Republicans to shut up and to prove them logically wrong. Do we want to be right, or win elections? There will be times when politicians should be angrily told to shut up, but facts framed as "reasons you are wrong" will not win the votes of individuals who hold different initial beliefs.

Abortion: Safe, Legal, and Rare

This might be a great policy outcome. It is not the worst frame, but it fails two framing tests. First, it fails to focus on women, linguistically keeping us focused on the conservative frame of legality and government reducing abortion. Second, despite focusing on abortion, it speaks to policy rather than a cognitive-conservative sense of sanctity. It is a good reactive answer to abortion-restrictors but not an ideal proactive liberal frame.

I trust women and I vote.

What is the core progressive truth near the topic of abortion? The progressive truth doesn't orbit around abortion but around women: "respect women" or "empower women."

Moral Foundations in Dissonance: **Authority, Sanctity and Faith**

Whom Can You Trust to Lead?

Many moderates and conservatives have community-building values that are best expressed with liberal policies and conservative rhetoric. Those who want power through division need the focus to be on two-dimensional caricatures.

99. "Abortion in Latin America: Miscarriages of Justice," *The Economist,* June 8th 2013. See the box labeled "Terminal Failure" listing global abortion rates.

They need a good-hearted churchgoer to *look* at a bought-and-paid-for lackey of the military-industrial complex who is defunding Head Start and buying missiles — and *see* "pro-life." The goal is to create division and get good people to stop listening to other good people, to make the other side seem to have no sense of shared values so that the only morally acceptable authority, the only leaders you can trust, must agree on this issue above all others. They win when abortion is a litmus test, defining the good guys and the bad guys across politics.

> In politics, the abortion frame isn't policy; it isn't even about saving babies. It's about whom you can trust to lead.

Authority Replacing Faith

Even if you believe that killing a fetus is killing a baby and the worst kind of murder, there are still contradictions in sending in armed men.

To a liberal mindset, we might see a typical story in the abortion debate as a woman whose birth control failed or was forgotten and whose rights will now be trampled. Cognitive-conservative minds are harsher about full accountability for any mistakes and so unlikely to back down within this framing. However, we have made the typical liberal mistake of talking policy instead of people: some women also choose to give birth in difficult circumstances. Republican policy violates their right to ultimately, carefully *choose*, rather than be told. There's no policy difference in this story: no abortion services are needed, but it's a very different world if you believe in freedom or faith. Liberals argue that abortion should be a matter of faith, not government: let's refocus there.

Example Progressive Story: Respect Women's Faith

Imagine this scenario: a woman who is pregnant from rape struggles with the decision to carry the baby or abort, then ultimately chooses to carry her child.

In Congressman Paul Ryan's world, this woman will have not made that choice; she will now be bringing a child into the world because she was forced to, because Mr. Ryan told her to and forced her to. Even if you believe a fetus is fully human, there are cases in which there would be no abortion — cases in which the state is committing a crime by cognitive-conservative values, continuing to apply force to the raped woman rather than even giving her the possibility of making what Ryan should consider the brave and faithful *choice*. Women are invisible to many of the Republican leaders: you can believe that conception is sacred and still realize that Paul Ryan doesn't respect women, doesn't see women as full human beings capable of faith, and doesn't even notice the ways

> Do I believe a woman pregnant from rape should have an abortion? I don't believe anyone relevant has asked me.

that he takes away women's rights — he wrote "The Cause of Life" without using the word "woman" even once.[100]

What if you believe that life begins at conception? Then Republican leaders are still treating women with disrespect, still violating the proper bounds of authority — by conservative values, not just by liberal standards. Can we create space for voters to express their sense of *sanctity* without grasping at *authority* over women? Can we tell stories that show the contradictions that come from choosing force over faith? Ultimately, these stories will also guide us to ways that government can nurture or help pregnant women who face hardships but would still choose to carry their pregnancy through.

Reduce the Wedge: Abortion as a Political Tool

Abortion is a major political issue, rather than only a religious one, because it divides good people. One of the best ways to bridge divisions is to work on a shared task together. If we find ways to reduce abortion-politics' use as a wedge issue, it will no longer be funded by the same political forces that want to cut maternal health care.

What steps can be taken to meet abortion-reducing and sanctity-confirming goals that would not be controversial among liberals? Can we seek and cooperate on areas of agreement?

Explore Questions Together

When you speak to people disturbed by abortion, ask them questions like the following: What works to reduce abortion? Have you researched which developed countries have the lowest abortion rates? What do they do?[101] *Ask real questions, and don't jump to answer them.*

Personally, I value the steps proposed here that increase options for women in ways that will let them choose fewer abortions. But this book isn't about abortion; it's about politics: the political goal is to unwedge our communities.

If they don't want to dig deeper and your conversation is nothing but the same arguments, consider if your goal should be to talk about something less divisive than abortion law. If so, this can be a good spot to redirect the conversation, politely offering to continue after they do research on their own or with you.

100. Paul Ryan, "The Cause of Life Can't Be Severed from the Cause of Freedom," PaulRyan.House.Gov. CognitivePolitics.org/ryan.

101. Note that US statistics are argued over endlessly. To sweepingly overgeneralize, blue states have cut teen pregnancy rates more, while red states have cut back on abortion after pregnancy. Both red and blue states are each using tactics that seem to work, while ignoring tactics from the other side. Politicization and partisanship is not helping the pro-life cause.

If they do want to answer complex questions, you'll find some of the lowest abortion rates in the most Socialist, pro-women's rights, sex-positive states. Sex-shaming and poverty increase abortions; giving women more choices (many more choices) turns out to be the best thing you can do if you actually believe that a fetus is a baby. I have not found pro-life people receptive to being bashed with these results. But inviting someone to look at what works best to meet their values without violating mine, or simply discussing that I've searched for this information and am curious what they know, giving them time to talk, reduces the divide between "us" and "them."

Frame the debate with your values: it is not Pro- vs Anti-Life, nor Pro- vs Anti-Abortion. Liberal leadership does not mean more abortions. The policy is not just whether the *government*, through *force*, will make the choice. Let the government provide Head Start, time off from work, and everything that the low-abortion-rate Scandinavian countries provide. And yes, let Paul Ryan as a private citizen pray in church for raped women to carry their babies. Being tolerant of choice regarding government force, while being pro-life in your faith and support for struggling mothers, is not a contradiction. Today, both are missing from the Republican platform, and Democrats are sucked into opposing the Pro-Life movement's narrative instead of advocating our own values.

The Nurturing and Empowering Frame Summary

A woman with a pregnancy she did not choose may have a challenging decision ahead. One side does not help her and does not speak to her faith — their only contribution is through the police enforcing the decision they have imposed on her. The other side aims to help: to create enough space in the material world that she can make a decision of her own faith without fear. She may choose to have a baby conceived in rape; she may face poverty if she has this baby: this must be her own faith-choice that she must be allowed to make. Our role is to support her and make sure the consequences of her choosing to have a baby do not include shame or poverty.

Tell a progressive story that makes more sense to a cognitive conservative than the cheap-and-easy version promulgated by the Republican politicians.

Abortion Politics versus Liberal Goals

What is your goal? For the abortion debate, agreement would be a miracle, but a realistic goal might be preventing abortion from becoming the key issue in deciding who is a good person or who is "other." Find ways to disagree on this issue and still

work together, still be one country. Even if abortion is the issue you care most about, you might be able to protect abortion rights the most by getting pro-life, pro-compassion swing voters to focus on and vote for maternal health care and support for single mothers rather than focus on and vote against the legality of abortion.

Pull It All Together for a One-to-One Conversation

- [ ] Start with active listening. Try to keep your cool with individuals. Give them a chance to talk. Possible questions if (like me) you're not patient enough to just listen:
    - [ ] What has worked to lower abortion around the globe? While I know some of the empirical answers — and they tend to be very liberal answers — I often stop with the question. It can be a good conversation-calmer, a good chance to change topics with an invitation to return to discussing abortion later.
    - [ ] How will you enforce this? How long would a woman who committed the crime of abortion be in jail? If you make it illegal for doctors, how will you prevent unsupervised medical (chemical) abortions? These may be leading questions, but the more you ask them as real questions that request the person to think about them and give real answers, the more you can shake up ingrained partisanship.
- [ ] Agree with everything you can agree with. Certainly some women suffer after having an abortion; certainly some women regret it later. These don't prove that the government should send the police. If you feel that abortion goes against your sense of what is right — maybe you personally feel that it is a difficult, painful choice, something less than murder but more than nothing — then share that. None of these beliefs even begin to give the government the right into a woman's uterus. Agree with every last bit you can before finding your truth and speaking it strongly.
- [ ] Speak your truth, not your opponent's opposite. I believe in trusting and empowering women. My truth has little to do with abortions. I have a lot to say about the way girls and women have been abused by our political and economic system.
- [ ] Use stories and metaphors that focus on women making hard decisions and needing support. Use stories that evoke a nurturing parent helping good people through hard decisions.
- [ ] The conversation itself can be part of the metaphor: Are you together in community, seeking to support women, or is the conversation an example of a world in conflict that calls for a strict father to restore order?

Anger Should Be Focused

This section has emphasized compassion and connection with people you know personally who are pro-life. With politicians, it is often more effective to show strength. Yes, when Mr. Todd Akins[102] is ready to force a raped woman to carry the rapist's child, claiming that women won't get pregnant from rape — shout. Tear down the men who make it central to their lives to take rights from women, or who make denial of women's rights a stepping-stone to power.

Attack them not for being pro-life in the compassion of their hearts but for being ready to use government power callously, for being ever ready to use force against women but too lazy to learn biology or find helpful ways to make the choice of having a child easier. If you really want to cost someone like Akins votes, attack him for forcing all women — including those who would choose not to terminate their pregnancy — to do it under force of arrest rather than through appeals to faith. But patience with friends, coworkers, and family members struggling with deeply held beliefs may eventually change votes.

> Don't tell voters they are not pro-life; that can't work. Do point out that Akins is pro-force, not pro-life; separate him from his votes.

Be angry at anti-life abortion-punishers. Just be careful to help people who believe in *LIFE* and even *LIFE BEGINS AT CONCEPTION* to disentangle themselves from politicians who oppose prenatal care and Head Start.

Win by Creating Space

Consider spending more time listening to people disturbed by abortions. We can respect their sense of sanctity and can help them feel heard even if we don't budge a centimeter on making abortion anything but a freely available choice. Combine listening with asking people their position amongst many more than two opposed labels, letting people declare themselves as believers in *LIFE* without forcing them to automatically oppose *CHOICE* to do so.

Allow people to believe what they believe, to know that you've listened, and to feel like you are on the same team. Separate honest pro-life voters from politicians like Akins; don't paint them with the same brush. Let people say, "I'm not like that" so that eventually their votes won't go to abortion-restrictor politicians.

Aim toward real discussions about policies that would lead to lower abortion rates and healthier pregnancies — policies that allow for genuine choice.

102. Kirsten Powers, "Todd Akin's 'Legitimate Rape' Claim a Peek Behind Anti-Abortion Curtain," The Daily Beast, Aug. 21, 2012. CognitivePolitics.org/akin.

Sample Conversations, Comments & Exercises

Sample Conversation: From Politics to Personal Truths

Let's imagine this hard story: A young woman in our community was raped and impregnated, and she is not ready to have the baby. She is scared. Imagine also she doesn't believe in abortion and is struggling with her choice. What are your first thoughts; what do you do to help?

In real life, few people will begin where the politicized reactionaries begin, shouting threats at her. We don't have to control the conversations and won't be able to: just ask the question and listen — don't focus on either agreeing or disagreeing but on connecting.

The most effective frame regarding abortion law is focusing on the woman who is struggling with a challenging choice. As soon as both participants in the debate are walking in her shoes, it doesn't matter if you're pro-life — "well I wouldn't have an abortion" — she needs help and nurturance, not government interference.

Engage Complexity

1. Consider your standard conversational approach about abortion. Write down the following:
    - What do you say to pro-choice liberals?
    - What do you say to pro-life conservatives?
2. Afterwards, listen to this man who was conceived from a rape: www.cognitivepolitics.org/exercise/life1. Review your responses as if this man were your friend. Do your responses make sense in this case? Are your responses to the abortion issue appropriate for everyone who is disturbed by abortion, including voters who might also believe in women's rights, or are you only listening to and responding to the loudest and most obnoxious anti-choice activists who can never be convinced?

Do your answers make sense in this context? Are we allowing ourselves to get so angered by dishonest politicians who *use* abortion until we forget that most pro-life voters are simply speaking their heart's truth? The men who want to be empowered as our strict fathers are leveraging an issue that is sacred in the hearts of good people. How can we keep dialogue open with good people with whom we disagree — and will continue to disagree with — on matters of faith and religion?

Focus: Choose One Small Goal

Imagine a good-hearted conservative Christian, a charitable person and good neighbor who believes that God brings life at conception. If you could encourage them to make one small change in their views, what would it be?

What small change would you make?

My small change might be a world where those people still called for a pro-life ethic from the churches, still held that life began at conception, and still said that unmarried people shouldn't have sex — but gave up on getting the government and police to be at the center of their faith.

Separate faith from government and power.

Brainstorm Labels That Create Space

What are all the ways you could name the movements that have labeled themselves as Pro-Life and Pro-Choice? Are there more descriptive names? For this exercise, try to avoid terms that are merely offensive like *anti-choice* or *pro-abortion*. Instead, look for terms that get at key ideas, more *descriptive* of each movement, phrases that help people on all sides feel better heard. An imperfect possibility is:

Women's Choice vs. Government's Choice

This is a very liberal frame, a fighting-frame rather than an agreement-frame. It makes the liberal point and might be a good choice for base-building, but it's unlikely that even vaguely pro-life people would ever use this frame or that it would become popular. What terms would add clarity so that some people who identify as pro-life would adopt a new term?

Exploring the Boundaries of "Us" and "Them"

A good way to break down "us vs. them" is using more than two labels.

A central problem for liberals in the abortion fight is the us-vs.-them divide it generates — this division is a way to win votes for politicians who don't represent ordinary people.[103] A key to progressive framing is to make it more complex, to get

people really thinking. One key to framing the abortion debate is simply to have more terms, including some that bridge the wedge.

Some pro-life people (by today's labels) really are well described as pro-life, while others are merely pro-birth or anti-abortion and often seem happy to be controlling women. Let's separate them: don't call the whole movement pro-birth; go case by case. Create more than one label, separating the pro-life block along its very real divisions. Can we create a space for people who are sadly and unenthusiastically accepting of choice — who wish women would not get abortions, and wish it very much, but are still not willing to violate their choice? Right now, the available frames guide that person to call themselves Pro-Life because that is what they feel in their heart and pray for. Liberals claim that all we care about is that person's position on the government, but we're lying to ourselves if we think our movement welcomes that person with open arms, or that the Pro-Life movement doesn't.

> What happens when you point out to pro-life people how many of its supporters are mere abortion-restrictors? The actual abortion-restrictors won't care, and truly pro-life people will say "that's not me." Create space for truly pro-life people — people who look after their neighbors, who want to nurture mothers and potential mothers — to separate themselves from people whose advocacy of life ends at birth. For saner politics, separate the decent people from the manipulative politicians; don't attack them until they circle their wagons together.

Continue the exercise to brainstorm new labels, aiming to fracture both sides into ever smaller groups. Especially look for terms that crisscross the current political divide, wrecking the boundaries of "us" and "them." In the drug debates, there are people very focused on harm-reduction: they see the damage done by drugs and want to get serious rather than ideological. What if there were a well-used word that included people who were pro-life without reducing choice? Where do people go if they believe in their own hearts that abortion is a significant and wrong choice, and want women to choose not to have abortions, but also want women empowered to make the choice?

What would happen if we created labels for people who were broadly pro-life and specifically anti-abortion but didn't want to use the government to force that opinion on us? Can we find a frame that includes all of pro-choice, pro-life, and pro-faith?

103. The politicization of abortion is also a terrible problem for people who honestly want to reduce abortion numbers because the issue is now always a fight instead of a cooperative give-and-take. There are many noncontroversial ways to reduce abortion through empowerment rather than force, but with two sides fighting, these opportunities are lost.

Imagine a car with all these bumper stickers:

Pro-Choice

Pro-Life

Pro-Faith

What is their frame?

I expect *PRO-LIFE BUT LEAVE WOMEN THEIR CHOICE ABOUT IT* is one of the most widely held positions on abortion. It often leads to voting Republican out of feelings of connection to the Pro-Life movement, even though it matches better to Democratic policy choices. People who feel deeply that abortion is bad, but don't want to use force against women who choose otherwise, have a comfortable *home* in the Pro-Life *framing* today. They feel at home in the party that loudly shares their distress at abortion — even if it is implementing policies they wouldn't agree with. They feel cold and disconnected to the party that keeps abortion safe, legal, and just as rare — but is unwelcoming to people who are distressed by abortions no matter whether they would force a choice on someone else. Can we change that?

Pro-Life at Prayer

US Out of My Uterus

The Republican coalition depends on a uniformity that cannot survive a framing that allows people to be pro-life *without* restricting choice. When it is time to write a platform, they cannot make space for *PRO-LIFE THROUGH FAITH (NOT GOVERNMENT)* — not without giving up on the whole abortion fight. It *must* be "us" and "them" for Republican political success. If we can turn up the complexity of the sound bites, welcoming people who believe in the sanctity of pregnancy but tolerate choice, we'll win elections.

How do you *welcome* people who have different and strongly held religious beliefs, but are perhaps willing to grudgingly tolerate the rights of others to have different beliefs? Can you create a political home for them? Do they know you are willing to listen?

My first brainstorms on expanded labels for the choice, abortion, life, and women's-empowerment debates are *at the end of this chapter (p.116)* and online at *CognitivePolitics.org*. Before you read my thoughts, please brainstorm your own and post your ideas online; help create new categories and come up with better names for the categories. An ideal frame would allow people with complex ideas about abortion and women's rights to nonetheless find a term that feels like a comfortable fit. We're not looking for nasty terms to replace pro-life and positive terms for pro-choice but real terms with more depth and more clarity.

Active Listening: Give People Their Voice to Gain Their Vote

Surveys of homophobia have found an interesting result: if you ask people who don't approve of homosexuality whether they support *CIVIL UNIONS*, they

are more likely to be accepting only *after* saying that they oppose *GAY MARRIAGE.*[104] If the only chance they have to express their distaste with homosexuality is civil unions, they'll speak their opposition. Give people their voice, perhaps to say something you don't want to hear, and it sometimes reduces their need to impose their views.

Similarly, many people are disturbed by abortion: if we give them a chance to say they oppose abortion *in some way*, if we merely do a good job listening to their opinion, that will often be enough — they don't really want to use force or imprison people. Sometimes expanding the window helps — gay marriage made civil unions much less controversial, and then once civil unions stopped seeming like the apocalypse, people relaxed and gay marriage became acceptable too. Sometimes creating new frames inside the current, polarized window will help, finding ways for people to quietly legislate *CHOICE* while still having strong faith in *LIFE.*

Give people their voice, help them feel heard even when they disagree with you, and they are more likely to rely on their voice rather than turn to laws and force.

Conversational Approach: Complexity, Depth, and Healing Divisions

If you have a friend or family member who cares about abortion, consider offering to spend an hour focused on their issue. Ask them what they want to explore, and along with what they want to look at, add these questions:

1. What are the steps that mean more pregnancies survive into thriving children? What has been tried? What works?
2. Which of these steps do you believe the government should take?
3. Which approaches have been most successful at reducing abortion?

If you actually do this exercise with someone you would otherwise argue with, you're likely to notice that both liberals and conservatives have many ideas that reduce abortion: a liberal might believe that empowering girls so they can talk about sex without shame and fear would mean more birth control, the government should provide health care to every pregnant woman, and there could be a religious or sacred voice (far from government) advocating taking responsibility and seeing life as sacred. A conservative politician flips many of these, with the church providing babysitting and nurturing while the government plays the strict-father role of saying "no."

Don't try this except at home. Democratic leaders need to lead, to get on-message with hard-hitting, repeated-frame sound bites. But off the TV, we can connect with depth.

104. David W. Moore, "Revisiting Gay Marriage vs. Civil Unions," Gallup.com, May 11, 2004. It's quite a large effect: in one poll, civil union support went from basically even at 49-48 to a 56-40 landslide. CognitivePolitics.org/civil.

If you spend time in allied conversation working on a *shared task* — sharing the task of brainstorming, coming up with all the ideas you can rather than arguing about each — this is a way for everyone to feel like they are part of the same *in-group*.

You can bring two attitudes to this conversation. You can try to win: "The Socialist countries are completely pro-choice and yet effectively more pro-life than you, and Red States have terrible abortion records. I win this debate!" Or, you can try to have a calm conversation from which everyone leaves feeling connected. You may not overthrow the other person's belief structure; they still may not value your facts as much as you do. What you can do is bridge the divide so that pro-choice people seem like responsible human beings to people who are being manipulated to see you as otherwise. Don't win points; share mutual respect so that in-group politics will collapse.

Speak from Your Frame

What frame do liberals use when we speak about women's right to choose and abortion? This exercise explores the ways we follow, or don't follow, George Lakoff's framing advice from the first chapter.

Find an online article about abortion, and read the comments.

Below are the two main frames used today. In both cases, as chapter 1 suggests, "saying no" to a frame still evokes the same frame. Count how many times advocates of each side use their own frame, and how often they try to counter the opposing frame:

☐ How many people from each camp try to say "no" to the other side's frame?

☐ Which comments would speak best to a moderate who felt distaste at the idea of abortion and simultaneously believed that a woman's right to control her own body was important?

☐ Do any comments on either side break both frames, or encourage allegiances besides pro-choice and pro-life? Is there a voice of reason among the commenters?

	Pro-Life Advocates	Pro-Choice Advocates
Life Frame: Abortion is/isn't bad enough to be criminalized.		

Choice Frame: The government should empower/restrict women.		
Other: Do any comments avoid the usual frames?		

Sample Comment on Abortion

Below is a comment intended to divert an online abortion article from a fight into a discussion. After that is a response to a *TIME Magazine* article about how successful the Pro-Life movement is. How do you think each would read to various audiences? Do you think either might influence someone who *feels* that a pregnancy is sacred to think twice about the political implications?

> What do you think of Finland? They have a much lower abortion rate than the US, with a very different approach than the Pro-Life vs. Pro-Choice fight we have in the US. If a woman wants an abortion, it's paid for as part of the free health-care system, and if a woman decides to have her baby, the government provides more support than in the US. Everything at the government level is way to the "left." But abortion has not turned into the same political conflict around women's rights, and instead, at the societal level, the life-is-sacred values have become very widespread. Now women there generally choose to avoid abortion, at least compared to the US. Abortion rates are much less than in many places where it's illegal. As a society, they are simultaneously much more pro-life and much more pro-choice than we are.

Longer Sample Comment

This was a reply to an article that focused on whether pro-life was winning or losing:

Start gently lacking clarity. Don't tell the reader which side your are on at first. Get them thinking, not reacting.

—**How much progress is being made in creating respect for the sanctity of life?** TIME Magazine takes a purely legalistic and punitive view of the pro-life question, caring about polls rather than life, legislation rather than results. —**The article assumes that pro-life people are purely about criminalizing abortion rather than actually lowering the rate of abortion.**

Reverse common accusations. Welcome "opponents" to be better rather than insult them.

Begin a story. Conjure a frame in which a woman needs nurturing help, not a police action.

There are other signs that would prove respect for life is increasing. —**When a woman is pregnant against her wishes and is struggling with the question of whether to throw her life upside down to carry the baby,** is her community showing up with offers to babysit? Does your community make sure she will have prenatal health care; do we respect or ostracise her? — **Will she have opportunities to finish her education and provide her child a tolerable economic life?**

Ask real questions. Note that some pro-life people will have good answers; the reader might be a Catholic who babysat for her single-mom liberal friend. Be curious and seek exceptions to your expectations.

This article asks only the easy questions: What is the government proclaiming? Who will win?

Break up in-group formation. Don't attack people's faith; target political manipulation.

—**Many countries have outlawed abortion** yet have much higher rates of abortion than others that haven't outlawed it. Being pro-life isn't a bumper sticker; there has to be more to it than that. What economically developed countries have low abortion rates? What works? If you've spent years either pro-choice or pro-life but don't know what pressures a woman to make a choice she doesn't necessarily want to make, or don't know what has actually worked in other countries to lower abortion rates, look inwards. —**If you don't know, a pro-life bumper sticker isn't enough to make you pro-life.**

Started Gentle. Perhaps end with more heat. Challenge readers to hold their own values with more integrity, rather than to mimic your values.

Help retake the commons! Internet comments have become ugly, draining hope. All it takes is one really good comment in each conversation to remind sane people that there are other sane people out there. Keep text ready that you can copy and paste, comments that add hope or good questions, letting people feel that there is sanity among the hyperpartisanship.

"I Statements"

Experiment with skipping past arguments, and simply and quickly say what you believe. For example, "I believe we do more good by offering help to women who are struggling with a pregnancy than relying on the government to try to force women who have not been convinced." This pulls ego out of the equation; you are not explicitly telling others they are wrong, merely adding your views. "I statements" are a great tool for influencing internet conversations, making it clear a sane center exists among the squabbles.

Looking Forward: New Labels, New Sides

How many ways can we redraw the map, breaking apart the traditional us vs. them? *On (p.111)* I asked readers to brainstorm and share new label possibilities; below are my current favorites. Most of these frames aim to feel right to the people who believe in them; only a few are marked as "attack frames" that will not be welcome.

Pro-Life >> Being *for life* means being *against* abortion, war, and the death penalty and *for* providing support when a pregnant woman or parent or child is in need. Prenatal care and programs like Head Start must be provided, either by the government or by the church but by someone. It is vital that pregnancies lead to birth: the tactics chosen may be up for debate. You might be pro-life with or without government enforcement of abortion restrictions.

Pro-Life through Faith >> It is not the government's job to be sending the police to force women not to have abortions, but it is the faith community's role to encourage women to make the pro-life choice. You believe that pro-life is the right choice, but you leave it to choice.

Abortion-Restricters >> Government is the key. Just as with other crimes, we need to respect the authority of the government, and the government needs to tell us what to do.

Pro-Consequences >> Some people focus only on punishment. The government's one role is to demand accountability and punish those who do wrong. If an unborn

baby dies because the mother can't afford prenatal care, it's her fault, not our collective problem. This "War on Women" group often isn't conscious of women. *Pro-birthers* is an appropriate attack frame. I would label the worst politicians *faith vampires*: if a woman is raped and makes a difficult pro-life choice, they don't help but want to take credit for her faith. This is a world away from my friends who are pro-life. Use the attack frames only to separate honestly pro-life people from politicians, not to lump them together.

Pro-Life through Wishful Thinking >> This is an unusual attack frame, a gentle prod for people who imagine a law against abortion will mean that people gracefully stop having abortions; they never imagine prison terms and back-alley abortions.

Abortion is no big deal >> A fetus is not a human being, not even close, and abortion should not be an issue. As a nation, we should be helping people who need help, not bossing women around.

Trust Women >> or Pro-Voice >> This is the progressive truth that overlays the abortion debate, rather than the conservative frame that this issue is primarily about the government and the fetus. We say trust and empower women across many issues. People can trust women whether they think a fetus is a lump of tissue or a sacred human life.

One of the largest demographics is *pro-life through faith*, having broadly pro-life feelings and beliefs but pro-choice thoughts and policy preferences. Today, many of these people are driven to follow faith-vampires and pro-birthers because of the way we frame.

Review: Political Goals and Strategy Amidst Sanctity Conflicts

The biggest threat to Choice is not people believing that life begins at conception; rather, it is *single-issue voters.* So the best step for the pro-choice advocates is often not talking much about abortion with people who disagree. Pro-life is only a political issue because it serves the interests of the wealth machine, which is callous toward women's rights but not going to spend political capital either way.

The best answer for the Pro-Choice movement is often to avoid this wedge topic at home; the answer to Pro-Life at Thanksgiving is to listen attentively and then talk about something else. I'm very much the kind of liberal who enjoys complex and

convoluted conversations, but this book's goal is not to win points in a debating contest. If we want to win elections for more compassionate and higher-integrity politicians, listening and moving on to shared concerns can mean votes will go to better leaders.

Meanwhile, many Pro-Choice groups see people like Todd Akins as a great recruiting tool, exposing the callousness toward women of politicians using the label "Pro-Life."

And they are right too. This book is focused on messages that aim at conservatives and moderates. Mobilizing liberals and feminists to fight back against the war on women calls for different framing than influencing swing voters.

The Republican Party's callousness toward women, including a widespread mindset about rape that sees problems with the victims and spends no time angry at the rapist, was very visible in the 2012 election. This was visible to many women across the spectrum, overwhelming Lakoff's standard framing advice: Todd Akins lost when people said "no" to his reactionary message, rather than "yes" to a proactive liberal message.

The 2012 election shows an effective approach: just as conservatives are trying to focus on (largely fictional) partial-birth abortion, progressives should focus on the callousness toward women of many male leaders of the Pro-Life movement. Ask right-wing politicians about rape and whether a woman can choose then; ask them at what point a woman is independent enough to follow her own faith.

The 2016 campaigns didn't focus much on abortion. But even in the background, it is still a key issue that delivers a large segment of single-issue votes. Many religious voters truly repulsed by a candidate who would mock a disabled reporter could still put abortion on the scales with everything wrong with Trump, and abortion tips the scales. Democratic political campaigns don't have much room to maneuver: they need to be simply and straightforwardly advocates for choice. Which means that if we want single-issue voters to look at the candidates as a whole, much of the bridge building will be at family dinner tables and through personal connections.

Chapter 7

Same-Sex Marriage: Weaving Community, Unraveling Authority and Sanctity

Looked at historically, homosexual rights is a stunning area of political victory for progressives. The current political fight began in San Francisco when the first same-sex marriages were welcomed in 2004, just a few election cycles ago. At the time, most people thought this issue was helping Republicans win elections, while a decade later Republican strategists find themselves struggling to satisfy their base but know it is a losing issue.[105]

Many progressives feel despair around our communication skills. Our messaging is so bad that working-class people keep voting for rich politicians destroying the working class. Gay rights has been quite an exception: same sex marriage went from barely conceived to widespread acceptance in a decade. How? [106]

Same-Sex Marriage: Frames, Values, and Goals in Transition

Historical Conservative Framing: Is Homosexual Sex a Mere Sin or an Existential Threat?

Why did the Catholic Church hierarchy go crazy over homosexuality yet get quiet about priests raping[107] children?

Before homosexuality transformed into a movement and a debate, people knew men sometimes had sex with other men (and women sometimes had sex with other women, but this drove the politics less).[108] Society took an odd approach to two men having sex. Soldiers in a foxhole could have sex and treat it as a shameful act to be

105. Nia-Malika Henderson, "How the GOP won on same-sex marriage," CNN, June 29, 2015. This article discusses Republican strategists' preference to avoid this issue in general elections whereas ten years ago it helped them.

106. For a review of the rapid early history of same-sex marriage, read "Same Sex Marriage Timeline," SFGate, May 18, 2008.

107. Committee on the Rights of the Child, "Concluding observations on the second periodic report of the Holy See," (United Nations, February 25, 2014), p5: "the Holy See has consistently placed … the protection of the perpetrators above the child's best interests."

kept secret, and society could tolerate that. Furtive sex between two men was a mere sin. But demanding the right to have open, caring relationships without shame was seen as a bigger threat than mere sex; this is when homosexuality became political.

It wasn't the sex itself that was a threat; it was the open breaching of social norms.

If you were a member of the privileged *in-group*, then a lie, a little corruption, or foxhole sex were always things to keep quiet: everyone sins. If you were ashamed of these things, kept your head down, and, ideally, prayed for forgiveness, then that was usually good enough.

Out-and-proud homosexuality challenges the conservative moral foundation of *authority,* while furtive homosexual sex or even raping a child merely dodges that authority: *love the sinner, hate the sin* requires a sinner who feels guilty, not someone proud of an alternative. *Cognitive liberals* don't have an innate sense of this *authority* and focus on actions and intentions. Even if an individual intuits that homosexuality is unhealthy or unnatural, a cognitive-liberal mindset isn't concerned with violations of sanctity and authority unless they also violate fairness or compassion.

Homosexual sex has always been happening; historically, homosexuals were often in danger of being individually targeted and sometimes the focus of organized hatred. But for many *cognitive conservatives,* when shame was replaced with *pride*, homosexuality transformed from a minor *sin* to a fundamental *challenge*. De-shamed homosexuality was seen as a threat to the natural order and to the authorities who previously defined the sanctity of the natural order.

Explore Liberal Framing: Community Redefines Sanctity

Most liberals do not understand the conservative frame on homosexuality and talk right past it. We are amazed at oddities like the Catholic Church banning *celibate*, sexually inactive but gay-inclined priests while being slow to respond to child molestation. But barring gay priests makes logical sense if priests are leaders who teach us about the ordered universe we live in, and homosexual desires are a symptom of being out of tune with that natural God-given order.[109]

108. Heinz Heger, *The Men with The Pink Triangle* (London, 1980), p61: "Homosexual behavior between two 'normal' men is considered an emergency outlet, while the same between two gay men, who both feel deeply for one another, is something 'filthy' and repulsive."

109. According to the "Instruction Concerning the Criteria for the Discernment of Vocations with regard to Persons with Homosexual Tendencies in view of their Admission to the Seminary and to Holy Orders" (www.vatican.va), men who "present deep-seated homosexual tendencies" and not only those who actually "practice homosexuality" cannot become priests. Watching the struggles

Using logic against religious views tends to turn into heated arguments. But once people have a gay friend — even a TV friend — they start to see homosexuals as people, members of their community and *IN-GROUP*. This struggle is being won largely thanks to Hollywood and regular people daring to leave the closet. Political and intellectual debates have not been key in convincing conservatives. Once lesbians and gay men were visible as members of the community that conservative values strive to protect, homosexuality in the abstract lost its threat.[110]

Sanctity values are derived from thinking with the parts of the brain responsible for disgust reactions (*chapter 2 -- p.43*), which evolved to minimize disease. Strangers bring disease to your community. Once people are no longer strangers, the underlying disgust response fades.

Unwind the Conservative Value-Knot: Authority Then Sanctity

It's natural for a liberal to begin with the conclusion:

> I don't see a problem with gay sexuality, and you shouldn't either.

But this is really the last step in a long process, not a starting point.

To a conservative mindset, the *IN-GROUP'S* authorities claim that gays are violating sanctity; violating sanctity defines them as outside the community, so their voices are easy to ignore. It's hard to tackle two moral foundations at the same time, but in separate conversations, both these approaches work:

Sanctity/Normalcy first:

When people know someone or feel like they know a TV character, homosexuality transforms from a taboo into a normal part of our shared community. But taboos only break down when people are not making a judgment. Sometimes, TV characters and friends of friends can be

Judgment/Authority first:

Most political campaigns can't avoid bringing up authority since their goal is to change the law. A political conflict is a bad time to shift someone's sense of taboos and sanctity. Instead, when someone believes that homosexuality is taboo and it is their job to judge, can you explore only

within the Catholic Church is an interesting window on conservative values of authority and sanctity, particularly with Pope Francis loosening the infatuation with strict authority. See: Alexander Stille, " Who Am I to Judge? Francis Redefines the Papacy," The New Yorker, July 30, 2013.

110. Anna North, "Knowing a Gay Person More than Doubles Support for Marriage Equality," Buzzfeed, March 15, 2013.

the most powerful influencers since they don't evoke the sense of authority or responsibility that a parent might feel. However, politicizing the issue will remind people of their existing views, instead of opening them to experience something new.[111]

whether it is really necessary for them to judge? If someone who is disturbed by homosexuality can merely be convinced that God may judge but they don't have to spend energy doing so, it both solves the immediate political needs and may ready them for future openings.

Note that the sanctity-first approach matches Lakoff's theories explored in the first chapter: tell your story, tell *only* your story (ignoring rather than negating theirs), and tell it over and over. And encouraging a letting-go of judgment hews closer to Haidt's advice to take other people's moral foundations seriously, politely inviting them to tweak a consideration of whether they or God are in charge of judging, rather than trying to overrun all their values and get them to agree with all yours in one conversation. I find this pattern across many issues: telling your own story in bold strokes works best with the undecided and away from politics — away from anything partisan or that forces people to make judgments. Your story works when people are listening without anxiety or a desire to be heard. Meanwhile, contentious issues require listening to another person's values while seeking connection first.

This advice is for people in your community and not for public debates between politicians. Politicians can win by putting their opponents on the defensive and making them seem out of date, but liberals win at home when we weave our divided communities back together.

See *Contrasts between Lakoff's Metaphors and Haidt's Moral Foundations -- p.46.*

Lessons Learned from Success: What Worked?

What might be considered the biggest victory by progressives in forty years came from two main causes:

1. *Pride.* Queer rights and pride were no longer protected by being hushed up. The larger progressive community became increasingly supportive of individuals who were proud and loud about it. We provided some support for countless individuals to be a combination of brave enough and safe enough to speak their voice: for someone's niece or grandfather to stop

111. Mark S. Granovetter, "The Strength of Weak Ties," *American Journal of Sociology*, Volume 78, Issue 6 (May, 1973), 1360-1380.

hiding and speak their truth. This has been an exception to progressive's tendency to ignore support for our own community. We exhibited the conservative *IN-GROUP* loyalty value, supporting individuals who took the risks, and it worked.

2. *Repetition of personal, human stories told by trusted messengers.* With support and with pride, millions of people have done the work individual by individual, both on TV and at home. This matches Lakoff's advice, though it was done mostly outside of politics. *Humans of New York (http://www.humansofnewyork.com)* takes this even further: it avoids being political except when a real person tells a story of how politics impacted their life — circumventing the standard team-membership lens that most of us use when viewing politics. This ultimately changed the definition of the *IN-GROUP* to include people who had been outside.

Practical and Effective Activism against Hate Politics

Homophobia involves groupthink and shame. These are the home base of right-wing authoritarianism, of hate politics and fascism. How do you fight authoritarian tendencies? When we look at the Holocaust, history shows that typical Germans who participated in mass murder didn't desire to be the most hateful person they could be: they became Nazis when they thought all their neighbors joined, and they only hated Jews when hating Jews was the accepted thing to do.[112] The Nazi leaders used media and organized protests to *normalize* hatred long before the Holocaust began.

To fight hate politics, we have to make the *OUT-GROUP* seem normal and the hatred abnormal. And we did. Hollywood, which often perpetuates stereotypes,[113] has in recent years done a better job displaying lesbian women and gay men as human beings. As have millions of individuals who've come out of the closet. Relatives, friends, and fictional characters who are gay and normal-enough, who are people you know and care about, have been destroying the feeling that homosexuality is a strange, foreign threat to society.

Support Your Community

People stepping out of the closet, telling their stories and willing to be in a spotlight were the core of breaking down homophobia. It's not required to have political leaders lead nor win debates. Presidents Clinton and Obama didn't do this — ordinary people did.

112. Trying to determine how much the average German desired to participate in Nazi hatred leads to arguments that can't be concluded. I expect even the participants never knew for themselves; hate and anger politics often run largely at a subconscious level.

113. Shareable Resource: J.F. Sargent's *5 Old-Timey Prejudices That Still Show Up in Every Movie* makes explicit some very obvious-if-you-look racist and sexist patterns in Hollywood. (Cracked.com, November 15, 2011).

Share pride across boundaries >> Allies like Parents, Families and Friends of Lesbians and Gays (PFLAG) play a huge role in making it safe for people to be publicly proud of who they are. Non-LGBTQ people making public that they are proud to share communities and families with LGBTQ members helps break down *in-group* borders.

Support our movement's activists >> Look at conservative think tanks: they support their interns, help them network, and help them find jobs when the internship is over. Progressive think tanks, however, have a reputation for providing less mentoring and less support.[114]

From Washington interns, to union frontline employees, to canvassers, the left forgets to look after our own. We burn our young activists out for short-term change. Gay rights is one of the few exceptions: people coming out of their closet *did* get support, and, correspondingly, this movement has led to our biggest victories. The research showing conservative demographics to have manipulable fears also shows liberals to be short on community-building or social-capital values. This shortage is not mere framing. We succeed when we change.

Many young idealists are introduced to organized left-oriented activism or politics as canvassers: young idealists join up for a cause, are used, and very often burn out.

Study anti-bullying campaigns >> Bullying among kids parallels the worst types of politics among adults. How do anti-bullying educators teach empowerment skills? How do they train students to notice when they need to look after each other? The most effective anti-bullying programs use "exercises to increase the empathy of bystanders,"[115] creating school communities where students look out for each other rather than rely only on adults and punishment.

Healthy conservatives seek a world where people are strong enough to stand up for themselves and each other. They believe in community-building social-capital values: not the fear, blame and hate politics of talk radio. There is a lot of space for us to work together here.

Focus on Stories and Personalization

People don't give up homophobia when their views or their biblical interpretations are attacked. They give up on homophobia when homosexual individuals (real or fictional) become personal, or part of their community. This happens most fluidly away from politics, where there are no teams.

114. *Next Generation of Conservatives (By the Dormful) (http://www.nytimes.com/2005/06/14/politics/14heritage.html)* The New York Times, Jason DeParle. June 14, 2005.

115. Stuart Wolpert, "Successful anti-bullying program identified by UCLA," University of California, February 3, 2016, UniversityOfCalifornia.edu.

Show Loyalty to a Community That Includes Everyone

Cognitive conservatives desire a nation where we show group loyalty. Yes, and I say that group includes the rainbow and doesn't include phobias. If enough voices are raised together, strong about values while welcoming everyone, then that can be made the consensus of the in-group. And people who seek the norm, the middle ground, will stop openly voting based on phobias. Liberals can offer to meet the needs of conservative group-loyalty values while getting the policies and tolerance we need.

Hopefully, the success of the same-sex marriage effort will show a path to unravelling other right-wing hate mongering. Ordinary people and small actions, even just watching healthier media, do make a difference.

Contrast with Less Successful Campaigns

When we show that abstracted homosexuals are actually real people and good neighbors, thus within the basic bounds of sanctity, we engage conservative values without necessarily understanding them. Conversely, when we list reasons every woman has a right to an abortion or argue for compassion in economics, we trigger and reinforce conservative values of sanctity or fairness on those issues.

Race and Class: Hearing the Wrong Stories

We've had slower progress in recent years reducing racism and face an increasing tendency to hate the working poor. These issues contrast with homosexuality, which is widespread within families — even Dick Cheney has homosexual relatives. America is remaining segregated around economics and race, and Hollywood dismisses working-class people and very often casts minorities into caricature roles. Subtle, often subconscious racism sounds mild compared to the overt racism of a few decades ago, yet often it makes the difference between whether a job is offered or whether a trigger is pulled.

Economics: Lacking Pride

Compare LGBTQ Pride with the liberal response in economics. During the ascent of liberal politics in the US, workers and unions led the movement. And people were proud to be workers. Blue-collar workers claimed to create all wealth; they didn't generally express a desire to become management. Today, the Democratic Party is merely charitable to blue-collar workers.

Speak Your Truth

Progressive politics had a major failure in fighting homophobia with *Don't Ask, Don't Tell.* We compromised our values and our truth — not merely making policy compromises to get a law passed. President Bill Clinton did not step up and say, "Gay and lesbian soldiers are people. Period. They're asking

to serve in our nation's armed forces, and we should honor them." If Congress had voted him down, there would still have been honor and clarity in saying that we were against discrimination.

Following polls is not speaking your truth, and it leads politicians to compromise their truth, rather than make compromises with opponents. President Clinton followed the polls that Americans weren't ready for gay men to be soldiers. If we follow the polls today, next year we will still be following the same polls. Liberals need to press our leaders and organizations to focus on framing that clarifies our truths, slowly changing what people think.

Bill Clinton could have said:

> Gay men and women who want to serve in our military are loyal patriots, deserving our thanks for their courage. The furthest compromise I can get out of Congress is "Don't Ask, Don't Tell," which I think insults women and men serving in our armed forces, and I apologize I couldn't get a bill with more dignity passed.

Progressives fail when we muddle our own values — for example, when Obama stops saying that every person in America should have health care or when Clinton says that gays shouldn't tell. You might vote for a compromise, but never pretend it is your truth.

Expand the Lessons

The success of the same-sex marriage movement shows one way to unravel right-wing hate mongering. When targets of hate are seen as complete people, they stop being the abstract "other." Get people from the targeted community into TV shows with decent roles: into stories. Provide support, and provide an echo chamber, for people from that community to speak about their lives with pride.

Defend Targeted Groups

Attacks on the poor >> Opponents will tell stories of the *lazy and irresponsible poor*, even as policies target the *working poor*. We need to tell stories of the working poor who contribute far more than they get: people who are not receiving the deal that Henry Ford's workers did, when a worker making a car was paid enough to own one. There are millions of these stories, and we need to tell them millions of times. Note that it is particularly helpful to tell these stories when people aren't thinking about politics! Create a culture in which everyone thinks about what it must mean to work for minimum wage, rather than a culture of unending political debates.[116] Activism may be as simple as watching a movie together, perhaps one whose key characters are poor or recent immigrants.

Bigotry often comes from a place of fear. Insults increase fear and separation. People's healthier values thrive when the fear goes away.

Trump targets immigrants and Muslims >> We need to do more than react to each of his hateful statements. The history of Islam needs much more exposure to balance current bad news. The Dark Ages and Crusade years were periods of history when the Islamic Middle East was more civilized than Crusading or Dark Ages Christian Europe. So it's clearly not religion but something more historical — and thus more changeable — that divides violence-plagued Muslim ex-colonies from more peacefully settled Christian nations. Introduce people to basic historical facts outside of politics, when they are not seeking to rationalize their political beliefs. Read history, go to an art museum exhibit that happens to be from an Islamic culture, or watch an action flick with a conservative family member about the Crusade years that has well-developed Muslim characters. Small actions of normalization add up, eventually making political change possible.

When and if you are in the targeted group, I'm not in a position to give advice; don't look to a book on framing.

If you are a member of the bigot's in-group, your place of greatest leverage is continuing to accept them in your shared community while demanding better norms for that community. If you are in the privileged group, don't unfriend bigots on Facebook, and also don't let their actions slip by unremarked. Simple "I believe" statements can help: "I believe we should treat everyone with dignity." Don't silence yourself if one remark doesn't transform them; persist.

Immigration: Share Your Family History

Keep it personal. For example, you could post to Facebook on the date a relative came to the US, talking about their struggles and the ways they were welcomed or not. Don't make it political so quickly that people only see the

116. The "nobles" of old — the knights, the warrior class — knew that the peasants worked like hell but simply decided that they were superior to the peasants. Now that the peasants can vote, more complex — and more fragile — ideas are required.

stories through their political lens. After stories like this are in a personal frame, the stories of our friends' families, then we can bring them into the political frame.

Create Deeper Change

How do we deepen this process for people who let go of one prejudice? Many people in my grandparents' generation started hating Jews, then blacks, and then gays — in each case, personal hate mixed with political manipulation. In some ways, this is a tremendous progressive success story: groups that have been hated for centuries are now accepted inside the fence. Still, past years' racism and anti-Semitism have morphed into homophobia, concealed racism, and Islamophobia. Can we replicate the same-sex-marriage movement quickly, every time hate politics appear? As people are letting go of specific old prejudices, what can we do to loosen people's general tendency to dislike whole groups of people? What runs deep in creating, or healing, prejudice?

Sample Conversations, Comments & Exercises

Keeping Score: Bible-Based Challenges

Many liberals think that homophobes read the Bible selectively and hypocritically. It is common to attack the homophobic reading by pointing out where the Bible discourages judging, or pointing out how Jesus spent no time on this issue, or pointing out the hypocrisy of imposing some rules from Leviticus and ignoring others. When does using someone's holy book against them work?

- ☐ Is the Bible one of your sources of personal inspiration?
- ☐ Do you quote the Bible to point out others' hypocrisy?
- ☐ Do you quote the Bible other than to point out others' hypocrisy?

How do you think your audience will see your use of their holy book? Are you sharing from within their community or attacking from outside? If you are right — if the Bible is unclear, or your opponents are being hypocritical in what they cherry-pick — under what conditions do you help your cause by pointing this out?

If you are using Christianity only to support your personal politics, not adjusting your politics to Christian teachings, then you will come across as using their religion. This won't convince anyone. Much of the liberal reputation for elitism comes from trying to score points even in one-on-one conversations; we are very often factually correct and hurting our causes badly at the same time.

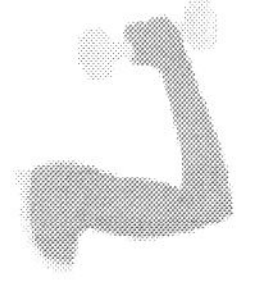

Shared and Unshared Values

Think about a recent discussion about same-sex marriage or a similar topic. What would have happened if you had tried the following? Experiment in your next conversations:

- ▹ Active listening "Yes ... and" technique. Once you can describe the values that the other person holds dear, can you repeat them back until they can hear their values from you? Then, make your values clear. Aim to create space for others to hear your values just as you hear theirs, even if you're not reaching any agreements.
- ▹ If the conversation is going well, ask the other person explicitly if they consider the sanctity values they hold to be more or less important than compassion. Remember that Haidt's studies find cognitive conservatives hold compassion similarly to liberals. You don't have to invalidate the values you don't share in order to turn attention to the values you do share.

Often, moderate-conservatives hold the values we share more strongly than they hold the specifically conservative moral foundations. But if liberals fail to engage the conservative values at all, we slip into sounding like opponents even when we have the same priorities.

Looking Ahead: Paradoxes of Social Capital

On both the left and right, we know that "it takes a village," but modernization is erasing our old villages. Tight-knit communities tend to support their members the best but exclude outsiders the worst. Modernity seems to be breaking up those communities — simultaneously and across many nations, old exclusions are breaking down while it's also becoming harder to get a neighbor to babysit. What used to be provided by neighbors is now purchased in a marketplace.

The small-town values seem to correlate with cognitive conservatism, and those values are unraveling — both the positive and negative values at the same time. Liberals are happy to see those values rapidly declining on issues like same-sex

marriage. But charitable giving is also correlated to church attendance — will we see positive community values decline at the same time as same-sex marriage becomes more widely accepted? Even when Republicans are winning elections, we're seeing self-interested libertarianism and Trump's angry rage supplanting small-town pragmatic conservatism. The community-binding conservative Moral Foundations are in decline, for both good and ill.

Cognitive-conservative values that help create a strong *in-group* seem to be correlated with church attendance, intolerance toward minorities, and increased charitable giving. Is there a way to disentangle these? It's my belief that if we can create a society where people have a sense of place and the opportunity to contribute, we'll have met the real values of conservatives and will be much more effective at helping people let go of the fear-based components of social capital.

Review: Pride and Connection

Same-sex marriage conversations are the opposite of abortion conversations in many ways. The more this topic comes up the better, and the current framing is already successful. Allies should keep posting pictures of cute same-sex married couples on Facebook and sharing stories that reveal the humanity of people who haven't been seen as normal. Help make what was not tolerated yesterday feel normal today. Share stories that stretch and exercise the compassion of your audience. Be an ally for Pride — in which people feel absolutely supported in being themselves — do the work to create a supportive community, helping individuals come out of the closet. If you want to win elections and expand rights, it also helps to have some gay and lesbian couples who appear otherwise normal to conservative voters, expressing those values that conservatives share and talking about supporting their families. In all cases, we know our values and talk without hesitation, with pride. If we could talk about underpaid working people with the same clarity, we could win on economic issues.

Recommended Resources

Webinar: How to Move a Conflicted Loved One to Support LGBT Dignity (http://vimeo.com/51161395). Watch Jonathan Haidt's theories implemented by a visionary political campaign. Hosted by Auburn Media, October 10, 2012. Link at CognitivePolitics.org/dignity.

Reviewing Violations of Sanctity: Shame, Sin, and Leadership

The issues of the last two chapters are rooted in sanctity values connected to sexual taboos and shame. It's long been obvious to liberals that the leadership of the Christian right — the people who talk about sex shame the most — are regular exhibitors of what they themselves would call sinful behavior.

Why is hypocrisy about family values not punished by conservative voters?

Exploring Different Mindsets: What Values Are Invoked if You Cheat on Your Spouse?

As usual for liberals, the values invoked are fairness and empathy. You have violated your agreement with your partner — *FAIRNESS*. And hurt them — *EMPATHY*. You might be worthy of forgiveness if you apologize to your spouse, if you make it better with her or him. Don't listen to an authority about how to be forgiven; ask your spouse what your path to forgiveness is. If you have a reputation for talking about the sanctity of marriage, that would make you a hypocrite, and liberals particularly dislike hypocrites. We don't understand how people like Gingrich[117] who seem to express egregious values in their personal lives can run as and be elected by family-values conservatives.[118]

To a *COGNITIVE CONSERVATIVE*, cheating on your spouse also violates the rules of society. You have violated the rules set by *AUTHORITY*, disrespecting your society and *GROUP MEMBERSHIP*. You particularly need to make yourself right with authority, perhaps with God and with religious leaders who represent Him. Of course we all sin. You can be a good person who was tempted and failed: that doesn't mean that proclaiming men should be faithful was wrong; it means you were a good leader with the usual failings in your personal life.

117. Jake Tapper, "Gingrich Admits to Affair during Clinton Impeachment," ABC News, March 9, 2007. CognitivePolitics.org/gingrich. LaCapria, Kim. "Clinton Impeachment House Speakers' Sex Scandals," Snopes.com.

118. Donald Trump did not particularly run as a family-values conservative and doesn't fully fit this pattern.

Many conservative voters seek leaders who can see and speak to the natural moral order. This leadership skill is important, even though we all slip from the ideals; we all sin sometimes.

Leadership and the Missing Consequences of Hypocrisy

People ashamed of the skeletons in their closet often find reasons to cast shame on others. Draft dodgers who favor war scare me much more than veterans who understand the costs of war and believe that sometimes we must pay those costs. Many politicians seem to have moral failings right in line with their favorite speeches yet manage reelection.

Attacking people in another group for hypocrisy just solidifies team boundaries. Agreeing to follow group social norms helps define the in-group, like a team jersey: "our team wears red shirts." If someone on the other team shouts that someone on your team isn't wearing the right color shirt, your team will just rally around your teammate.

> It's ineffective to attack a conservative value just because a leader fails to uphold it. Either respect the value — and point out alternative leaders who do uphold that value — or challenge the value on its own merits.

What might work to get hypocritical politicians out of office?

Alternative Leaders

One way to separate cognitive-conservative voters from hypocritical leaders is to point out better conservative leaders. Cut down the size of the steps we take in each conversation: Don't aim to convince Trump supporters to become Democrats, right now, in one conversation. Instead, learn about decent conservative leaders who actually follow the values they claim to hold, and inject those people into the conversation.

Spotlight Respect

A second way is to switch from shaming leaders to respecting voters. Don't attack someone for supporting a hypocritical politician who talks about but doesn't live "family values." Instead, express your respect to the person you are talking with who has implemented those values. If someone is a veteran, thank them for serving: don't frame your message that they are as bad as the chicken-hawks who want their vote; merely leave the implication that those politicians don't deserve their vote.

Inoculation

When a cognitive conservative (or anyone) has chosen their team with its leader, you face tremendous barriers getting them to break with their team and repudiate their leader. Instead, prepare early and sensitize people to the worst

kinds of hypocrisy before a specific accusation is leveled at a specific leader. We will be much better off with leaders who live their values. For conservative leaders, that should generally mean people who were ready to volunteer to serve in combat if their country needed them and who have followed what they claim are good family values.

This means that in conversations that have nothing to do with particular politicians, we should talk about the value of leaders willing to pay costs to support their beliefs. If you're a hawk, did you serve in the military? If you favor peace, will you stand up during times of jingoism or just hide? Saying "Cheney avoided the draft and Gingrich left his wife" is a request for someone to repudiate their team and their leader, so they will look for reasons to defend them. Instead, inoculate against the behaviors of chicken-hawks and self-entitled alpha males rescued by their parents' wealth, until everyone agrees and looks out for those behaviors without having betrayed their own team under pressure from your team. I wish my party would nominate people who oppose wars from the beginning and not wait till they are unpopular, and that your party would nominate veterans.

Sanctity and Pollution in Politics

Sanctity and pollution values are difficult to define. First, we're not talking about actual pollution. The studies don't show evidence that either liberals or conservatives feel more exalted by natural beauty or more disgusted by an actual oil spill. Rather, can a culture or an institution be sanctified or polluted? Once a physical contaminant has been washed away, do you still feel a sense of pollution? Do you respect taboos?

In surveys, sanctity/pollution values are often held as a single set, as opposite ends of one line. Cognitive conservatives care about that line, and cognitive liberals don't recognize it. In politics, it's helpful to divide sanctity issues from pollution issues. Some of the worst politics come from politicians holding groups of people to be polluted. Today, gay people, Muslims and immigrants are variously targeted. Yet the same core-value set seems to help build community — for example, to increase charitable giving — when people are finding sacred values in their own lives and their own communities. In political conversations, it's helpful to treat issues that invoke sanctity very differently from those used to evoke pollution values.

The conservative value of sanctity/pollution underlies both abortion and gay rights. Pregnancy is seen as having sanctity, a positive value that is violated by abortion. This contrasts with homophobia, which starts with a disgust response, seeing homosexual sex or homosexual people as polluted. I expect that sacred values are much less likely to respond to pressure. Social pressure, especially if it is coming from within their own demographic, can be effective at embarrassing people to pull back from focusing on pollution. When we're not talking about politicians but voters, it's probably a good idea to be careful about attacking sacred values; instead, look for ways to get the policy you need without asking others to let go of what they see as beautiful and true.

> Acceptance of same-sex marriage is spreading rapidly, but Americans are calling ourselves "Pro-Choice" far less than twenty years ago.[119] Why do you think liberals are winning one culture-war struggle while losing another?

Remember that perhaps 80 percent of the electorate will care about sanctity and pollution values at least a little. Strong majorities will care about the cognitive-liberal values of compassion and fairness *more* than they care about taboos, but when the most-left 20 percent leads the conversation, we often fail to speak to the other values at all.

119. Lydia Saad, "'Pro-Choice' Americans at Record-Low 41 percent," Gallup, May 23, 2012. CognitivePolitics.org/choice41.

Chapter 8

American Exceptionalism: Shared Views That Define an In-Group

Exceptionalism and never apologizing are big deals to many conservatives, while these topics are often invisible to liberals. The idea of American Exceptionalism, that there is a natural order in which America is special, is often repeated by right-politicians. It evokes in-group pride for many, many people, far beyond the conservative base. Most of us want to feel pride in our country, but American Exceptionalism has subtleties that leave liberals out of the loop.

Exceptionalism: Frames, Missing Frames, and Goals

Conservative Political Strategy: **Create a Sensitized, Defensive Group Identity**

Mitt Romney wrote *No Apology: The Case for American Greatness.* The title sounds like a progressive caricature of stiff, fragile conservative pride.[122] Donald Trump's theme "Make America Great Again" sounds a similar tune, and a few years earlier George H. W. Bush regularly talked about his need to never apologize.

> "I will never apologize for the United States — I don't care what the facts are."
> — George Bush Sr.[120]

> "I will never apologize for America."
> — Mitt Romney[121]

Liberals tend not to care about or understand the Republican obsession with not apologizing. How did apologies become an issue? Why do Republicans feel a need to say how "great" America is, over and over? Republican leaders have run their talking points through focus groups and know they work, so how does the "no-apologies" frame help their election campaigns?

120. Wikipedia's "George H. W. Bush" entry lists eleven(!) quotes on the theme of never apologizing. Accessed Dec 16, 2016. CognitivePolitics.org/never.

121. Paul Stanley, "Romney at Clinton Global Initiative: 'I Will Never Apologize,' " The Christian Post, September 25, 2012.

122. Mitt Romney, *No Apology: The Case for American Greatness* (New York: St. Martin's Press, 2010).

The *no-apologies framework* is crafted to guide people who feel pride in their nation — which is most of the electorate — to see liberals as "outsiders." It is not about the details of history. Rather it has two steps:

1. Bloat people's pride >> Encourage people to feel tremendous pride in our nation. Nations are good or evil, with us or against us, and America is the greatest. Unrestrained pride is used as a marker of group membership.

2. Then threaten their pride >> Evoke another group that completely disagrees with you and sees no reason to feel any pride in America. Create a caricature that everyone not in your group is just as negative about America as you are positive. Once people are fearful and on the defensive, it is easy for liberals to wound that bloated pride and become "outsiders" to a merged American and Republican *in-group*.

Looked at from a linguistics perspective, constantly saying "no" to apologizing is an apologies framework.

We should give { no / an } **apology.**

In other words, the purpose is to get people thinking about apologizing; it's not intended to get people to think proud thoughts.

This tactic works best when opponents play along, responding to bloated reasons for pride by telling patriots all the reasons that their pride is wrong.

Today's Liberal Framing:
America Is Complex; Notice and Fix the Problems

Liberals have a wide range of perspectives on patriotic pride. Democrats range from self-defined patriots who feel that this is the greatest nation on earth to people whose primary consciousness about America is its racism, its treatment of Native peoples, or the CIA's murderous work in places like Guatemala, Chile, and Iran. In general, these views fit under a very broad liberal frame: America is a big, complex country; we should feel pride for the good stuff and apologize for, and fix, our problems.

This complex frame does not generate a clear answer to the conservative frame.

Liberals Caught in the Trap

What do we do with the horrible stains of racism, murder of Native peoples, and unnecessary wars? What politics are built from the stains? The problematic politics is when we just say "no" to the other side. Republicans broadcast the message that America is so perfect we should never apologize for anything, and so liberals argue against that, pointing out imperfections in American history. Our facts might be right, but we are reinforcing a counterproductive frame.

We fall into a trap whenever we fight against the idea that people should feel pride in their own nation. Our facts in any particular case might be right, but it doesn't even begin to matter at election time.

As Republican leaders proclaim a level of faith in America that more than borders on idolatry — treating our nation as Immaculate — many progressives have gotten shy and embarrassed at expressing our pride in American ideals. Just because Republican leaders will never admit a blemish doesn't mean that we need to ask Americans to feel *no* pride in a country that does have many things to feel proud about. If you want to create positive changes and win elections, you can't ask that 51 percent of the electorate reach ego-free nirvana. Help people feel pride but for healthier things.

> Do tell your truth.
>
> If your family has suffered and you tell personal stories, your truth is a powerful frame. Be careful of framing, however, when you are not telling your own experience: avoid impersonal laundry lists of complaints or seeking things to complain about if you do live a relatively privileged life. When you tell stories of suffering that didn't happen to you, share the voices of people with direct experience rather than voicing your own judgment.

This parallels the framing around unwanted pregnancies, in which liberals want to *EMPOWER WOMEN* but often focus on the conservative frame of *THE ACT OF ABORTION*. When it comes to pride in America, demanding that people judge this nation or saying that *AMERICA ISN'T EXCEPTIONAL* — saying "no" to the Republican frame — is a counterproductive way to frame. And silence lets Republicans invite moderates into their story of America. So what do we believe in?

What's Your Story?

What's your story of what is special about America? Do you express primarily what you see as shameful, what you see as worthy of pride, or a mixed reality? Do you share a sense of community with others who express pride in your nation's accomplishments?

Your story:

Failures of the Republican Frame: Truth and Demographics

When people think America has nothing to apologize for, they're visibly on the blindly white side of the Three-Fifths Compromise, the broken treaties with Native Americans, or invasions in Latin America.

It's a fairy-tale version of America that insults large demographics. Unsurprisingly, these demographics are currently voting against Republicans in large numbers. American Exceptionalism has been used to attract many white males to the Republican Party, often despite their economic interests, especially since the Vietnam War. But it increases the distance between the Republican Party and many people who aren't white, even if they are cognitively conservative.

Political Lessons When frames are carefully or subconsciously intended for white audiences, make sure other audiences hear their words. Let history and their own words speak for themselves. For example, put Romney's *No Apology* between a book about Nixon's support for Chilean dictator Pinochet and another about slavery.

How can Democrats avoid taking the blame for facts that hurt patriotic voters' pride while both speaking the truth about history and spotlighting the Republican lack of consciousness of nonwhite history?

The Frame Evoked by "No Apologies"

The "no-apologies" frame seems to follow Haidt's Moral Foundations: cognitive conservatives *SUPPORT THEIR IN-GROUP,* see their nation as *SANCTIFIED,* and seek *LEADERS WHO RECOGNIZE THIS.* But it is a frame that, at first glance, seems to ignore George Lakoff's advice and leads with the word "no."

When Democrats say "no tax relief" it looks like the conservatives are trying to relieve us; when Republicans say "no apologies" it makes it sound like Democrats are constantly apologizing. The Republicans are following Lakoff's advice: they are evoking the frame of whether we should apologize by saying "no" to it, creating a frame for liberal thought on America's role in the world. We need to have many

voices clearly describing a widely shared progressive frame if we don't want the Republicans to define our views for us.

The Progressive Frame: Replacing Fairy Tales with a Textured Story

Conservatives evoke an American Exceptionalism that is similar to a Santa Claus story, a fairy tale. We can replace this story simply by having a better one. Find your idealism and turn it into a real story. Rather than attack the conservative frame, simply replace it, and let it die of its own shallowness. Help conservative-minded individuals feel more loyal to real American history including both our ideals and failures.

What calls itself American Exceptionalism in modern American politics is not a healthy conservative ideal.

Fairy-Tale Exceptionalism

Conservative values are to work hard and take responsibility. We were not handed a guaranteed victory. Real people risked and sometimes lost their lives for American independence. Real people shed blood, sweat, and tears — and even paid taxes, conserved resources, and recycled — to defeat the Axis powers. The "exceptionalism" frame fictionalizes them; it pretends our successes were nearly magical. It implies we are a democracy simply because we are America, not because people made sacrifices. If slavery was unavoidable — if slavery is not something America should apologize for — then so was Washington's exhausted army crossing the Delaware River.

This *American Exceptionalism* erases sacrifice and hard work and just says, "we're better; we're almost doomed to succeed because we are America."

American Exceptionalism has no obvious policy implications: it is used by conservative isolationists and interventionists alike. It's pure framing.

Which is more patriotic: to teach high school students an idealized version of history, or a real one as balanced and true as possible? Do you frame your approach as patriotic, or do you avoid that word?

A Patriotic Frame That Doesn't Judge: Hard-Work Exceptionalism

As in many other framings, the best place to start is where we agree. Unlike abortion, where there is often deep disagreement about what is sacred and so the most effective tactic is often active listening, we already agree on much of what adds to America's greatness. Go ahead and say it!

Judgment Frame

Lakoff talks of the need to repeat our stories, our frameworks. So what is our ideal America?

I think the rules for America are the same as for the rest of the world: arguing about whether our history is cleaner or dirtier than other nations' — giving us a final grade — is a silly, unhealthy task. The whole exercise of *judging* whether America is a superior or inferior nation is a conservative frame.

Avoid making final judgments. Instead, tell stories with depth. If judgment needs to happen, let the person you are talking with do the judging. Whenever possible, describe what should have been done and create space in your stories for the people who did the right thing. Far too many of this country's founders wanted or accepted slavery, but Thomas Paine, Benjamin Franklin, John Jay, and Alexander Hamilton were some of the few famous leaders who pushed for abolition. And other less famous people fought harder; there were struggles that weren't taught in my history class in which someone got the Northern states to abolish slavery, people took big risks to create the Underground Railroad, and others resisted the Fugitive Slave Act.[123] Describing the people who chose to do the right thing, even when they lost, puts those leaders who didn't in an appropriately sharp light while you can still focus on the positive.

The Republican frame is a judgment frame: America is great (or not); America should not apologize (or should be apologizing). Saying *NO* to Republicans within their frame is counterproductive. Instead, let's say that America has a rich history with a lot to learn from, and patriots should ask what they can do to make their country a better nation. Someone else can argue about overall judgments: give me real, complex history worth learning about, worth more than a label.

Focus on the difference between an intrinsic *God-given Exceptionalism* and a *hard-work exceptionalism*.[124] We look at the same revolution and history, but some see it as handed down from *authority*, as something intrinsic like a Hollywood movie in

123. "Resistance to the Fugitive Slave Act," Encyclopedia.com. Accessed February 3, 2017.

124. Is *hard-work exceptionalism* a liberal frame or a neutral one? It encourages real research and independent thoughts, making your own judgments: so if you think that those are liberal values, you can call it a liberal frame, but I could imagine conservatives saying it

which the good guys simply have to win. Whether we say "yes" or "no" to this frame keeps us in an authority frame, a judgment frame.

These are two competing stories. One encourages complex thinking and introspection and a sense that America was built through the efforts of real people. The other encourages mindless groupthink, implying that America is a miracle, an act of a Higher Authority.

Hard-Work Exceptionalism

Hard-work exceptionalism focuses on leaders like Jefferson, Paine, and King and the ordinary people inspired to risk their lives for ideals. They could have done worse: replace just a few of the early Founders with a few modern politicians and there might not be anything we'd recognize as the United States of America; we could have had both kings and slavery. Or things could have been much better: more ethical founders could have stood more resolutely against slavery. We made this country exceptional; it wasn't handed to us from an authority. Our frame isn't concerned with judging or authority but with learning and improving.

I don't think that honest cognitive-conservative people need the Hollywood magic story, but they do seek a story of America worthy of pride. It makes sense to have a nation with enough pride to have social capital, to be willing to sacrifice if necessary to defend the country or pay taxes for schools and railroads. For progressives to build majorities, we need to pull the threads from our history that are worthy of pride and rebuild group loyalty in a healthy way. Attacking the pride of conservatives will just cause them to circle their wagons: we need stories of American patriotism and pride that treat people as adults, inviting them to find pride in a complex America.

Create a Shared Story

Despite our differences, Republicans and Democrats look to many of the same heroes. People across the spectrum quote Jefferson, for example. We were the escape from European feudalism and warring kingdoms, introducing the democratic revolution to the modern world. We were the big exception and the world's rescue from fascism and the insanity that swept the planet in the mid-twentieth century.

If a conservative feels that your patriotism is feeble, get ahead of them. Go ahead and say every last thing you agree on; say everything you can think of that makes the American ideal a great ideal. Know more history than they do. For example, Thomas Paine was the person who did more than any other to make the American Revolution a popular revolution rather than elite vs. elite; he's a shared hero who was very far to

is really a conservative frame for the same reasons. I don't think this is important to answer either way. The *hard-work exceptionalism* frame stands in opposition to the shallowest of ideas coming from the Republican Party.

the left. Talk about him. Yes, include your pride in the Abolition, Women's Rights, and Civil Rights movements and more as part of the "real America." Don't list these competitively; don't make the progressive story something outside the American story. Instead, share the sense that we all should agree on these. Don't try to win points against the person you're talking to, but be part of the same welcoming, unbounded in-group that confidently defines an American ideal worthy of pride.

Romney does not think he is being a racist when he says the nation that drove the slave trade, or empowered dictators like Pinochet and the Somozas, or slaughtered women and children at Wounded Knee has no need to apologize. He isn't looking at the list of facts and saying, "oh well, there's no reason to apologize for slavery." To cognitive conservatives, it's not that the list of historical facts has been weighed and balanced and America found worthy but that the exercise of weighing and balancing is inappropriate. *In-Group Loyalty* precludes spending time focusing on facts unwelcome by your group; loyalty precludes wondering if you should apologize for something America has done. So, we can't fight that frame with just facts.

> Trump is explicitly racist while other politicians are not so easily categorized as either racist or not-racist, but the solution is the same: inviting their potential voters to share in community with us while we set healthier norms for our shared community.

You may be able to mock one person's archaic views to an audience, but you can almost never convince someone that their pride is simply "wrong." Instead, you have to define what we *should* be proud of. Build up a positive picture and push American policy toward that ideal. Create a new pride first, leaving the old hateful or angry pride to fade.

Create a story of mutual cooperation. A story where ordinary people created America despite abuses by the powerful. It frames a bit to the left of Lakoff's nurturing-parent story: a nurturing sisters-and-brothers story. Share a story of pride in ordinary people beating back the feudal overlords, slavers and monopolists, and include the horrifying failures as stains.

When Is It Helpful to Bring Up America's Failings?

If you feel tempted to share a list of things that America has done wrong, ask yourself if your audience would do research? If no, you would just be blasting your opinion, scoring points in a game with no referee. If yes, point them directly toward the history. But don't overwhelm. Pointing a student toward *one* historical instance is much more powerful than a barrage of lists lacking detail and context.

It's easy to find framings that say "no" to the Republican frame that America is immaculate, such as lists of the countries the US has invaded. One example is *"From Wounded Knee to Libya: A Century of U.S. Military Interventions" (http://academic.evergreen.edu/g/grossmaz/interventions.html)* by Dr. Zoltan Grossman. But how many people who aren't already bitter about US policy — how many people who want peace and a just world and to celebrate the Fourth of July — are going to take this list and start studying each case?

When conservative and moderates see this list, what they see is an attack on their pride, an attack on their in-group. These lists may solidify people who agree with you, building a bitter, small liberal *in-group*. But when you barrage moderates with lists of unwanted facts, you just create separation and encourage them to circle their wagons under more welcoming conservative leadership.

Exercises

Warm-Up Exercise: Facts That Lead to Pride

For five minutes, say everything about American history that makes you proud.

Treat it like a meditation: No, this exercise is not to list all the asterisks and things foul with this country. If you can't, sitting by yourself, tell an amazing story about the amazing side of American history, explore why you *want* to be angry. And there are damn good reasons to be angry. But you can be much more effective at creating change, much more effective at showing other people where the ideals of democracy and equality have not been our reality, sometimes horrifyingly so, if you are able to answer the question of what makes you proud without needing to answer the question of what makes you ashamed or angry *in the same five minutes.*[125]

125. This book is written for liberals across a wide spectrum, some who are very angry about America's historical role in the world and many who aren't. This is a book about framing and communicating; I purposefully won't go deep into US history.

Use *Active Listening* to Seek Areas of Agreement and Connection

With conservative relatives, ask them to spend five minutes telling you everything about America that makes them proud.

This isn't a great place to end, but it is a very good place to begin: a warm-up that will prepare them to hear you. Listen for what you agree with, and reinforce every area of agreement before you move forward.

> Low self-esteem is a major contributor to young children smoking. Attacking their self-esteem because they smoke is counterproductive. If people are voting Republican because their faith and comfort are shaken, shaking it more is a dangerous tactic.

Most of the things that make even conservatives proud of America fit quite well within progressive values. Many conservatives are proud to be the Party of Lincoln. Let them get it out, listen to them, and encourage them to make weak stories stronger.

Practice Shared Pride as a Story; Separate Ideals and Stains

Practice telling a story of your *idealized* America that is human, real, and worth feeling pride for — for example, the ideal of Democracy, the Jeffersonian ideal of equality in which every family had fifty acres of the means of production, the slow and courageous struggle for freedom and civil rights. Despite the many stains on this story, practice telling it as a story of pride in which every failing *is a stain* and not the central story.

Tell the story of democracy, equality, abolition, expanding civil rights, and the ideal of widespread abundance.[126]

Create a story of "us," both at our best and when we fail. For the exercise, catch yourself whenever the story becomes a "them" story. There are likely to be times for hard-hitting truth, but people need a story of pride, and American liberals have fallen out of practice with telling our ideals in a proud story. Practice a story that begins:

This is what I believe in about America

---

126. The Republican leadership no longer believes even in the middle-class ideal or "two chickens in every pot." Neither at the policy level nor in their rhetoric do they think that every adult American deserves a job with more dignity than earning a deflated minimum wage working for Walmart's billionaires. Abundance is a story of hope — a little tricky to tell in this era of McMansions followed by collapse followed by McMansions — but what does an abundant nation look like to you? I would modify FDR's vision of abundance with something more sustainable and more focused on replacing the community connections that were common eighty years ago. But for me, FDR's vision is a good starting point.

Tell a story of heroism, Thomas Paine, Thomas Jefferson's ideals and perhaps even liberal mercy for his failings, the Abolition and Women's Rights movements, Eleanor Roosevelt, Malcolm X, and Martin Luther King Jr. Tell it from the bottom up, describing what you feel proud about instead of accusations — tell the accusations only as the shadows and stains, at least for this practice exercise.

If you can tell this story better than Bush or Romney can tell their "cranky old man who doesn't apologize" story, Thanksgiving politics are yours. You'll have broken the in-group vs. out-group boundary, showing that you have a reasonable sense of the sacred.

Mesh Tactics with Achievable Goals for Each Audience

William Blum wrote *Killing Hope: U.S. Military and C.I.A. Interventions Since World War II.*[127] Who might benefit from a listing of times that the US was in the wrong? Think of whom you might discuss politics with, then divide them into these categories or add new categories:

1. Who is idealistic and fact-oriented enough that they would absorb the information and become more committed to changing US foreign policy?
2. Who would not be surprised at a long list of atrocities but would become more burned out rather than inspired?
3. Who would recoil and become more firm in their belief that their conservative political group is an "us" and you are an anti-patriotic "them"?

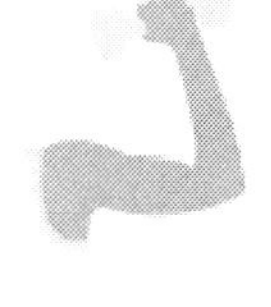

Find Something to Honor

Create a list of actions in American history that particularly upset you. Then, for each, find someone who opposed it. Take a moment to research and find names and stories worth sharing.

Share your new stories at *CognitivePolitics.org/recast_and_honor.*

Build Bridges Using Nonconfrontational Shared Activities

When worldviews are far apart, the first step is to build bridges. With a conservative, read a book on Thomas Jefferson together: wonderfully

127. William Blum. *Killing Hope* (Common Courage Press 1995). Blum takes the diametric opposite of "never apologize" with his stark list of US interventions. *Available online (http://www.thirdworldtraveler.com/Blum/US_Interventions_WBlumZ.html).* Howard Zinn's *A People's History of the United States* carries much of the same factual information in a format that more people will be able to absorb. Blum, Romney and Trump are using the same frame focused on whether America has done terrible things we should apologize for — are we great or not, yes or no? Zinn is using a completely different frame — it would be more honest and more interesting to include more stories that were previously left out of our history.

complex history that makes simplifications difficult and gives lots of space to agree. Healthy, human conversations that have give-and-take *without consequences* are a prerequisite to talking about current issues involving another's *core beliefs*, where egos are tender.

American Exceptionalism is about framing — this contrasts with other issues like abortion that involve real policy disagreements. This chapter mostly turns back to the first chapter, seeking an alternative frame that doesn't just say "no" to the conservative frame. The key conservative value is *IN-GROUP LOYALTY*, but it's neither easy nor important to change that value in order to reframe. Communication skills are key — both having our own story that doesn't noticeably contradict theirs and listening actively to seek areas of agreement.

Authoritarian Goals:

Create a simple story in which American pride comes from an innate status-quo, given by a Natural Authority, to "Real Americans." Today's leaders will implicitly claim that authority. The story is used to define an in-group, people who will support each other no matter what.

Progressive Goals:

Draw together a large majority of Americans with a story that centers on hardworking people who cooperate, and slowly succeed, in creating more and more of a democracy while seeing racism and military adventurism as stains in our shared story.

Considering Audiences

I don't think this story varies as much as others, whether you are talking to a far-conservative or a moderate. Unlike homosexuality or abortion, there is less fundamental disagreement. We are generally not arguing with or contradicting conservatives but simply deepening their version, making it richer and more real.

All we have to do is tell a richer story and we've won: a story with no in-group and out-group, one that creates space to think instead of rote respect for authority.

Review: Reality, Framing, and Judging

Is America a nation worthy of our pride?

Whatever your answer, this question evokes judgment. We have to let go of *overall* judgment — yes, say what you see as right; say what you see as wrong. But if you add up the rights and wrongs and try to give a grade to the country's history as a whole, you'll have an unwinnable, unending argument.

Progressives running for office should tell a story that has some hope of being electable — in my opinion, a compassionate story is often more powerful than a harshly true story that is frighteningly judgmental. Harsher truths also have their place: look for ways to combine both truth and reconciliation, not just anger or despair.

There are some questions with no easy answers; there are times when the best frame to win an election means means looking away from the truth. Framing to win elections might mean calling America a "Great Nation" by counting slavery and genocide as worth less when "judging greatness" than focusing on our experiments in democracy.

I don't think we need to speak with one voice, having one answer from everyone "left" of center. It is part of a president's job to look at America from a positive angle, to build pride in this nation as we are. It would do no more good to have them spend all their time focused on past failings than to have someone struggling with alcoholism stay focused on the worst moments of their bad years. There should be a liberal voice from a party that has a chance of winning elections — and that party should get "on message."

There should be other voices, and the people who speak about America with pride and compassion should also create space for raw voices of anger and justice. In my personal hearing, the harshest and most dissociated criticisms of America have come from other middle-class white males speaking on others' behalf. Dissociated anger crowds out angry voices that have a right to be heard, and it interferes with efforts to build political power that can make a difference today.

One of the themes of this book is that you don't create a worldview in one conversation. It's good to feel pride in your nation's accomplishments some days and good to hear harsh, challenging voices on other days. Putting the vast good and the

vast bad on a scale and trying to measure and judge them simply isn't a helpful thing to do, no matter which way the scale would tip.

Resources and Toolkit: Activism without Judgment or Apology

Avoiding the "apologies" frame doesn't mean whitewashing. Instead, it could mean guiding people to the history that drives your judgments about America's role in the world, rather than pushing your judgment.

- [ ] Share visions of America that focus on people who tried to do the right thing, whether they succeeded or not. One easy way is to gift copies of *A People's History of the United States* by Howard Zinn. See *CognitivePolitics.org/books.*

- [ ] If you talk with high school or college students, know what historical events drove your own views, and simply encourage them to write papers about those topics, coming to their own conclusions. Studying relatively recent history in places like Chile, Nicaragua or Iran can help students in the US develop their own informed views on American Exceptionalism.

- [ ] One way to seek shared values with family members who have different political views is to read or watch history on subjects where you might find some agreement. For example, Thomas Jefferson expressed values that neither he nor we have done a good job living, but reminding ourselves of this idealism is one step in the right direction. Instead of shouting at a family member who claims not to be racist but voted for Trump, invite them to step into their claim, and invite them to join you to watch a video about Civil Rights or Martin Luther King Jr., perhaps *Freedom on My Mind* (1994)[128] or *Freedom Riders* (2010).[129]

128. *Freedom on My Mind — One Woman's View of Civil Rights and Personal Change* is available online or by DVD via http://www.clarityfilms.org/freedom

129. *Freedom Riders* is available from PBS at *www.pbs.org/wgbh/americanexperience/freedomriders.*

Chapter 9

Economics: Compassion and Fairness Don't Mix

Do those with economic authority earn it? Do our paychecks reflect our contributions? What do people deserve? For people struggling with low-paying jobs, is the key value compassion or fairness?

Republican leaders have been twisting economic reality until hardworking people who are struggling believe they are being taken advantage of by those below them, deflecting anger from Wall Street and CEO pay. Meanwhile, the people the Democrats intend to champion, people who work hard and earn little while their CEOs earn hundreds of times as much, often feel that the Democrats pity them.

> "No matter how you slice it, the rich do the heavy lifting when it comes to shouldering the national tax burden."
> —Curtis S. Dubay[130]

Economic Frames and Goals Around Fairness and Compassion

Cognitive-Conservative Working Class: I work hard. I am a responsible contributor, doing what I'm supposed to. I feel like I'm doing more than my share. I pull my weight, so my struggles in life must be caused by someone not contributing their share and leeching from me.

Conservative Ideology: You get paid according to your *real contribution*. CEOs do contribute hundreds of times more than ordinary workers. We live in a world of scarcity, and you earn wages or get rich only through voluntary transactions in which someone is happy to pay you for your contribution. If you're not

Cognitive conservatives intuit that the status quo is mostly fair — *If you need help, it must be because you have failed.*

The Democrats appear to pity your struggles — *Do you want that pity?* Will you identify with a party that pities you?

130. Curtis S. Dubay, "More People Should Pay Taxes," The Heritage Foundation, September 19, 2012.

getting paid much, it signals you're not contributing much, so work harder or find a better job, but don't beg for help.

Democratic Party Today: People are struggling, paid terribly, or can't find work. It's a sad situation, unfair, deserving of empathy and pity. Democrats mush together a desire for *COMPASSION* and real *FAIRNESS*, as if those were the same value. When we talk about economics, we tell one story that includes both a struggling drug addict who can't hold a job and someone doing important but underpaid work. We mix the values of compassion and fairness. At the top of the pay scale, we take it for granted that a CEO is not really worth 300 times as much as other workers … it's so obvious to us that we don't say it out loud.

"Help is on the way!"
— John Kerry[131]

Old Left Framing: Workers create all value. CEOs, Wall Street, and stockholders *redistribute* that wealth from the people who created it. We live in a world of abundance where all needs can be met if parasites don't create artificial scarcity and keep us from working and being paid for the value we create.

The frame that *workers create all wealth* was in the air at the time of progressive ascendancy.

Today, establishment Republicans are undermining working people while Democrats are pitying them. Unions historically gave working people pride; today, no thriving movement does.

Failures in the Liberal Frame: Mixed Moral Foundations

Typical conservatives and liberals disagree in a different way than most liberals think we do. Liberals think conservatives lack compassion. But the rhetoric of *COMPASSIONATE CONSERVATIVE* was welcomed by the moderate-conservative demographic. Instead, the key difference, the one we're blind to, is *FAIRNESS*. Most of us have often heard, but don't always address, the conservative fear that throwing money creates the wrong incentives and doesn't really help. Unlike the sanctity-related issues in this workbook, we don't have such different underlying values but simply perceive economic facts differently. This perception can be changed with focused stories and examples of how the economy really works.

131. "'Help is on the way,' Kerry tells middle class," CNN, July 30, 2004, CNN.com

Democrats fail to separate the two values we hold: we want compassion for those unable to contribute enough to equal their basic economic needs, and we want fairness that workers and CEOs be paid according to their real contributions. However, when we mix these messages, it sounds as if we are pitying working-class people as unable to pull their own weight. That's not what we mean, liberal activists know that's not what we mean, but we don't make the message clear to people who don't already get it.

> Do proud working-class people want your compassion or pity? Even if the Democratic Party's economic message is not condescending, it is close enough that political opponents can make it sound that way, as if it were charity for people who have failed.

A CEO being paid 300 times what a worker earns is seen as a bad thing. Is it a bad thing because the poor worker has developed too few skills and therefore isn't much of a contributor to the economy, needing charitable help — while the CEO doesn't really *need* but did *earn* their large salary? Or is the core problem that the system is rigged, and the workers have too little power while the CEOs have too much power when wages and salaries are set? It's too early to talk about compassion if you don't agree between these realities.

Goals for Talking About Economics

Progressives need to go on the offensive about real economics: that people who provide the goods and services count, that there is currently abundance, that we should not be desperate. If we're desperate, something is wrong. Let's find it.

✓ Separate the conversations that are driven by compassion from those driven by fairness, and be very, very clear which value you are emphasizing at any time.

✓ Talk about the real economy and real contributions, not dollars.

Progressive Economics Around Contribution

American savings should become American factories giving workers jobs that let them contribute to our needs. If Wall Street executives were making millions coordinating our savings into capital investments in a way that created more jobs and more wealth for other people and they were just getting a cut, that would mean they were contributing. But when they make millions for moving jobs overseas, there is something more deeply wrong. The problem isn't people earning very large salaries or bonuses; it's people getting paid large amounts without contributing to overall wealth.

Today's Conservative Framing: A Path from Pride to Shame to Blame

> "If it were the case that the rich had grown richer at the expense of the poor, thereby making them poorer, then we would have reason to be concerned. Something would have to be done not to equalize outcomes, but to address the unjust means that the rich had used to defraud the poor."
>
> — The Heritage Foundation, a conservative think tank, which argues that this is not the case[132]

Underpaid people are struggling, and therefore their pride is fragile. Republican framing experts are playing two games: One is to increase shame and just slightly twist the Democratic message so that it hurts the pride of people who are struggling. The other is to take that shame and give it an outlet: to guide people inclined to trust authority into blaming people "below" them such as the poor and immigrants.[133]

Blame doesn't require consistency or logic. Immigrants are attacked in one moment for working too hard and taking away jobs, attacked in another moment for being too lazy and relying on welfare.

Cognitive conservatives lean toward trusting authority and power: that even if there are a few exceptions of greed and cheating, most millionaires and billionaires obtained their money through hard work — every dollar they have was given to them when someone freely chose to pay them for what they offered. It's earned; it's fair.

Most people I know feel like they work hard, whether they are paid badly or well. They contribute, or they wish they could find a job that gives them a chance to really contribute. If they are unemployed, they want to work. Democrats want us to be charitable to anyone poor, including people who are incapable or lazy. Republican Party strategists make sure that hardworking underpaid or unemployed people hear the Democrat's message of supporting those who don't contribute.

> I personally do not enjoy thinking of myself as needing charitable help — if I'm struggling, I have pride. I'll struggle through.

132. David Azerrad and Rea S. Hederman, Jr., "Defending the Dream: Why Income Inequality Doesn't Threaten Opportunity," The Heritage Foundation, Sept. 13, 2012. CognitivePolitics.org/defending. This is a good example of conservative framing. Are conservatives framing this about empathy or fairness? Do you think Walmart is getting rich by building an economic ladder for hardworking people, or is it damaging the economic ladder we had a generation ago?

133. Notice the similar patterns of simultaneously increasing pride mixed with shame: The *No-Apology* frame evokes that someone is accusing you and waiting for an apology. Meanwhile, the *Contributor* frame makes people feel like they are failures if they struggle and then offers to restore pride by giving them someone to blame.

We All Believe in Care and Fairness: Misunderstandings on Contribution

> "Conservatives have figured out their moral basis, and you see it on Wall Street. It includes: the primacy of self-interest."
> — George Lakoff [134]

Lakoff is going against the evidence that conservatives give more to charity and their communities, on average, than progressives.[135] There are billionaires who get rich by having desperate people work without health care: yes, that's the primacy of self-interest. There are clearly many Republican politicians (and plenty of Democrats) pushing the self-interests of Wall Street. But ordinary cognitive conservatives turn to the "strict father" when their sense of *FAIRNESS* is crossed. Many often-Republican voters are *excited* by the "compassionate conservative" frame, not excited by the "self-interest" frame. They are as willing as anyone to reach into their pockets if they believe the cause is just. And perhaps more importantly, when it comes to framing and winning elections, they don't see themselves as holding self-interest above all else. If you make that accusation without a solid story, you just prove to them that you don't understand them, that you are "other."

The problem is not that *CONTRIBUTING-CLASS* conservatives lack compassion. Instead, we've hit a moral-tastes land mine in which they intuitively trust authority and power and, in turn, *intuitively* trust that Walmart contributes to the economy proportionately to profits. Progressive attacks miss their target when we argue as if

134. George Lakoff, "How to Frame Yourself: A Framing Memo for Occupy Wall Street," Huffington Post, Dec 19, 2011. CognitivePolitics.org/primacy.

135. Arthur C. Brooks' 2007 book *Who Really Cares: The Surprising Truth About Compassionate Conservatism* argues that conservatives are more charitable than liberals. This has led to much squirming in liberal circles as they try to explain it away. One of the better-known examples is Michele Margolis and Michael Sances's, "Who Really Gives? Partisanship and Charitable Giving in the United States," August 9, 2013. SSRN: https://ssrn.com/abstract=2148033.

The abstract of "Who Really Gives?" explains that "at the individual level, the large bivariate relationship between giving and conservatism vanishes after adjusting for differences in … religiosity." They argue that this means that conservatives are *not* "more generous." In other words, yes, conservatives give more to charity, arts, and church than liberals give to charity, arts, and PBS, but we will not call them more generous because their giving is inspired by (or at least correlated with) their religiosity. I've seen this specious reasoning echoed repeatedly in liberal blogs. It is similar, in many ways, to Pro-Life arguments that conservative states have lower teen abortion rates because a lower proportion of pregnant teens have abortions, even though liberal states have reduced the total number of abortions just as well with sex education and access to birth control.

conservative voters consciously believe in the primacy of self-interest rather than the primacy of contributing your share.

Dependency Is Destructive

Conservatives as a group believe that giving help, especially automatic help, creates dependency. It is destructive of human dignity and self-discipline. This is not the primacy of self-interest. Conservatives freely give (slightly) more to charity and their communities than liberals. If you show up at a church needing help, you are more likely to get it than by showing up at a university. Conservatives neither like nor trust government. None of this is the primacy of self-interest. Yes, political movements have been led by people whose policies push for the primacy of their self-interest — conservative movements led by the self-interest of the wealthy and powerful. But to pretend that self-interest is the conservative metaphor is both unfair to middle- and working-class cognitive-conservative voters and is a misdirected and ineffective way to change their minds.

Conservatives feel an intuition that liberals will create a nanny-state that will bankrupt hardworking people and turn the poor into overgrown children.[136] I think liberals in the 1960s made some mistakes in this direction — both materially and psychologically focusing more on charity than on creating a path out of dependency — and we learned some lessons. Do we actively listen to conservatives and answer their intuition in words and stories? When conservative intuitions point at a real problem, do we just answer that Republican policy would take us back to a world with much more misery and poverty, or do we engage their ideas and model how we want them to listen to ours?

The conservative economic metaphors are not built upon bad *values*. Cognitive conservatives are not lacking compassion. The problem with the conservative story is not the values but the facts: typical working-class people are begging for jobs which would allow them to contribute far more than they seek to consume. We need to show conservative voters that Walmart workers — part of the *47 percent (p.164)* — are contributing. And that Walmart billionaires have mostly learned how to pay people less, a financial game that doesn't create real wealth. Walmart billionaires are not actually contributing; they are costing and not creating jobs. It's the billionaires, not the Walmart workers, who fail to contribute.

When Democrats try to help those Walmart workers, they tend to propose policy shifts that would increase the incomes of those workers and provide health insurance. This is a worthy idea, but it is not the same as noticing that low-paid workers contribute and deserve dignity. Trump's victory came with no clear policy proposals,

136. J. Bradford DeLong, *"Shrugging off Atlas"* (*Democracy: A Journal of Ideas*. Spring 2013, No. 28). This book review explores the fallacies in the conservative focus on a "moocher class."

but he played to both the pride and shame that many people feel about their work lives.

Definition: Contributing Class

Are you doing something that someone needs? Can you describe what you contribute: Do you teach or heal? Do you bring joy? Do you build or provide something people value? Do you wish you were contributing more but can only find less meaningful work?

> "To be effective, your movement must be seen
> by all of the 99% as positive and moral."
> — George Lakoff [137]

Liberals see Walmart billionaires profiting in large part from their dominant economic power over honest, hardworking people. And if you believe that story, fighting a living wage would be an indication of particularly foul values. When we pretend that the logic we see is also what conservatives see and so their values are the opposite of ours, we are being unfair to ordinary cognitive conservatives. And interpreting their values incorrectly makes us ineffective at countering the conservative metaphor.

Applying Nonviolent Communication: Uncover Shared Needs

Chapter 3 discusses the Nonviolent Communication technique of putting connection and needs above strategy. Economics is a great place where our deeper needs are more powerful and often more similar, and so this is a better place to stitch our communities. p.65

Minimum wage is a strategy. Campaign for a higher minimum wage, but don't expect it to start good conversations among people who are already opinionated. For me, minimum wage is a strategy to meet two of my values: *compassion* for people who are stuck in bad jobs and *fairness* since I think most people with weak bargaining positions are treated unfairly. Still, I can imagine many other economic changes that would fulfill those values but not involve the minimum wage.[138] Seeking out and discussing your deeper needs, rather than the political strategies you think will achieve them, can get better conversations started.

137. George Lakoff, "How to Frame Yourself: A Framing Memo for Occupy Wall Street," The Huffington Post, updated Dec 19, 2011, *TheHuffingtonPost.com*.

138. For an exercise exploring the difference between needs and strategies, see CognitivePolitics.org/strategies.

If you believe that the Republican proclamations about helping working people are merely shallow slogans, get people who have bought the slogans talking. Find your shared needs, talk about stories instead of numbers, and share the reasons you came to your conclusions rather than trying to get others to lose an argument and accept your conclusions.

An Effective Progressive Frame: Economics of Contribution

What if labor creates almost all, or even just most, wealth? What if making the stuff we need, healing the sick and teaching the kids, what if that is the economy, and other jobs are taking slices of a pie baked by makers, farmers, builders, teachers and healers? What if there is plenty of work needing to be done, and Wall Street profits today come from destroying jobs as much as creating them? CEOs and advertising executives and Wall Street are not contributing what they take out of the real economy.

Many hardworking cognitive conservatives, including some Tea Party and Trump supporters, would answer the above questions somewhat the same as the left. Liberals are effective when we use frames and stories that focus on real contributions rather than monetary ones: Who makes what we really need? Use real examples, have many voices using the same examples, and repeat regularly.

Your pay and profits are only loosely tied to your real contribution. If people want to eat strawberries and you pick those strawberries, you're making a real contribution; you have earned health care and a place in our society: this isn't charity. If you want to eat strawberries, in this economy the person who picks the strawberries will get paid almost nothing, while advertising people, investors, and Wall Street manipulators will all get surprisingly large cuts. It's not a question of compassion but fairness.

What metaphors come to your mind when you hear the term *CONTRIBUTING CLASS?*

If you do a necessary job and are not paid a sufficient wage, then there is a "redistribution" happening away from you. You are making a real contribution of *a fair day's work* and not getting a real distribution in the form of a *fair day's pay*. You are producing real, needed goods or services, and yet you're not able to afford a similar share of real goods and services. The modern economy does not provide jobs

for everyone who wants to work and does not pay people according to their real contribution.[139]

Picking strawberries is definitely *contributing class*, and a CEO guiding a team to create a useful product more efficiently is also contributing. But advertising junk food to kids or shuffling jobs overseas while leaving trained workers unemployed is not contributing. Often it won't be by job title: a divorce lawyer who helps angry parents focus on their kids' needs could be a huge contributor, while their colleague who encourages revenge isn't at all. I think most of us desire to be contributors, but some subcultures of greed lose track of that, and many working-class and service-class people are not given the chance to contribute much. An economy where people are allowed to earn a comfortable living while contributing seems like a straightforward demand and goal that should speak to most Americans.

Progressive Framing Strategies on Economics

Separate conversations about economic fairness from those on charity or empathy >> Many progressives believe in government-run charity: if you can't work, we want the government to lend you a hand, and even if you're just lazy, we still don't think you should actually starve. But that's charity and compassion, not economics. If you argue compassion within a conversation about economics, you create space for the conservative metaphor: Walmart's owners are great contributors, paying more than their share of taxes, while their workers contribute little and should thank the owners for their jobs.

Never mix compassion and fairness when talking with cognitive conservatives. Know that the Republican message machine aims to twist your message to one of pity. Therefore, you might explicitly say "it's not a question of compassion; it's a question of fairness" at the start and end of conversations about CEO pay or similar economics.

Talk in real terms, not money terms >> If you create something other people need, you contribute. If you contribute and can't afford health care, you are being taken advantage of. Don't allow the abstract word *efficiency* to float by unchallenged: Bain Capital found ways to pay people less or fire them and find someone else to do it cheaper.[140] In this case, they didn't create new value nor help workers create more with less; they merely squeezed

139. This book is about framing, so we can't go too deep into economics, but briefly, if Wall Street were efficiently allocating resources then people who wanted to work would have jobs. If they're not efficiently allocating resources, they're getting paid not for contributing but for extracting wealth.

140. Tom Hamburger, *"Romney's Bain Capital invested in companies that moved jobs overseas,"* The Washington Post, June 21, 2012, WashingtonPost.com

profits away from the real contributors. Money was extracted; nothing was made more productive. There are other examples, such as Henry Ford or Steve Jobs at Apple, in which a story told in real terms would show efficiency and creativity at the top that benefited the economy. Unfortunately, the economy today is increasingly weighted toward extraction, toward paying workers less and toward too-large companies buying competitors instead of competing.

This is a good place for the "Yes, And..." conversation >> Be careful not to argue against more than you mean to, so you can get your real point across. Yes, Henry Ford and Steve Jobs created tremendous value and enlarged the economic pie. Ford helped create the American Middle Class. And today, too many CEOs spend their time sending jobs overseas, and too many Harvard graduates expend their genius just to extract money on Wall Street.

Never mush together fairness and compassion when talking economics. Talk about either, but talk about them separately.

Sample Conversations, Advocacy, and Exercises

Sample Conversation: Focus on Underpaid Contributors

> I hear you saying that our economy is in trouble, that productive middle-class people are working too hard and carrying more than their share while others are getting a free ride. I agree something is amiss. The 47 percent who are paid so little that they don't have to pay federal taxes includes janitors and grocery clerks and substitute teachers and Walmart employees. Are those the people you are upset at? Are you saying that people doing hard work for so little pay that they don't have to pay taxes, that they are at the root of our country's ills?

> How do you define contribution? To me, contributors are people who provide the things I want. I want the food on my table. Someone had to pick the strawberries. Does it make sense to you that we live in a world with enough abundance that you and I should be able to eat strawberries sometimes? So, shouldn't the person who picks the strawberries have all the basics of a decent life? It's not a job you have to study for, though it sure isn't an easy job, so I'm okay with the idea that a doctor who contributes more is able to own a bigger house. But are you saying that the people who provide the things you actually want aren't real contributors, that you can eat strawberries and be okay that the person who picked them doesn't have a decent if small home or health care?

> What I see is that people who do contribute more than their share are not paid enough to buy their share. Meanwhile, Wall Street, where in theory people get rich in exchange for helping distribute capital where it's needed and helping the economy run smoothly for other people, is getting rich for a very negative contribution, driving the economy into the ground and misallocating capital.

How to Discuss Inequality

Compare the two images below: first a map and then a chart about inequality. What does each say to you? What would each say to moderates and conservatives?

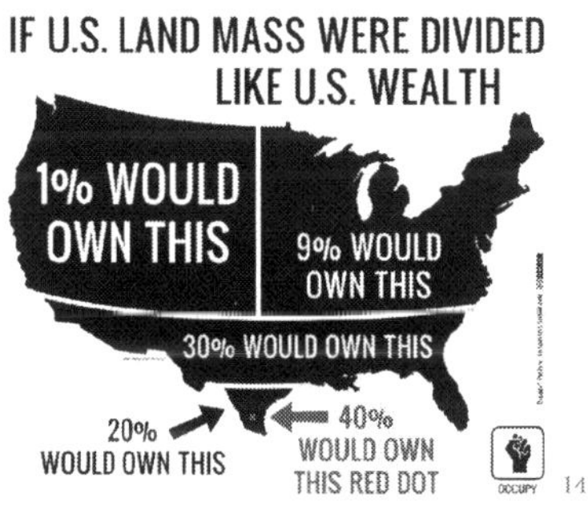

[141]

Figure 9.1:
Inequality is Unequal Meme

A liberal interpretation:

Lower-earning people are making too little money; this is unfair.

If conservatives disagree, it's because they don't care.

A conservative interpretation:

Worsening inequality must mean that a productivity gap is growing. The rich are producing ever more, while the lower-earning half of our country falls behind. Growing inequality *is* a problem: liberal and lazy values have infected too much of the country, and they aren't keeping up. Worse, they are now, unfairly, hoping that the rich who already pay more than their share of taxes should cover their lag. We must solve this: those falling behind need to be challenged to work harder and take more responsibility.

The map confirms liberal beliefs but doesn't challenge underlying conservative views about fairness.

141. Occupy* Posters and designer Stephen Ewen. This image and others are available for purchase as a poster or t-shirt from the artist, or under Creative Commons license, at *owsposters.tumblr.com*.

The following chart displays changes in productivity and hourly wages for production/nonsupervisory workers since 1948:[142]

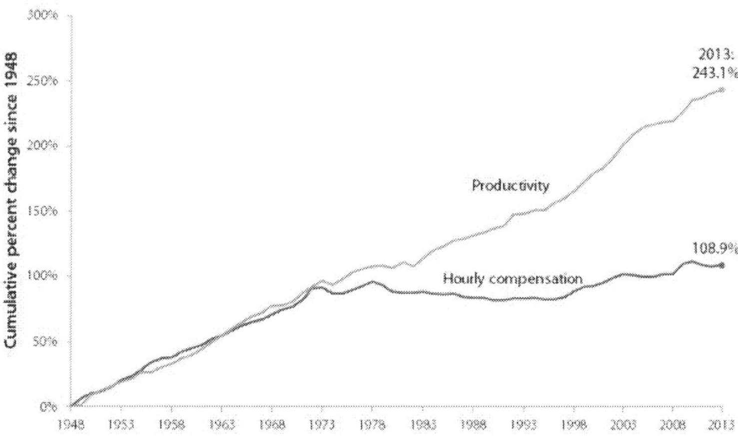

Figure 9.2: Inequality is Unfair Meme
This image, and further data, are under a Creative Commons license by the Economic Policy Institute. Shortcut to share their powerful page: *CognitivePolitics.org/swa.*

Instead of focusing on the unequal outcomes alone, the Economic Policy Institute is exploring *FAIRNESS*. Something has changed in how our society honors the traditional relationship between the wealthy and the working class. Liberals might think that capital always has been unfair to labor, but even if you think things were fair under Eisenhower, then they are not fair now. Workers are more productive than ever — but the owners of capital and inheritors of wealth have found a way to hold on to all the increasing wealth.

Conflict and Lakoff's Framing
Lakoff encourages us to express our own metaphors, while Haidt encourages us to listen to people with different values. I'd like to combine these: tell your story conscious of where the disagreement comes from. If we tell a story of high inequality by itself, conservatives can say this is the cost of efficiency. The more clear we can be about crony capitalism, the more we can draw people who believe in honest work for fair pay to join us.

Practice Exercises: Hope and Struggle

Write a point-by-point refutation of "What Occupy Wall Street Is Getting Totally Wrong" by Steve Chapman.[143] CognitivePolitics.org/chapman is a shortcut to the article.

142. "Cumulative change in total economy productivity and real hourly compensation of production/nonsupervisory workers, 1948–2013," *Economic Policy Institute*, Web. Updated June 26, 2014. CognitivePolitics.org/swa.

First, write out the points he is making in a list, and then refute those specific points — avoid discussing points you assume conservatives make. Do you think "the 1%" has created the wealth it holds? Can you subdivide the top 1 percent not just by wealth but by contribution and noncontribution?

John Steinbeck said poor Americans "don't believe they're poor, but rather temporarily embarrassed millionaires."[144] How do *you* talk to someone optimistic but economically struggling, and begin to get them to align with working people rather than millionaires, without damaging their optimism?

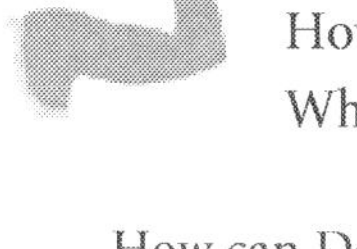

Imagine you are a therapist offering pro bono counseling to an exhausted mother who works for Walmart plus another part-time job to raise her kids. How will it affect her mental health to blame Walmart for her problems? What will lead to the most hope and resilience?

How can Democrats or liberals encourage hope and resilience without encouraging loyalty to imaginary future wealth?

Conversations: Expose Dissonance between Laissez-Faire and Contribution Economics

Adam Smith wrote against the entrenched powers of his time. But a simplified laissez-faire theory[145] vaguely attributed to him is used to prove that any interference in the market — any effort to balance colluding billion-dollar companies negotiating with individual working people — will have severe negative impacts. The questions below aim to loosen the grip of this frame.

> "They who feed, clothe, and lodge the whole body of the people, should have such a share of the produce of their own labour as to be themselves tolerably well fed, clothed, and lodged."
> —Adam Smith[146]

143. Steve Chapman, "What Occupy Wall Street Is Getting Totally Wrong," *Chicago Tribune*, Web. November 06, 2011. CognitivePolitics.org/chapman.

144. Details of this quote are disputed as discussed at http://en.wikiquote.org/wiki/John_Steinbeck, but nonetheless Americans seem to have long rejected the nobility of poverty.

145. Adam Smith is often associated with laissez-faire, a slogan — not a theory — favoring minimal government interference in the economy. However, he saw other sources of interference in a free market besides government, such as monopolies and collusion.

146. Adam Smith, *An Inquiry into the Nature and Causes of the Wealth of Nations.* (Gutenberg.org, 2009).

Abundance: Scarcity Is Artificial

The question below is probably unanswerable to free-market "true believers," so keep asking it, and listening, encouraging conservatives to wander into more realistic answers.

> According to capitalism and free market theory, what you might see in the first pages of an economics book, the more land, labor, capital and technology we have, the wealthier we should be. While environmentalists warn about the future, today we use far more resources with more capital and better technology than ever. So if we don't live in an abundant world economy, what went wrong? If we produce so much so easily, why don't we have enough? The numbers for welfare just don't add up as a major cause, and the trends started long before FDR. What are the deeper causes of joblessness?

Free Trade: Visible Failures of Free Market as a Theory

According to capitalism and free market theory, free trade should — basically it has to — make both nations wealthier.

> Do you think that free trade with China has made America stronger? If you feel like free trade is making ordinary Americans poorer, doesn't that mean that the whole theory is off-kilter?

America's Economy Thrived during the Progressive Era and New Deal

> Before America's ascension in the twentieth century, the Progressive movement broke the monopolies and empowered working-class people to have unions that could negotiate at the same scale as their bosses. Working people were able to take home more of their share of their contribution, the rich took less false profits than ever, and America thrived like no other nation on earth.[147] The Progressives broke monopolies and Reagan broke unions: When did America thrive?

Thanksgiving Table Gratitude: "Real" Contribution

What has the economy provided you today? Who made that contribution?

147. A good quick intro to Progressive Era economics is available at Wikipedia: http://en.wikipedia.org/wiki/Progressive_Era#Economic_policy. The Progressive Era is a good subject to recommend to students seeking topics for papers.

One of the signature goals of this book is improving political conversations at the Thanksgiving dinner table. A good place to start, very much in line with the spirit of the holiday, is to look around at the goods and services that make that dinner possible. Don't bring up politics as you do this, which will make people defensive and go for their usual talking points. Just give thanks and mean it, and bring the focus to real people.

> Who picked the cranberries? Who cleaned the turkey? Who packed and drove your food? Who stocked the shelves? Who ran the cash register? Who cooked? We want to thank them. They made our Thanksgiving meal; do they also all have homes and time to share a Thanksgiving meal?

If you look at what we give thanks for, much of it is contributed by underpaid workers — often immigrants without green cards with very few rights or unpaid family labor. Reinforce this reality away from politics, pointing it out where there is no controversy until it is a solid, shared frame that even conservatives will bring to political discussions.

And, as always, try to approach conversations with real curiosity — the questions as written can easily be leading questions, so be cautious to ask them with openness, hoping to hear real answers and new perspectives.

Sample Talking Points: Two Takes on Capitalism

The section below is my template for leaving online comments on economics. If you like the approach, you're welcome to write and share your own variants.

Below is a progressive frame on fairness and contribution. Since it's about fairness, I'll leave compassion and charity for another conversation. Avoid forcing people to choose between the usual teams.

> Election after election, we struggle around two definitions of capitalism. In one version of capitalism, if you are doing a job that needs doing, providing value other people need, a functioning free market will return that value: provide you with at least the basics of healthy food, decent shelter, and health care. A fair day's wage for a fair day's work.

Good conservatives think they are fighting for this kind of capitalism. Welcome them.

In another version of capitalism, you get what you can negotiate for in a market where you have to compete with powerless nonunionized teenage girls in impoverished, patriarchal countries — if you are a worker, not a CEO. A market where CEOs are paid 300 times what you are paid — they are friends with the board who decides their pay. A market where Wall Street extracts immense wealth from the economy even when they make terribly wrong investment decisions. A market where you can create value, do things someone has to do, and be called a "freeloader" by the people who are managing to pay you almost nothing to do the hard work that makes them rich. In Adam Smith's world, if you were more efficient, you got paid more. Today, you or your coworker might lose a job where you were efficiently producing and contributing to the US economy, and the CEO or Wall Street firm that fires you will get paid even more for firing you.

Democrats have a big advantage when framing economics: a century ago, progressives had good policies and good framing, so today we simply need to reinvoke what worked then. Get the idea that "workers create all wealth" to define one edge of the debate, to counterbalance the idea that we are all paid what we are worth and create space for debate. Our message should be that the working class creates wealth, not that we pity them and want to help them.

Is capitalism about being competitive and producing what people need? Or is it about paying people less and skimming from other people's contributions? Which of these patterns describes the richest CEOs and biggest Wall Street firms today?

Introduce new ideas. Don't demand that people change teams now; don't shove your ideology against theirs.

Romney Played with Fire: The Economics of Contribution

Candidate Romney is one of my favorite sources for making the conservative frame visible. While Reagan very smoothly reframed economic reality, and Trump just talks about his dealmaking skills, the 2012 election was full of framing mistakes that exposed conservative contradictions.

> "There are 47 percent of the people ... who believe the government has a responsibility to care for them, who believe that they are entitled."
> —Presidential Candidate Mitt Romney, 2012[148]

148. Corn, David. "SECRET VIDEO: Romney Tells Millionaire Donors What He REALLY Thinks of Obama Voters," MotherJones.com. September 9, 2012.

Romney lost in part when he failed to understand the Republican advantage in economics debates: much of the electorate near the 47 percent income line doesn't want the Democrat's pity. His comments about contribution were insulting many of the voters whose dignity usually causes them to suffer Republican rule rather than accept Democratic pity.

He also opened up what might be the best possible Democratic frame: contribution. If we transform the contribution talk from abstract dollars to real contributions, the billionaires will not be seen as having contributed what they've pocketed.

Trump, unfortunately, frames smoothly. While Reagan encouraged people to be hopeful, Trump welcomes his white supporters to feel like they are cheated and deserve help. This is similar to how I've heard Republicans attack Democrats, saying the Democrats offer free stuff. That isn't my experience of the Democrat's message, but Trump is making it explicit for his own supporters. He's trying to make white voters feel ok with their needs — this is a reversal of normal conservative values. Both Reagan and Trump had frames oriented toward people who were struggling; neither Romney nor Hillary Clinton bothered to do the same.

Review and Recommended Resources

There are many charts that aim to explain what is going wrong with our economy. Charts showing disparities in wealth or CEO-vs.-worker pay are very common and tend to enrage liberals. However, many conservatives intuit these disparities are proportional to disparities in productivity. Their starting assumption is that the inequality problem is caused by people at the bottom being lazy and unproductive, while liberals quietly assume that those same people are underpaid.

The Economic Policy Institute (EPI) often produces work that challenges rather than ignores conservative thoughts. This includes the *productivity chart (p.160)* and Lawrence Mishel's more detailed article *"The Wedges between Productivity and Median Compensation Growth" (http://www.epi.org/publication/ib330-productivity-vs-compensation/)*. The EPI is a great resource to keep on hand for social media discussions.

Trump 2016: Deflating Strongman Politics

"A Strong Presidency: More Complex Than Left and Right" (p.87) exposes different flavors of conservatism often glossed over by liberals. Under Trump, we're watching American conservatism transform.

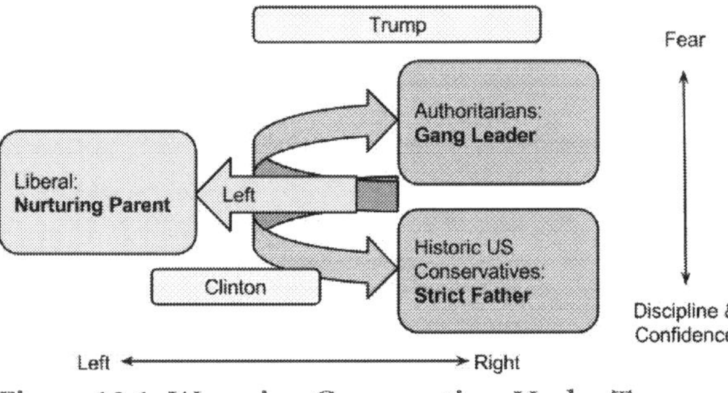

Figure 10.1: Wavering Conservatism Under Trump

Metaphors

What are the metaphors behind the Trump movement? The strict father encourages you to be disciplined against temptations, to avoid the easy way out. When I talk to conservatives about the strict-father metaphor, they often resist the idea of an intrusive father as their metaphor: they want a less-active government that respects everyone's capacity for self-discipline.

That doesn't sound like Trump to me. Trump promises to make deals for you, defeat your enemies for you. He'll stand up for you because you can't stand up for yourself. He certainly doesn't ask for discipline — what he wants is loyalty. This is not a strict father preparing you for an independent life, but a gang leader offering you the goods in exchange for your unconditional loyalty.

Opposing Trump means switching people back to metaphors of family, responsibility and discipline, while carefully avoiding the *our-gang vs. your-gang* metaphors. Both nurturing-parent and strict-father metaphors imply we are one family, while gang metaphors divide us.

This is difficult: It is very easy for *our-gang* to be disgusted with Trump and go on the attack. He deserves it. But partisan attacks feed him; we feed his metaphor of being the gang leader of all the people mocked by you or liberals or the establishment.

Move conversations back to parent metaphors: focus on responsibility, self-discipline, and cooperation — where your handshake is a promise. As much as possible, leave Trump out of the conversation.

Moral Foundations of Trump

Trump makes a mockery of conservative moral foundations. He is the One Leader; he makes a mockery of sanctity and demands only loyalty — he might as well be a left-wing slander of conservative values. Many conservatives know this: in November, their only choices were to stand up for their

own values or to stand against liberals. Much of this book is premised on the idea that if we were in better communication with quiet conservatives, enough would have chosen to stand for themselves instead of against us.

Communication and Connection

Shaming Trump supporters increases separation. Can you hold out the option of respect? Aim to reconnect us all with our own better values? Try asking real questions: What makes you proud to be Republican? What does conservatism stand for?

The gentler and slower you go, the less you try to leverage these questions into immediate demands to repudiate Trump in a contest of your will against theirs, the more likely you can be effective.

Trump has been the only candidate speaking to the fears of people who grew up privileged in America and are now being sold out. Be merciless about what they deserve, and Trump has their votes. Many people who voted for him didn't like him, but felt unheard by the rest of the system. If you're on the playground and don't like bullies but one will stand for you if you get behind him, what choice do you have?

Only Trump stands up for my community.

Trump is a spoiled, sexist, racist, greedy, unprepared liar.

Figure 9.4: Disconnect

Active listening, asking questions that avoid policy but get at why people are frustrated and scared, and just letting them share their feelings are the first steps to letting people feel like they have an option besides Trump — people with options will reject him.

Authoritarianism and Loyalty

This book was taking form well before the primary season, but *Shame and Blame Empowers Unethical Leaders (p.80)* unfortunately fits perfectly. The key to breaking up authoritarian movements is never shame: we cannot mock Trump until his supporters find their confidence and leave.

What can work is a simple invitation to in-group loyalty somewhere else. Find and reinforce shared affiliations. If you've served in the military, talk about that, and remind Trump supporters they have another home. If you run a business, talk about how Trump screws contractors. If you've ever had problems with lawyers, talk about how Trump sues. In every case, be careful to draw the lines so that people can join you, so they feel welcomed rather than feel attacked along with Trump.

Away from the rallies, many of Trump's voters turn to him only because they feel he is their only option: give them a new home.

Moving Forward

Politics is often a place where we forget other life lessons.

In the wake of the 2016 election, I feel angry, I feel dismayed. I think judgmental thoughts.

2016 saw a lack of respect on an extraordinary level. A widespread willingness to blame minorities for every ill. Even Trump supporters who claim to be against racism have generally acted with a willingness to write off the lives of immigrants and refugees and minorities without ever bothering to learn their stories. Blame and hate have been focused not only on politicians but also on ordinary people who have little control over politics.

I'm angry because I need to trust that my country is far beyond that callousness.

If what you're feeling is anger, own it, meditate on it. If you are angry; what do you need? If you are angry, what exactly has you furious? Being angry that someone voted for Trump is too big to grasp, and too late. How can you break it down?

We need to find out why other people feel a lack of respect. Know what you need; find out what they need — slowly but with persistence. It's been a long time since American politics was done with open hearts and even a basic willingness to listen. Our old patterns are not working.

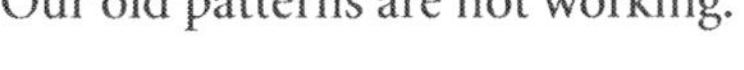

We have to win elections. And if being right was enough, we would not have a President Trump. If we are going to respect the people most likely to suffer under Trump, we can't just be right. We will have to find a way to connect with enough people who voted for him.

What requests can you make of people who voted for Trump while claiming that they are not racist? What requests can you make of people in your community who are not engaged? What requests can you make of the people you agree with, of yourself?

We don't have to convince Trump nor convince people who thrive on bullying. Politics is loud; they are loud. Notice the quiet people whom no one is listening to.

Remember that most people hate politics today, the whole thing altogether. They hate loud Trump supporters and loud Clinton supporters blasting away at each other. No

one intended for internet algorithms to echo the most obnoxious voices the most, but today that's what we all face. Ask, invite your friends to share their thoughts with you offline; offer to listen rather than blast your own views. Quiet people's votes count just as much as those of internet trolls and bullies.

I hope *Cognitive Politics* leads many of us who haven't been involved in politics to get more involved — and to seek out people who vote differently than us who also haven't been expressing their voices loudly.

Therapists guide people through divorces. Entire professions and countless self-help books guide us through difficult conversations in our personal lives. We've barely begun to try to bring these approaches to politics. I hope you'll experiment with the ideas introduced here and join me in creating a community that explores and shares new approaches.

Add your voice to the conversation at CognitivePolitics.org

Appendix I

Review: Progressive Tactics and Strategies

Following is a quick overview of strategies used throughout this book — a useful list to skim before engaging on a new issue.

☐ Moral Values: Know Which Value Is Being Triggered

Consider what values are alive for the other person in your conversation. Engage those. For example, if they are focused on the sanctity of human life in a fetus (value: sanctity), and you counterargue with choice (value: freedom), you're likely to anger them that you are not listening. Or, if you argue for more help for the poor (value: compassion), you'll frustrate even a compassionate conservative who has absorbed too much (false) information about the poor as lazy (values: fairness, responsibility).

☐ Practice Active Listening

Merely acknowledging another's opinion doesn't mean you have to agree with it. Simply say something like, "I hear how much you care when you talk about the sanctity of life starting at conception."

☐ Explore Needs and Values Before Strategies

Start by sharing your values and by seeking other's values before discussing any policies. For example, don't begin a conversation about health care talking about what the government should do; start with stories about people needing health care. Try to have shared values unfold into your policy conclusion. Listen with curiosity for other solutions to your needs besides the ones you propose; your listening is the best way to be heard in turn.

☐ Don't Assault Another's Worldview: Introduce Small Ideas That Cascade

Don't ask people to overturn a lifetime of views in one conversation. Instead, share and focus on one small point that helped lead you on your path.

☐ Consider Possibilities: Reconsider Your Goals

Consider nonpolicy goals, like breaking down the way conservatives are being taught to see liberals as the enemy, or helping someone notice that the hot-button issues are not the ones that should decide our votes.

☐ Bridging In-Groups: Avoid Shame, Blame, and Fear

When idealistic youth find out about the US role in overthrowing democracies in countries like Guatemala, Iran or Chile, many will separate emotionally from US nationalism and identify instead with a dissenting left. They'll find pride in their new loyalties rather than feel shame for their old loyalties. For someone whose identity is wrapped in patriotism, inducing shame with no place for a proud alternative will get you nowhere. People comfortable with their worldview do not become more compassionate under attack.

☐ Avoid Triggers: Begin Conversations to Invite Thought Instead of Reaction

Questions are often better than answers >> Who was the first scientist to wonder if global warming might happen? Which countries have successfully lowered abortion rates and how? Questions give people ownership of the answers they discover.

Do activities that put you in someone else's shoes >> Wonder what other people are thinking. What would you do if you and your family lived in Syria? Would you stand up to ISIS? Would that mean you'd become refugees?

Evoke problem-solving thinking >> Ask open-ended questions that lack a conclusion, or don't be clear about your views. Others can't automatically disagree with you until they've figured out your point. "Who Would Jesus Bomb?" might be pro- or anti-Christian or something else entirely. "Trust Women" might be pro-choice ... but it's not clear, so a reader will need to think about it. Open-ended messages get someone thinking about a subject, rather than knowing that you are on one side and they the other.

Approach problems as a team >> Start at the beginning; solve the problem with the people you are talking with. How might you solve the health care crisis? Ignoring Washington for the moment, how would you solve it? Creating team dynamics is a way to outmaneuver our usual political rationalizations.

Pull your voice out of "winning" >> Echo others' trusted messengers. Don't quote the Bible at a Christian unless you are a believer — let them hear the same message from someone they trust who really holds those views.

Pull your ego out of "winning" >> Let people hear your message without a need to agree or disagree. One of my favorite approaches is to simply have a conversation on a bus or at a cafe where others can overhear you. This works well for controversial and detailed stories like US imperialism or global warming. Talk for ten minutes, going over details. People who would shut you out the moment you told them that the US was behind Pinochet's dictatorship will eavesdrop happily, paying attention.

Appendix II

Prepare: Explore Goals for Your Conversations

What is possible in any one conversation?

Are you trying to influence

- ☐ the person you are talking with;
- ☐ an audience; or
- ☐ both at once?

Frames and Stories

- ☐ Inspire your listener(s) to switch metaphors.
- ☐ Help them to see something different within their own metaphor.
- ☐ Change topics from wedge issues to ones that evoke cooperation.

Moral Foundations

- ☐ Can you change your listener's moral tastes in one conversation — for example, to believing that *"gay sex is fine"*?
- ☐ Can you guide them to a different chain of their own unchanged values — to something like *"my job is to love; God's job is to judge"*?
- ☐ Evoke reciprocity and fairness by listening to the other person first.
- ☐ Reinforce shared group membership as citizens, humans, and family members — replacing and releasing *IN-GROUP* formation around political parties.

Policy: Expansion or Agreement

- ☐ Expand the window of debate: "labor creates all wealth" defines a clear left-edge, widening the economics debate, creating more space to meet in the middle.

☐ Find a policy solution you can both agree with. For example, the earned income credit rewards people for their work effort in a way that avoids many conservative criticisms of welfare.

Bridge Group Boundaries

☐ Listen and let the other side feel heard; use active listening.

☐ Emphasize areas of agreement.

☐ Work together, perhaps on something completely unrelated to the conflict.

Change Group Boundaries

☐ Draw group lines that encompass everyone: replace political problems and group formation with a focus on solutions. For example, target corrupt politicians together, or help troubled families in your neighborhood.

☐ Draw group lines that crisscross expected liberal and conservative lines:
— Make choosing life easier through babysitting and Head-Start type programs.
—Fight Wall Street corruption without being specifically left or right.
—Ally with libertarians on gay marriage or drug legalization.
—Ally with more traditional and religious conservatives on "a fair day's wage for a fair day's work."

☐ Emphasize boundaries that divide the conservative big tent, especially aiming to demarcate the unholy alliance between greed and religion.

☐ Tunnel under the existing boundaries: welcome and ally with healthier grassroots conservative values and impulses that are not being implemented by leaders and mass media on that "side."

☐ Simply be kind and attentive: slowly erode hate politics.

Appendix III

Practice: Slogans and Bumper Stickers

This section will look at bumper-sticker messages and similar short slogans. What values and frameworks do these slogans trigger, challenge or change? This is a quick way to review messaging, finding practical ways to implement cognitive science theories and effective communication techniques.

Declaring Allegiance to Your In-Group

Often, our first instinct is to go on the attack. This might help with in-group empowerment or identification but usually alienates everyone who doesn't agree and defines them as an out-group.

News for Dumb Fux

I think therefore I don't listen to Rush Limbaugh

Framing: These slogans violate Lakoff's framing rules: every time you say "Not X," you get people's neurons firing about X, thus reinforcing X. These make Fox and Limbaugh the representatives of conservatives. These bumper stickers are the "DARE" of progressives: for years we've known that "Dare to Keep Kids off Drugs" programs, funding police officers to go into schools and tell kids all the trouble they'll get into with each drug, mostly act as introductions to all the drug options. Insulting Fox or Limbaugh in general, without comedy, merely advertises them.

In-Group Loyalty: These slogans imply that my liberal *IN-GROUP* doesn't watch Fox, so if you are on the conservative team, you should.

Alternatives: What approaches let you create space for one shared agreement with people who often disagree with you? Perhaps:

MSNBC makes liberals dumb; Fox makes conservatives dumb.
Boycott both — read real media!

Boycott MSNBC & Fox
Read a newspaper!

Polarizing Messages: The following slogans define liberals and conservatives in opposition to each other, increasing separation, gaining at least as much group cohesion for the opposition as for your side. Liberals hate it when conservatives let angry voices go unchallenged; we should realize that gleeful conservative-bashing intrinsically violates progressive values and is also destructive at election time:

Slower Minds Keep Right

Don't Pray in My School and I Won't Think in Your Church

Vote Republican: It's Easier than Thinking

New Allegiances: Invitations to Healthier In-Groups

Racist People Suck

"Racist People Suck" is different. It declares an in-group or loyalty group of all people who don't like to consider themselves racist (a very large majority, even if subtle racism continues in much larger numbers), and it reinforces that group membership calls for agreement against racism. This fits with theories of authoritarian thinking, that authoritarian followers prefer to be in the great big in-group. If enough people are against racism, then authoritarian followers will want to fit in.

Hate Is Not a Family Value

"Hate Is Not a Family Value" is not "saying no" to the frame of "family values." Rather, it is celebrating that frame and pulling it back out of partisanship.

Conservatives have spent large budgets to run their slogans through focus groups. They have gotten the message out to activists about how to phrase key ideas. This is challenging for organizations: preaching to the choir is the best way to get donations but detrimental to the movement. We need to push liberal or compassion-focused groups to get more serious about messaging that speaks beyond the boundaries of people who already agree with us. If you are a member of an organization that develops messages only for their choir, speak up and request materials designed to slowly convince people who are not likely to be donors anytime soon.

Evoke Thinking: Subtle and Humorous Approaches

I've found the following slogans to be quite effective at getting people thinking and talking. They reinforce a fundamentally progressive view of the world but with enough humor to bypass resistance and get conversations started. They don't aim to define groups, and they focus on values rather than politics, even if it is only a short logic-chain to politics.

Well-Behaved Women Seldom Make History[149]

Homeland Security: Fighting Terrorism since 1492[150]

Politicians should dress like race car drivers. At least we'd know who their corporate sponsors are.

Consider the "race car drivers" slogan. It's barely ideological, though it does emphasize the progressive idea that politicians are bought by corporations rather than corporations being owned by politics. To my ear, I expect most conservatives won't hear it contradicting their values; it is exposing many of the problems that honest Tea Party members are upset about, and so it can draw us together. It gets people thinking in the frame you want — a tremendous job for a bumper sticker.

Associate Your Goal with Shared Values

I'll believe corporations are people when Texas executes one.[151]

I find this quote funny. But many Tea Party members who believe strongly in the death penalty might not have formed beliefs about whether corporations are people. To them, this association pulls in the wrong direction, encouraging division by party line: if you have always believed in the death penalty, you should now believe in corporate rights too.

Avoid making opposition to corporate rights — which could potentially cover individuals from the Tea Party to Occupy — into a partisan liberal issue to "score points."

I'll believe corporations are people when I see one pray in church.

149. "Well-Behaved Women Seldom Make History," original quote by Laurel Thatcher Ulrich. Get a *t-shirt at Northern Sun*.

150. Get a *t-shirt at Northern Sun*.

151. "I'll believe corporations are people when Texas executes one." Get a *bumper sticker at Northern Sun*.

Conversation Openings

Seek ways to start conversations without triggering the usual political defenses.

Start with Shared Values

Find all the areas of agreement. If you have a car full of left-wing bumper stickers, *start* with a positive, pro-community message, one that identifies your *IN-GROUP* as a broad community:

Give Blood	Vote for your grandchildren	Eat well, feel well

After you show that you share deeper values, less political people are more likely to care about your opinions.

Simply Express Your Values

Don't place yourself in opposition.

Bicycle
Organic

Echo *In-Group* Messengers

Quotes with positive values from messengers that conservatives will appreciate are great for email signatures or Facebook posts. Don't wield quotes as weapons to attack another team; just echo what you agree with.

I was a stranger, and you took me in.
"A business that makes nothing but money is a poor business." — Henry Ford

Less Clarity => More Thinking

Who Would Jesus Bomb?

This is one of my favorite t-shirts. People wonder if I am Christian, if the shirt is pro- or anti-Jesus. This lack of clarity confuses people and makes them think. Politicians need clarity and three-point plans that fit in sound bites. But if you're not debating, if you're not leading, then anytime you can make people think complex thoughts, you have a better chance to get them to see a new perspective.

Exercise: Messaging Review Using Bumper Stickers

Imagine you are a good-hearted person who since childhood has leaned slightly toward a cognitive-conservative mindset. You care about your church more than politics, and you tend to vote Republican more than Democrat but think of yourself as open. Find some bumper stickers on cars owned by progressives, perhaps at a co-op: How do they influence you?

Try this short checklist:

- ☐ The person identifies with a group I identify with.
- ☐ It does or doesn't make me wish a strict father would impose order.
- ☐ They share a sense of sanctity with me, or at least decency.
- ☐ They do or don't like me and my friends.
- ☐ They have no idea why I think what I think.
- ☐ They want to score points against my friends or religion.
- ☐ It makes me think.

Last Note on Slogans and Bumper Stickers

Often, we try to score points against the other side: it's fun to point out misspelled signs at Tea Party rallies or find the dumbest things any Republican candidate anywhere has said today.

Remember that much of middle-America is disgusted by politics. They're likely to trust whoever seems calmer and least likely to yell crazy things at them; whoever is more likely to give to charity, join the PTA, or donate blood. If you want to win votes that will help the working poor or give women more choices, "scoring points" goes against your goals. Actually doing good work, rather than just getting sucked into the world of framing and politics — bringing a small amount of politics to a larger dose of direct action to create the world you want to live in — is where the real power lies.

Appendix IV

Engage: Reclaim Common Spaces

Don't Feed the Trolls, but Don't Let Them Define Your Neighborhood

There is a lot of hate speech on the internet. We've learned what not to do about hate speech: looking back on Nazi Germany, historians find a small number of people full of hatred making a lot of noise. When the brown shirts marched, countless people disgusted by them left the streets; the moderates stayed home and watched from windows, *feeling isolated even while they vastly outnumbered the hateful.*

Trolls beating people up online may be trivial compared to being actually beaten. But I'm bothered that the only well-known advice for dealing with disruptive tactics is "don't feed the trolls," advice that seems to match everything decent Germans did wrong as Nazis rose to power. So let's begin to explore: How do we take back the public spaces? How do we avoid "feed-the-trolls conversations" while also not ceding the public forums to hate and anger? Can we find ways to add voices of sanity to the blogosphere, another option besides being silenced or getting into shouting matches? This appendix is quick advice for engaging online, subverting the shouting-match paradigm. Some of the advice is oriented toward toning down partisanship, some toward helping all the sane people watching the online battles feel hope that the other watchers are sane.

Consider what is missing when *anger speech* takes over the commons. Readers get a feeling of isolation that leads to apathy and hopelessness. Countering this doesn't mean winning all the points brought up by every troll. It means separating trolls from a sane center.

Find Openings for Online Engagement

> To counter trolling, you don't have to convince the people leaving angry or hyper-partisan comments. To take back public spaces, you simply give the sane center a voice so that other readers don't feel isolated and hopeless.

START GENTLY LACKING CLARITY >> Force "active listening" by being unclear whose side you are on and where you are going.

CLEAN UP YOUR SIDE'S AD HOMINEM ATTACKS >> Defend the "other side" from false accusations or unwarranted attacks. They don't help your cause — notice them and take responsibility; it works. Integrity breaks down the sides and lets you carry the middle — much of modern politics on the web is, or could be, won by the people who are simply able to make their points without coming across as jerks.

Be the one sane voice in each crazy conversation,
so the nonparticipants feel a hopeful connection to someone.
Create a "side" that everyone seeking hope,
decency or community feels invited to join.

No matter whom they are aimed at, tactics like name-calling are particularly damaging to frames that call for hope and trusting community; these tactics help ideologies that thrive on fear. Stepping out of your role of trying to score points for your team also helps break the opposing team's metaphor.

CREATE MORE SIDES >> It can't be us-vs-them if there are three or four ideas. If left-loyalists and right-loyalists are screaming at each other, advocate another vision; advocate for community.

Increase Thinking

ASK REAL QUESTIONS >> Ask with curiosity, hoping to better understand where they're coming from. Ask open-ended questions that draw people to introspect. Listen to the party-line answers until they run out, and then keep being curious about the roots of their beliefs.

BEGIN A STORY WITH YOUR METAPHOR, AND LET OTHERS FINISH IT >> Lakoff's advice is to conjure the frame or metaphor you want. Leave it to others to think through the implications of the metaphor or story you've begun. Let the conclusions be their own ideas as much as possible.

SKIP THE CONCLUSION >> Leave parts of your argument unfinished. Make it less obvious which side you are on. People can't think and run their automated argument

defenses at the same time. For example, "Trust Women" might be pro-choice, but it's not instantly clear. It gets people thinking with the metaphor you prefer and lets them own the conclusions.

Define a Large and Welcoming In-Group That Advocates Decency

Fight hate speech from the center >> Invite readers to see a moderate, sane and widespread middle. Don't imply that hate speech is conservative or turn it into a liberal-vs.-conservative battle: isolate the haters. Don't encourage decent conservatives to hate you as a liberal more than they detest hate-speech trolls.

> You might say, "I don't think real conservatives agree with you, just trolls on the internet."

Authoritarian followers seek the middle >> Bullies seek to be normal within their *in-group*. Especially if you're an ally of a hated group rather than the target, you can help best by speaking up consistently and clearly, redefining normal rather than pushing the bully into an in-group that doesn't include you. If you unfriend or isolate them, you're not helping the people whom they target.

Don't let trolls represent anyone >> If a comment is hateful, aim to isolate the troll with a quick comment like:

> I don't think you represent real conservatives.

Trolls often aim to get conservatives to circle their wagons around the crazy or hateful points; you need sane conservatives to side with you against hate. Invite people to hold real and decent values, even if those values are different than yours. With Trump's style of politics on the rise, it's particularly important for progressives to understand how we can influence conservative politics in positive ways.

Encourage Healthy Conservative Moral Foundations

Appeal to conservative values >> If your audience is conservative, consider if your policy goals can be achieved within their value frame.

Encourage a loyalty check >> Someone doesn't have to completely agree with you — as long as you're not yelling at each other — in order to notice when their deeper values are being used by politicians.

✓ are religious values inspiring and changing politics,

✓ or are political goals using religion?

Cognitive Politics Isn't Just About Conservatives

Cognitive science is teaching us more than just what is wrong with the other side.

Many liberals feel like we're the little kids in the schoolyard, being bullied and getting our lunch money stolen by the Republicans and *Fox News.* Yes. The thing is, they're not bigger than us, and we outnumber them, and yet they're still stealing our lunch money. Why are all the wedge issues initiated from the right?[152] Why aren't we smart and disciplined enough to split good-hearted conservatives from the self-interested and greedy ones?

> The Democrats' core challenge is to inspire people whose economic interests are poorly represented by the Republican Party but who have natural tendencies toward cognitive conservatism.

And under it all, that's not merely a call to arms: it's a real question. What about the cognitive-liberal mindset has left us unable to handle schoolyard-style bullying, even as adults?

This book aims to show liberals a bit about some of our shortcomings, which are framed as tactics because a book about shortcomings wouldn't get read. Tactics and framing aside, when we create healthier liberal politics at the root, when we integrate politics with community-building values, when we show that we know how to help people without creating runaway bureaucracy, then we'll attract many more moderates to vote with us.

Moving Forward: Compassionate Politics versus Pragmatic Politics

At the core of a healthy-liberal vs. healthy-conservative debate, we find compassion vs. pragmatism and realism about growing strong individuals in strong communities. Much of Berkeley would begin to give every homeless person here an apartment, until every homeless person in America moved to Berkeley and our homeless program collapsed.

If you define conservatism as the pragmatic and grounded alternative to compassion without boundaries, there is no significant conservative party in America today. My hope is that by crushing the aspects of the Republican Party that grew out of the Southern Strategy and feed on anger, while simultaneously respecting and sometimes learning from the community-building moral foundations that ordinary conservatives truly feel, we can create space for a grounded, pragmatic, community-building, and antiauthoritarian cognitive-conservative party.

152. Gay marriage has evolved into a wedge issue that benefits liberals. But it was initiated outside the discipline of the Democratic Party and was initially seen as likely to hurt Democrats when Gavin Newsom brought it to the national stage.

Index and Key Concepts

About the Author: Stephen Cataldo

Stephen is a social entrepreneur and software engineer currently living in Berkeley, California. When encountering organizations in conflict, he has often been the person to quietly hear both sides and aim to bring about a new consensus. Currently, Stephen facilitates *strategic planning amidst conflicting visions* for cofounders, social enterprises, and nonprofits.

In lieu of regular book readings for *Cognitive Politics,* he facilitates workshops on conversations across partisan divides.

Next year he hopes to partner with a conservative author to write a parallel book for cognitive conservatives who seek to express their values to liberals in deeper and more effective ways. He is also seeding a start-up for liberals and conservatives to improve dialogue through a "fair exchange" of listening, with an expected beta in mid-2017.

For social media, workshop, and consulting links, see: *CognitivePolitics.org/bio*

Made in the USA
San Bernardino, CA
06 May 2019